On Tour With Shavetail

Christopher Devitt

William L Devitt

William M Devitt

… Fathers of war proof!
Fathers that, like so many Alexanders,
Have in these parts from morn till even fought.

– William Shakespeare
Henry V

SHAVETAIL:

Old army slang for a newly commissioned second lieutenant. From the practice of shaving the tails of newly broken mules that they might be distinguished.

THE TRIP

THE TRIP

Introduction

Daddy

This is really the story of three trips. The first was from August, 1944 to January, 1945. It covers the places in western Europe in World War II that I was in while serving as a US Army infantry lieutenant. I've written a book about this, "Shavetail: The Odyssey of an Infantry Lieutenant in World War II," from which I have included quotations.

In discussing the first trip (August '44 to January '45) I have concentrated on the seven locations in which my company of 190 men (E Company, 330th Infantry Regiment, 83rd Infantry Division) participated (fought) while I was there. Six of the seven most memorable locations are in or near Germany's Hurtgen Forest, a few miles east of Aachen. The seventh is in Belgium's Ardennes Forest, a few miles south of Liege.

The second trip took place in July, 1988. I had just turned 65 and had retired from my job. My wife, Mary, and I had decided to fulfill a wish we had had for years, namely, to visit England. We were both Anglophiles, with Mary ahead of me in the Anglophile contest. I decided also that after our time in England, we would visit the same locations (as in the first trip) in western Europe where I had been during the war. Mary, who had spent her time during the war in high school and college, showed no enthusiasm for tramping around far off destinations in France, Luxembourg, Belgium and Germany. Nevertheless that became part of our 1988 trip. Mary, although less than eager to visit the sites, was always a good sport about it.

Sadly, Mary, my dear wife of 54 years, died on October 20, 2006, after a long battle with Alzheimer's. She and I had eight children.

In the summer of 2007 I began to think of taking a third trip — this time with three of my sons in tow, hoping to visit the same seven battlefield sites and later to write the story of the trip. My original plan was to go in the summer of '08. But after much thought, I recalled the words of "September Song," reminding me that at the age of 84, "the days dwindle down to a precious few." So the trip was pushed ahead to October '07.

Three of Mary's and my surviving four sons (Chris, Sean and Willy) were able to come. Our middle son, Nick, had died in an accident in 2001. Our fourth son, Matt, could not make it. Our three daughters, Mary, Anne and Dolly (our nickname for Sarah), all had children in school. And so it goes.

Some time after I had started writing, Chris and Willy thought to have a say. Hence, the three authors.

So this is the day-to-day story of the third trip, together with my remembrances from the first two.

Willy

We would be off then, to the Old Country. We would feel a bit of the sweep of history, and history is why we were going. Our father's history, everyone's. Who could escape it? Mr. Joyce famously said that history is a nightmare from which I am trying to awake. For the time being we would remain fast asleep in the land of those now mythic crucibles — Waterloo, Sedan, Verdun, Passchendaele, Normandy, Ardennes and bloody Huertgen — site of our father's own trial by fire, by blood. Now as much a part of his children's histories as his own.

"The past is never dead. It's not even past." — William Faulkner

CD

Prologue:

Twas early of eve,
Late in the day;
Hard off the daily toil, travail and trouble.
I caught the call. Daddy it was.

He would return to the battlefields of his youth. He would need help. He thought of his sons. Who or whose should come? Or would?

Surprised and shocked
And flattered and frightened I be.

"Must do it soon. We're dropping like flies. Don't know how long I've left," says he.

"Don't be silly. You'll be buryin' me," says I.

"But I've decided," says Himself.

So back and forth by phone it was
For the several weeks or so.
Who could, would go;
What play, how pay?
Whatever then are we to do?

So, somewhat hang-dog shamefully,
Always perfectly painfully,
I fought the pending looming funk

Of endless aeroplane (No Smoking), unfamiliar awful rented automobile, dithery reserved hotel booking, inscrutable itinerary, and … maps and maps through itty-bitty squinty magnifying glass.

Am honored and excited and afraid.
But not so strong as you might think
And nor that I would have one think.

What if I break down, freak out or fuck up?
Not merely faintly embarrassed,
But to out and out dead ass dishonor oneself before the public, God, Brothers, Daddy,and fucking all and sundry!
So I sought to get out of it, dodge the bullet, but I couldn't. Though had I done, the regret would coat and soak me all my sorry days.
So then and there it was:
Die cast.

… The first day of recording
My recording.
This whole thing would be a test
To see if I am to be tested.
Allons, allons mes enfants!
Forward through fog at speed!

Morning Chi Kung,
Breakfast,
Capital day.
On my way,
Out and about,
Twist and shout.
Places to go,
Things to do.
Trousers to buy,
Shirts to try.
Un-stash the cash,
Unleash the hidden Krugerrands.
Nuthin' to it but to do it.

The question is:
Is anything being recorded?

I can't really tell.
Is it anything worth recording?
Is anything ever worth recording?
I don't tell.
I won't.

And on to the gymnasium:
13 minutes of hit the heavy bag,
13 minutes of bicycle to nowhere,
13 minutes of row without water,
13 minutes of elliptical sorta skiing,
13 minutes of the hand crank what's-it,
13 minutes of stair stepper inverse escalator,
And then we'll try a little something else
And then that will be that
And on to the next.

Speed back from gym.
Run up on Dear Wife Marilyn.
On her way out.
Ships pass in the night.
Who invented this kind of life?

Saturday night, someday something.
Isn't it special? Isn't it grand?
So time to get the good drink on.
Solitary sit in backyard.
Jack up the night; wind up the day.

Come the dirge dusk surprisingly soon in muted minor key. Like when you finish a chapter and start another, and somehow it seems precipitate.

The stark soon trip looms large in threat.
The shadow lengthens and deepens.
Crisp autumn leaves begin to fall.
Wind-whoosh flutter-flap through arbor.
Daddy loves me (I think).
I hope he knows I love him too.
Try to stand up, stand up tall ...

Parlez-vous français?
Sprechen Sie Deutsch?
And God only knows what the hell,
The bloody English will say.

When anyone on the playground had a candy bar or anything worth having at all, everybody would throngingly cluster about and urgingly say and shout:
"You know me, you know me."
Good great God, please help us.
You know me, You know me.

Zephyrus whispers sweet breath softly
Into and through and to the old oak tree.
Door slams, horn sounds, child cries.
The slow sub sound of an idling motor.
I hear a human step up or down steps.
I warily watch the alley.
The squirrels are searching. They catapult their nuts – clump, clump, clump – like big fat-splat raindrops.

I'm blinking,
I'm drinking,
I'm thinking.
Ain't that plain, so plain, just plain but plain to see.

Sey hey, let's go.
It's Saturday night.
Live.

Sunday morning. Up'n at'em. Autumn equinox.
O, looky looky 'cross the road:
Gal from a glossy magazine ad adjusts her shirt.
A little tweenie dog with her (might be a Chihui) small as our Gracie; dances, preens 'n' prances.
'Sposed to be nice today, or so they say.
Should be nice every day,
Weather-wise, if nothing else,
Climatologically speaking.
If Nothing Else.

But I've but to amuse myself, get some gas, grab a paper, entertain some fun. Out the door and out-of-doors.

Run down breakfast. Le petite déjeuner or Frühstück. One of those things.

Down to the river, sweet sunny day, but it is no longer summer – for today is the first official day of fall. That would be the autumnal equinox. Fall into the familiar secluded spot. Hidden beach on bend of river. Play some yoga, kung fu, chi kung, a little stick play. There won't be many days left like this in the season or maybe even ever.

What else to do in one's waning day? Call a friend? Who would that be? Chase the girlies? But God forbid. (To the married man, that is proscribed.)

Forbidden fruit, eh Mama?

Off the river, down to the gym. O alas, the pool, the outdoor pool is closed with the passing of the period.

Fall back to the friendly river.

Orange amber sunlight skips off silver water.
Whooshing wind sounds through sweeping swaying arbor.
Brother geese and ducks bob and weave.
Something swings and clangs on a boat.
Come now the squeaky-clean tourists.
Meself, I'm just passing through.
Then back to the backyard brooding.
Evening hard upon us like a hold-up.
Shadows lengthen, stretch like pulled taffy.
Dimming hard light stripes through the trees.
Warm as cooling tapioca.

I wonder and worry about the impending ordeal. The cup, the chalice, the Grail. Can I survive the high up breathless flight, the Euro-drive stick-shift breaking-back day, the toss-and-turn far-from-home sleepless night?

Be I too old? Too worn out? Too broken? Too always full of pain?
Has the road then lost its luster?
Life's allure never now the same?
Shame … Shame.

I hear an air conditioner perking.
Drips and drops make moist below.
Purple flowers here, yellow flowers there.
Black shadow leaves dance on off-white garage door.
Summer's delinquent grill sits and rusts.
Must needs cut grass once more.
Ramshackle patio furniture might see the snow.

What can our Father be thinking?
To ponder such Homeric quest.
Three sons lined up to form the crew –

And God alone only knows what.
Hope to entertain amusement,
Or even the out and out fun.
Un petit divertissement,
(Is that unworthy of the Endeavor?).
Pray humbly that I can make it.
But short of that – ailing, failing –
Maybe I can fake it.

Mark it. Something, like a boat, will come about. It always does.

A man goes to war. Then takes his soft sons that they might see.

Hard riding, fine fellowship, good humor, the odd argument here and there.

Un petit divertissement.

It's a shootin' match. Anything likely to happen. It beats me what. But it's bound to be bloody telling.

For good or for ill.

Get yo' money down.

Daddy

Chapter One
Tuesday, October 9, 2007
Minneapolis-St. Paul Airport,
Gatwick Airport and Dover

In World War II, I was an infantry platoon leader (a lieutenant) in Western Europe. My combat time was largely three weeks in December, 1944 in or near Germany's Hurtgen Forest and one day in the Battle of the Bulge in Belgium (January 3, 1945). If three weeks and a day seems like a short period of time, I must ask, "compared to what?"

In early December '44 our rifle company of 190 men walked into the Hurtgen Forest to take on the German defenders with their deadly artillery and small arms fire, and who were protected in log-covered foxholes. My platoon of 40 men was part of the 190. After three weeks, only 50 battered infantrymen (10 of my platoon's 40, including myself) were able to walk out. Ours was a risky business.

Two Purple Hearts plus several near misses were signs of what I and my men went through in the three weeks and a day. My four months in an army hospital after the second Purple Heart was a pleasant contrast to the "short" period of death and mutilation.

My combat experiences described above are an important part of the story being told here.

On October 9, Dolly, my youngest daughter, drove three of her brothers, Chris, Sean and Willy, and me to the Minneapolis/St. Paul airport to board Northwest Airlines flight 44 non-stop to Gatwick Airport near London. Dolly asked me to call her on October 20. I said "yes," and asked her why. She reminded me that October 20 was the anniversary of her Mama's (my dear wife Mary's) death, one year earlier.

Chris, Sean and Willy are good sized fellows, running in age from early forties (Willy) to early fifties (Sean and Chris, the oldest). This was probably the first time we would be traveling together since their childhood days when the entire family (mother, father, eight kids and St. Bernard dog, Flora) would pile into the Chrysler station wagon to spend a day or two in northern Minnesota's mosquito filled lake country. As father, I was the biggest of the bunch. But time brought change. By the time of our trip to Europe, I was the smallest of the four.

The flight was without incident, but was one hour late arriving in Gatwick. My cardiologist insists that I walk for half an hour *every* day. So, I resolved to make three 10 minute walks inside the plane while in flight at some 20,000 feet in the air at a speed of 600 miles an hour. I did it.

But that's not as easy as it sounds. The big, powerful four-engined plane was filled to capacity with people. Both of the plane's sets of windows had rows of seats (three seats to the row) running next to the windows. Between the two window rows was a center section with six seats per row. There were two aisles by which the passengers could get in or out of their seats – one aisle between the center row and each of the two window rows.

The boys and I were seated in the center section for the nine-hour flight. My plan was to make the three 10 minute walks back and forth along the aisles, totaling my prescribed 30 minutes. Simple and easy enough. But not nearly so simple and easy as it seems. The aisles were so narrow that two people would have to squeeze in order for one to pass the other. I don't know how or why, but both aisles seemed always crowded with passengers going to and from somewhere or other, though I suspect that the toilets were the favorite, probably only, destination.

However, my problem was how to walk for ten minutes three times at an uninterrupted rate amidst the planeload of human flesh.

This reminded me of my worries in 1954, when taking the Minnesota bar exam for law school graduates which, upon passing, qualified them to be lawyers (the main reason for going to law school). The written exam took place on three consecutive blistering-hot July days in a non-air-conditioned classroom at the University of Minnesota law school. Twenty percent did not pass. I made it. I remember wondering and worrying that I might not pass. My anxious wife and my two little boys needed a passing grade. Also my job with a law firm was contingent upon passing the test.

Somehow, together with the worrying, my memory brought me back to 1944-45, when I fought against the German Wehrmacht in the Hurtgen Forest in Germany and the Battle of the Bulge in Belgium. It was a deadly time, but I made it through. Just before the bar exam, my worrying let up a little. I told myself, “That damn bar exam can’t be so tough. They’re not even shootin’ at ya.”

I don’t recall how I was able to complete my half hour of walking on the plane. But I think I had in mind, “They’re not even shootin’ at ya.”

I sat back in my seat and realized that the last time I’d been on a plane was with Mary during our trip in 1988. While on our flight to England in ‘88, a young German boy and his mother sat directly behind Mary and me. The boy kept pushing the back of Mary’s seat. She quietly asked the boy to stop. He continued to push. Mary began to lose her patience.

Mary, who with eight children of her own, was no rookie when dealing with kids, finally turned in her seat and said to the boy in a definitely increased volume, “KNOCK IT OFF!”

The German boy probably did not understand the meaning of Mary’s words, but he surely understood her intent. He stopped immediately.

Our flight reminded me of the Pilgrims journeying in the year 1620 from Plymouth, England, to Plymouth Rock, near present day Boston. In 1620, Northwest Airlines had not yet introduced transatlantic flights, so the Pilgrims were obliged to take a boat—a slow boat—over the Atlantic Ocean to the future state of Massachusetts. The trip took a month, or was it two or more? I don't know if any of the passengers in our plane complained about the one-hour delay. But I do know that the Pilgrims would have laughed at length at the idea of complaining about a one-hour delay in crossing the Atlantic Ocean.

Even more laughable (and impossible) to the Pilgrims might have been the story that someone walked 20,000 feet above the ocean while simultaneously traveling at a speed of 600 miles an hour.

Before leaving on the trip I told the boys I'd be taking notes at the end of each day about what happened that day. I even gave each of them a note pad. I told them that I intended to write a story about the trip and that a few on-the-spot recollections by all of us about meals, people, historical sites and other items of interest would be helpful.

My note taking lasted two days. I have not yet summoned the audacity to ask the boys for their notes. I'm sure that their negative replies to me would indicate that there is something in their genes which hinders their note-taking skills.

Willy

The comings and goings of air travel are distinctly unpleasant. Landing at Gatwick, quite the anti-climax. Deplaning, walking briskly and with quite a few cares in the world, through massive, various and endless terminals, reading all manner of sign, maneuvering past fellow shell-shocked travelers, negotiating the ins, outs, ups, downs, whims and whams of modern London's second largest transport hub, all the while lugging, dragging and otherwise humping bags of luggage, most of which will never be used. I believe in the British Army this is known as *yomping.* So we yomped. And yomped. Ever onwards towards London Bridge tube station. And what of Buckingham Palace? And Big Ben? Piccadilly Circus and the mighty Thames?

No time for that, it's hurry on boys, hurry on! We're off to the Continent and must needs get there bloody fast. There's no time to tarry, pack up your troubles and ye olde kit bag, what ho! Rough work afoot, lads! Up, Guards, and at 'em! To France! En avant! The Yanks are coming! Hurrah!

Guess what?

I'm having a smoke.

France can wait.

Heading south on the train. England flies by. Mile after mile of red brick council flats, high-rise tower block housing estates, grey everywhere, with the occasional burst of green. Of this pleasant land. Rail staff bring carts of coffee, tea, wee sandwiches. Chris and I traveling separately from Daddy and Sean, having paused for the cause, we're around twelve minutes behind them. Remarkably precise this British Rail. We chat and joke with the girl with the cart. Such a civil people. It's true. Switching trains at Charing Cross. Waiting on the platform. They huddled in here by the tens of thousands during the Blitz. The Jamaican and West Indian rail staff the friendliest of the friendly. It's "mate" this and "cheers" that. Another train. It's been said all Englishmen lead lives of quiet desperation. And I feel I've been here before. My Anglophile mother. Died one year ago this month. "Play the game." Hastings line. Tonbridge to Tunbridge Wells. Calling Folkestone. Kent to the coast, lads. Roll on Dover.

CD

Up 'n' at 'em Tuesday 9 Oct 07

Today's the day the grand journey begins.

A little kung fu warm up exercise, early morning breakfast, and O my God, I've forgotten to get the fake cigarettes for the aeroplane ordeal. E-cigs, they say they say.

But any-who,

What Ho!

The daft and blazing brilliant day.

Anne with Willy aboard by to pick me up. We're rolling. We're on our way to Daddy's to stage. Check the gear, straighten the straps. Knuckle down, buckle up. Down and dirty buck up. We're under way. They're racing! Pop smoke; sey hey.

Anne: EEee Hhaa!

Hi Ho – Gun's up – We're off!

We're on the road.

We under way,

Be there today.

Except we really won't. It'll be tomorrow or the next day or some time in the near or distant future, God willing, the crick don't rise, and …

So on.

So here we are: Change of direction and vehicle. Dolly at the wheel, Daddy riding shotgun, Brothers Sean, Willy, and finally me – CD; all squished and squeezed in the back.

Yo hubba-hubba yea hey-hey!

The great, grand and good sort of day.

Goodbye goodbye.

Four Heroes at the fly yard
Sit round and wait.
On parle le français.
Scarf down the odd airport snack.
And now the flight's delayed.
And then what?

Brothers Three and Daddy
So patiently wait to wing.
A330 aircraft poised off-stage to sing.
Be-seated and besotted,
We roll exquisitely slow.
Come on, come on,
Let's do it, do it – go.
Small talk, joviality, bonhomie.
Sean runs to take a pee.

Iron tube grabs some air.
We're rollin'- rollin'- rollin'.

Little pictures on the little TV screen or computer monitor or some such explain how to wiggle one's fingers in order extricate wanted or needed information from this magical machine. I, of course, can't figure out about the headphones nor how to liberate the remote, or (again) some such device, from the housing on the chair.

Oooo ... I'll use some time.
We're off and running.
Wow!

Flip flop fly'n.
Cocktail hour.

Double vodka, beer back.
Better get two.
Wouldn't wanna get caught short.
Ain't we got fun?!

The little airplane food dinner.
The little bottle of wine.
But I never dine and drink at the same time.
Though they try to tame, to civilize me,
I'm just not havin' it.
But then, one might make the exception.

Little movies on the little screen.
Astonishing and confusing.
Headphones, handset, molded plastic.
Disregard and meditate.
Daddy close to blessed sleep.

Case the room and check the talent.
Watch that one – Line me up.
But bathroom stall be pretty small.
Ten Thousand Foot Club must wait for another time.

Fly high, fast and furious.
Non dormiunt in darkened cabin.
Willy and I manipulate and play (guess you call it that) with electronic devices.
Try to hear the music;
Try to sleep the sleep.
Succeed in the former;
Fail at the latter.

Sky high, free and fast –
We're gettin' there.
Fastball 600 miles an hour.
Plane pitches gently like a rocking chair.
Eyes burn as in a forest fire.
Never could sleep when in motion;
Never learned the knack.
And the motion brings tomorrow:
London, Dover, Calais;
Plane, train, taxi, rent-a-car –
Ride.

The dope the Good Doctor gave me must have worked to some degree. I'm neither dyin' nor freakin' out.

Ground speed: 928 kilometers per hour. (Really?) Were we actually on ground, we'd really be burning rubber.

Engine drones and rumbles, lights flicker.

AC patrol forgot to crank it up, so the temp is OK.

I snicker.

I could dance.

Tin plane commence to jump'n' jive.
Real happy to be still alive.
They say fasten seat-belts
But I don't care.
No such thing as fender bender
Up here, out there.

Daylight assaults.
We swim in fog.
More obfuscating muddling cloud.
A little light enters the cabin.
Break of dawn before the ...

Sleepy Girl across the aisle stirs.
People slowly start to move.
Quickly down the row to the head.
Bustin' through the mourning fog.
We're Gettin' There.

Willy watching "Wag The Dog,"
But I lack the attention span.
Focus. Focus!
Pretty girl sidles by.
My eyes burn like tear gas in an army boot camp toture.
Shut 'em down, Shorty.

Plane wings west to east.
Sun springs east to west.
We joust with Apollo.
Sunrise holds the breath ten minutes.
Fly girl serves us some kind of something:
Breakfast, petit déjeuner, Früstück.

Touchdown in Jolly Old England
And ain't that just that.
Willy and I beg split for smokes.
Call it a rest stop.
Daddy and Sean forge on.
After the "aaahh," we beat feet too.
Jump train for Dover
And think things fine –
Separate But Equal.

But nothing is fine. Not now. We've gone and separated ourselves, and with no code or plan to recover. The whole European Theater could be blown.

Half the squad – with grim-set jaws, hurry headlong on.

Half the squad – after crossing an ocean in the air, in desperate want of a smoke.

Could one not wait?

Willy and I corral a train to follow Daddy and Sean to Dover where we hope to reunite. There's plenty of room to stretch out and watch the colorful English countryside flash by.

A middle-aged woman pushes a tea trolley by.

"Thanks, but no thanks."

Too anxious for fear of the failure. And what's to become of the Old Man? But at least big Sean is with him. And Willy, as I watch him watch out the window – stout heart – seems calm and self-contained.

We now approach Dover by rail.
We're on the way;
We on the money.
On the channel.
Look, there's blue water,
The white cliffs of Dover.
There they are.
And there they are too –
The long lost kinsmen,
Lost but now found.

Sean variously, furiously, telephoning at the terminal. Daddy chatting with all and sundry. He seems to be quite the hit. Willy scuffling and trying to help. I lean on my stick.

Announcements and pronouncements aplenty, sometimes involving security. That would be in German, in French, and in English. I can grasp but a little. But what the Hell – I even often miss the boat in my mother tongue. I think it fun and funny. Let's keep our sense of humor about us, lads, and our sense of fun.

Strange flashy flashing lights that emanate from novel noise-making machines have the English of Dover here. Mechanical gambling of some sort. There are pastries and confections, and newspapers; and wandering, bustling, yet friendly – very friendly people. Much as this might grate an Irishman, the English seem a civilized lot.

We're Gettin' There.

But We Missed The Boat.

But for the smoke, the plan awry.

And we'll not make Calais tonight.

So what to do and where to stay?

I know. And know how.

"Come on, Willy, let's go!"

Walk around, walk about, swing hips and shoulders, trust to chance. Feels so fine after the Great Sit. Dover seems a sweet town. There are little apertures high up in the cliffs that look like doors. Maybe someone lives there.

There – The iconic English red phone booth. (Goes with the bus.) Goof and make photo art. And art is all it is – The phone inside now gone.

Smile!

Book at the County Hotel, just off the coast by the sea. Rejoin the gang. Everybody happy. Move in. Hallelujah.

Down to the gilded hotel bar.

For which I've always had weakness.

We, all of us, sit at the shiny, stylish, civilized bar and order shiny, stylish, civilized drinks.

Spirited discussion: boxing.

Meet a neat man there in the bar – lightweight to welterweight. Richard Hughes, he said he was; claimed he fought some pro.

Title shot – Contender maybe.

Live it up, baby.

“The Germans, what they were trying to do ... to get to Antwerp, you know, on the Belgian coast and cut off the English army who are on the north side, and the American army on the south side. Well, they were not successful. But I, I was in that, that Battle of the Bulge – the story that I wrote, fellas. I was there just one day, but ... And I've written a book, but there's more to the story.”

“That's 'cause you got hit.”

“Yeah, on my chin.”

“Hey.”

“On my chin.”

“Thank you, thank you.”

“Thank you, sir.”

“Thank you, sir.”

“Hey yeah, hey yeah.”

“I go into over detail.”

“Yeah. Yeah, yeah.”

“So I'm showing these fellows ... they've read my book ... and I'm showing them where I really was, see, where it really was.”

“Your friends who fought the war …”

“Huh?”

“Your friends who fought the war, your friends from the war. When you think of them, your friends of the war ...”

“Ah, they're dropping like flies, my friends. Two years ago four of them died. In my high school class ... I went to a school in Minnesota ... there were 95 students, so it wasn't a very big school ... and yeah, we're dropping like flies ... but there are still a few of us around and we see each other."

"Are they trying to get rid o'ya, then?"

"Huh? Uh huh. Huh?"

"Do they try to get rid of you?"

"They do, they try, yet here I am."

"Yeah, that's the spirit.""

"Yeah!"

"Yeah!"

"Yeah, that's right."

"And what, then, of the others?"

"Well, another, a good friend of mine, a classmate of mine in high school, was killed on Okinawa. You've heard of the big battle? It was right before the end of the war in the Pacific"

"Yeah."

"And after the Germans had given up on this side of the world ... and this friend of mine was killed about ... just a few days before the fighting stopped ... which was the last big battle of the whole war. He's my age. He was 21 years old. Went to high school with him, and a nice boy, and from Minnesota too."

"Yeah."

"And uh ... So I still think about those things."

"Yeah. Of course."

"If you didn't think about it, there'd be something wrong ..."

"Or you'd be inhuman."

"Yeah. That's right. Well ..."

"God bless ya. Memory ..."

"Yeah."

"Thank you."

"Yeah, yeah."

"Good memories or bad memories ..."

"Yuh, yuh."

"But that's life, isn't it?"

"Here's to memories – good and bad."

"Aye!"
"Here here!"
"Hey!"
"Hey hey hey!"
"Hooray."
"Yeah."
"Drink up."
"Hey, what happen to Willy?"
"Where Willy?"
"He not here."
"Went out for a smoke."

Mumble, whisper; close the book.
A saxophone you'd yearn to blow
Heralds soundtrack throughout the scene.
From somewhere, can't say where.
I'll remember this all my life.

Daddy

Chapter Two
Wednesday, October 10, 2007
Gatwick Airport, London and Dover

We landed at Gatwick an hour late—about 10:30 a.m. Our plan was to take a train or bus to London Bridge Railway Station, then another to Charing Cross Station, and then a third to Dover to catch the ferry to Calais. We thought we should get to Calais (across the English Channel from Dover) by 5 p.m. in order to pick up our rental car before closing time. But time got away from us. Every move took a little longer than I had figured. By the time we reached Dover we were ten minutes too late to take the last ferry.

I had not figured a one hour delay in our flight. A second hour was lost when I learned (too late) that the French time (Calais) was one hour later than the British time, meaning that I had lost two hours in my calculations.

We had lost a day in our excursion by missing the first night of our reservation in Normandy. But the result was not all bad. We were able to see some of Dover, a city rich in history going back easily to William the First (the Conqueror) and including World War II, when Dover was the English city separated by only 32 miles of water from Hitler's thought-to-be-invincible armies waiting in France to cross the English Channel to overwhelm the decimated British Army.

We stayed in Dover in the County Hotel. Our two rooms had contained a trouser press, an item I've never seen nor heard of in any American or other hotel. In the bar, we met and talked to a former professional lightweight boxer – Richard Hughes. The boys enjoyed talking with him, and later that evening we saw him at the restaurant where we had dinner.

The hotel seemed similar, except for one, to all the others

we occupied on the trip. It was on a busy street in the middle of the city leading down to the seaside with its numerous ocean-going vessels.

With its grey brick or stone construction it appeared like an old building. But since I'm describing an English building as "old," it will be well to define "old." As an American describing an American building, I'd put an old building as in the 50-year range. But for an English building, with their history and possibly a building or two dating back a thousand years, I think "old" should begin at the range of 150 to 250 years.

The hotel's front entrance was almost touching the busy street. Busy street, narrow sidewalk, front entrance. It was five floors in height with one elevator to take us to our rooms on the fourth floor. A little to my surprise, the elevator was self-service (without an elevator operator), so at least part of the hotel was not old.

Although we had not yet rented a car, I wondered where one would park. I'll never know.

The entire experience at the hotel was excellent. We were treated as guests and not as by a landlord renting rooms for a night. The staff were courteous and friendly. And I'm happy to say that the treatment we received in every hotel on the trip in England, France, Luxembourg, Belgium, and Germany (except one) was equally as courteous and friendly.

The one hotel which was unlike the County Hotel in Dover was the one at Gatwick Airport outside of London, the last hotel on the trip. It was the only hotel we visited near a big city. Everyone was efficient. They had our reservation and had a large room ready for us. Unlike all the smaller hotels, upon leaving the large airport hotel, I left feeling that our treatment had been less friendly, even impersonal, as though we were strangers receiving the treatment for which we had paid a fairly handsome sum.

This could have been outside New York, or Chicago. All of the other hotels on the trip were in or near smaller communities. I think that people in smaller communities are friendlier and nicer, and I vote for them.

Dover. We had not intended to spend any time in Dover. For me it was merely the nearest place in England across the English Channel from France, about 30 miles of water. I'm sure the city and its environs are filled with historical sites including an ancient castle or two. But we had neither the time nor the inclination to explore historic Dover.

Although the boys and I on our 2007 trip did no driving in Dover or any other part of England, I cannot forget my driving experience in Mary's and my 1988 trip. Mary graciously, or possibly wisely, let me know that I should do all the driving.

I was aware of the English custom of driving from the wrong side of the car on the wrong side of the road. Before leaving, I asked a friend who had just been to England how he had managed the driving there. He assured me that it would take a little time to adjust to the English system, but soon I would get used to driving there.

In 1988, Mary and I spent two weeks driving in England, but I have never recovered from my constant fear of driving on the left side of the road from the wrong side of the car.

The plan was to take a ferry from Dover to Calais, about an hour's trip. The ferry boats seemed to me to be ocean liners which were designed to make the trip memorable and relaxing. Lounge chairs overlooking the water were in plenitude on the decks. The passenger could just relax and enjoy seeing the ferries going in the other direction toward Dover. For the more ambitious traveler, the ship provided numerous short time distractions such as restaurants, bars, game arcade, and gift shops.

But the ferry was not the only way of crossing the 30 miles of channel to Calais. I think a few have swum across. We skipped that.

Comparable to the ferry is the hovercraft, which is a boat that does not float on the water but hovers a foot or so above the water propelled by a downward and forward blast of air. The crossing on the hovercraft takes half an hour and seems similar to a short airplane flight. I had taken the hovercraft once before and the most memorable thing was getting on and off the craft.

That "once before" was in 1988 when Mary and I took the hovercraft from Dover to Calais. Neither of us enjoyed the ride. It took half an hour and it seemed we had just got settled in our seats when it was time to get off. We were on vacation and didn't want to be rushed.

On the positive side, Mary and I might have considered the bragging we could do when we got home. Some lying would have been necessary. We could brag about crossing the English Channel from Dover to Calais on the magnificent vessel called a hovercraft which saved us a half hour's time over using the dingy, slow moving ferry boat.

I don't recall if either of us did any bragging after we got home. But if we did brag, I'm sure we would have made clear that we would have much preferred a one hour cruise on a delightful ferry boat.

Within the last several years another method of crossing the English Channel has been developed – a tunnel under the channel water from Dover to Calais. I think it is restricted to use only for railroad trains. To me a most interesting element of the underwater tunnel is its name— "the chunnel". The English, with their dexterity with the English language, saw the relationship between the English Channel and the undersea tunnel and came up with chunnel, the perfect word for what it is. (I hope that, after the foregoing explanation, some curious investigator will not discover that the word, chunnel, was invented by some person from a faraway place such as Timbuktu— in Mali).

Even if I have the derivation of the word "chunnel" wrong, I still believe that the English people happily have produced some of the best writing in their English language.

This is proven by a man from Stratford upon Avon named Shakespeare who between 1564 and 1616 did some writing.

My most memorable impression of Dover occurred after we had boarded the ferry and pulled a mile or so offshore. At first glance the rightly famous white cliffs of Dover seem to thrust skyward out of the water. In places the cliffs show some yellow or brown. A second look shows that the cliffs are not in the water, but that the town is located on the land between the cliffs and the water. In the water, next to the shoreline, are endless lines of ships, from ocean ferry boats to single engine sports ships. But to me, a visitor, when I think of Dover, I recall the compelling white cliffs.

Willy

"Fuckin' bloody 'ell! Alright, then!"

Chris and I fumbling with hotel room key. A pint-sized bit of local color comes wheeling round the corner declaring oaths.

"Scared the piss outta me, mate."
"Ah, sorry, man. Just checking in here."
"Yeah, alright then."

There would be more with this amusing character later, and pints would be had, of that you can be sure.

Exiting the train at Dover Priory, a small old-timey station of the sort you see in old British films from the '40's. Not very cosmopolitan. Scouting up and down the platform, and here's Daddy and Sean. And it's on again. Much hauling of gluteus maximi to the ferry port terminal for to cross the water to Calais.

Exhaustion sets in as staff are consulted, phones dialed, and French operators are largely unhelpful. Je ne comprends pas. You see, we have a boat to catch and lodgings booked and we are big men from America and we are frightfully tired from travel, so if you could find it in your heart to assist us in embarking on one of those fine big boats I see down there, scoot across that 'lil olde stream, hop in a car so we can drive around for a few more hours— that would be just swell. Merci.

No one home at Hertz Rental. Dashed extraordinary manner of conducting business, what! Time running out for the last boat. More telephoning. Sean hard on the case. No one can get the phone codes right. Why not? It's just over there... I try my hand and request assistance from the friendly

Brit terminal staff.

"I'm very sorry to bother, but my telephoning abilities seem to be wanting just now, ha ha. Might I encroach on your good offices to phone Hertz Rental, the B&B in Dives-sur-Mer, or whomever this phone number represents?" Sweet natured Brit girl attempts contact, fails, attempts again, fails again.

"Hmmm... Odd. They won't answer their phone. Sorry, sir."

We sprawl over chairs and sofas in a big circle, luggage strewn. Considering comestibles, potable libations and a jolly good nap.

All present: "This is nonsense."

All present concur: "Quite."

CD and I out the door, up the street, look for lodging.

"Looky what I gots."

"Ah, now there's your man every time."

A silver flask of Russia's finest is produced from me backpack, tobacco ignited and locals accosted for info. Lodging and respite, thanks. Much good humor and fellowship with these open and friendly denizens. Good crack for sure. A brief history of one chap's life here in Dover, a rundown of all the coastal hotels for a couple miles and a solid recommendation for the County Hotel. It's "cheers, mate," and I regret not offering him a wee nip, though I reckon he'd already had sufficient.

We check out the digs, approve, say we'll be right back with two more and it's off to the ferry joint for to fetch Daddy and' Sean, who seems to be snoozing. Very sensible activity, that.

We tramp up the main coastal road, luggage in tow, Daddy limping a bit but game, the rest of us not doing so hot either.

Check in at County H, rooms assigned, doors opened, bowels moved, asses planted. Daddy and Sean downstairs, Chris and I up. Smoking allowed. Oh the civility!

Getting dark now, surely the cocktail hour is at hand.

Chris, Sean and Daddy repair to the hotel bar, I up the street in search of further libation. For a rainy day. Of which there must be quite a few of in this quiet quaint port town. Here's the off-sale. Some of this and a bit of that. Pakistani clerk helps me with my money, we have a good laugh. Pounds Sterling, dontcha know. Back down the street with me brown paper bag. Feels natural, this town. I could live here.

Back at the hotel, up to the third floor, deposit the rations, do the needful, and back down to the bar in a jiffy. A jiffy I tells you.

Daddy holding forth at the bar flanked by Sean and Chris. And who's this? Why, it's Richard Hughes from Essex, first encountered vulgarly proclaiming his fright at the sight earlier that night of two men of might from America trying to gain entrance to their newly rented and modestly appointed room.

"Say hey! I know you! How are ya, man?"

"Oy, mate!"

Drinks ordered, gin & tonic for the Old Boy, Guinness for the lads. The crack is general. Daddy regales with war stories. He was here. 63 years ago. To cross that very water there outside the window. In defense of this cheery island nation. And human decency everywhere.

Sadly, Hughes hasn't heard of the Battle of the Bulge, never mind the Huertgen Forest. This 30-ish Scots-Irish bantam. A former fighter, now training kids in a youth boxing program. Seated at a table with his uncle, bearded and ruddy cheeked, jovial and eyes twinkling from his lager. Hughes, shaved head and emphatic, pontificating on the greatness of Muhammed Ali in the ring and out— oh aye!— maintains Ali in his prime would crucify Iron Mike Tyson in his— a source of contentions various and voluble.

Our man's a southpaw.

"Yeah me too," say I.

"Yeah? I'll go a round or two with ya, yank!"

"Jeez guy– didn't know it was that kinda party!"

Laughter, another round of the brown, slam 'em down

and it's out on the town. Saying our cheerful goodbyes.

Daddy: "I was called back for the Korean War, too."

Hughes: "That's it. No more wars for you, mate."

Sauntering up the street Looking for a bite to eat. We happy few! We band of tipsily squiffy brothers. And our king. Aimlessly ambling, peeking in shop windows, immensely pleased with ourselves. Goodish greetings to all in the town square.

"What's good, mate?"

"This is good. Right here."

Young chap and his girl, sitting at a table outside a pub. This agreeable October evening.

We tip on in. The joint is jumping. Small bandstand but no band yet. Uptempo Irish music plays from the jukebox. Long bar of polished wood and elegant paneling on walls to match. And there's Hughes and his uncle, with a table full of friends.

"Christ, can't get away from you lot!"

"Ha ha, great minds, and all that."

We find a table, more drinks, and yes please, the fish and chips I think. So nice here. I'll just stay and stay. Uproarious laughter from a large table of Canadians. Much good-natured ribbing when I can't find the latrine.

"Hey yank! Little lost there? Ya need some help in there too?"

"I knew Americans were dumb but jeez– c'mon!"

Back to our rooms, the first sleep in 24 hours. Aye, a grand evening.

Early next morning. Up and at 'em. But first a bit of this. Mixed with orange barley water. From the Pakistani grocer. Nasty stuff. No wonder Jane and Michael Banks in 'Mary Poppins' didn't want their nanny smelling of it. Open wide my window. Cool air with a bit of the chill. Smell of exhaust and diesel. The huge port's at full throttle. Less than a mile away. The Channel. CD doing Tai Chi. I reclining in window sill. Watch the big trucks roll on below. Breakfast at nine.

All gathered in the large dining room. Stout, pretty Greek girl serves us eggs and rashers, beans and fried tomatoes, toast, tea and coffee – comforting hot, blandish English fare but sure we devour the lot.

And now it's time to catch our boat. A quick cab to the terminal, a shuttle bus to the port, and now we shall go across the water. Europe. Land of big armies and bigger wars. Once upon a time. We too come for war, in a way. Daddy's memories of it compel us. We will cross this water not for carnage and slaughter, but to bear witness to those places at which this old man, once young, nearly gave the last full measure. And surviving that inferno. A bride. Daughters three born to him. Yes, and five sons too. And here some are now. Ready to cross over. To places where memory and legends told become utterly real. For us. Our father's sons.

So it's goodbye white cliffs of Dover, hello old Calais.
We are Big Men From America–
we comes not to harm,
but merely to charm.

CD

11 Oct 8 AM

Awake to gray high Dover day.
Sit soft on sill, watch out window.
Major trucking motorway.
Beaucoup trucks and traffic below.
Stiff-boned, better-do-it, yoga.
Daddy and Sean not yet moving.
Willy and I up'n' at'em.
We pause together to ponder:
What do the English consider breakfast to be?

The proper English breakfast with bacon and sausage and tomato and egg and toast with biscuit and yogurt and orange juice and coffee, and a friendly pretty pregnant girl joking and being, well, just plain chummy and English. Daddy finds beans and tomato funny to break the fast. I gently tease him just a taste. All of us content and clubby, rested and raring to go.

Check out of the County Hotel.
Sit on valise on cobble in sun out front.
Pace the pavement, wait for taxi.

And then All Holy Hell breaks loose – We're about to be killed right now! Now, my mind knows of the odd English driving orientation, but the initial visceral onslaught sure puts a mitt on my mug. Standard American stuff, I suppose.

Laugh it off and look out the window.

Dover, Dover – Busting industry and cutesy touring conjoin. The little wending, winding cobblestone streets with bars and shops; the people oh, so friendly as to caricature. Then the harbor. There are giant cranes. The big boats blast their big boat horns. Sounds something evocative, but I don't know of what.

Hustle bustle. Colorful Euro tourist bus. Grab hard and sway with tight Euro turns. Lug the luggage. Stand in (or is it on?) line. Customs. Stamp the passport.

There's a stylish youngish woman traveling alone with briefcase in conservative, but well-cut, but sexy tight business suit and skirt. She's confident, haughty even,self contained. I take her to be French. I try not to stare.

We're havin' some fun now.
We board the boat.
We're havin' some fun now.

Aboard we cache our stash
And huddle and lounge about.
Tentatively trot out the fractured French.
Buy the drink and somehow manage.
The wind whistles wildly on deck.
Pull down cap, pull up collar.
Men of the world you see we be.
We're in the movies now.

Plenty of shipping on English Channel.
Beautiful day to break your heart.
Plenty of sun, like a shiny penny.
Smooth sailing (as they say).
Lots and lots and lots of shipping.
You almost need a traffic cop.
The storied crossing of the English Channel
Which I've always wanted to do.

We all take turns on deck photographing one another, leaning on the rail and practice posing against the blue-green-gray of the sea. The wind is brisk. There are high spirits and much whooping fun, but it feels good to retreat below decks, out of the seeming gail (which, of course, we know it really isn't).

Anticipation and expectation –
Like little chump children we be.
Happiness – the operant mode.
With each and each, and each other.
With the world at large and for ever.
With our own bad selves, it would seem.
And me? Et moi?
I don't really know what this means.

Make Calais. Lug the luggage. Stand on line (or is it now in?). The customary customs. Lounge around, cluster about, lounge around some more. Got to get the rental car, which to find and procure proves a tricky enterprise, but Daddy's perseverance and Sean's cleverness carry the day.

Someone's got to do it, don't they?

The Bad Bad Beemer.

The bags, of course, won't fit. We cram 'em tight and fold ourselves achingly in, as into a tiny tin. But we're on a roll. On the road to Melange. (And mightn't it be just that).

Sean at the wheel; thank God not me. Daddy says he'll drive a bit but we won't let him. Willy doesn't drive; he won't. I will probably be shamed to take my turn, and this I fear. I'll certainly get lost and likely kill somebody, probably us.

But Sean at the wheel; and thank God, not me!

Doin' well and feelin' fine,
Feelin' feelin' very fine.
Standin' tall and lookin' good,
Shoulda been in Hollywood.

God's Very Own Beautiful Day.

Rollin' rollin'.

Call me jelly; I'm on a roll!

A16 to Albertville. Through flat farmland into rolling hills, then to craggy cragginess.

Get lost and double back. Get lost and double back. Toll booths – throw euros in the basket, just like dollars through Chicago.

Make our way at length into a little town. It's the off-season now, mind you. No one there. A few straggling bright shining lights remain.

Caught on a game board, don't know the rules, rushing round and round again and again, sometimes backwards, never knowing when the stop or where the end; and fighting not to get angry, not to go mad, not to be killed; but sometimes OK anyhow anyway.

The twisting, winding, wending streets.

So where the hell we go?

Drive and drive and drive. Sean pushin' the wheel pretty hard.

Drive around. Roundy round.

Into the roundabout like Boston.

Double back. Switch back.

Faint tense and tired and tuckered now. And maybe more than faintly.

Find a little restaurant. Young guy there. My brother's attempt at French scares him. Defers to his sister – sweet little blonde girl, maybe seventeen. She has no English. I have the French I have. Find a phone to call but once again we lack the card. Only l'argent, no carte.

Drivin' drivin', once again.

Roundabout and roundy-roun.
Push hard on the stick.
Burn the rubber, smoke the clutch.
When I was young I liked this stuff.

Find another restaurant. Nobody in there, just and merely one guy, un gars. Oh joy! Joke the dude. Could use a drink, the bite o' buzz. Buy some wine, toss out Euros. Tip big. But against the local Value Added Custom.

Daddy not drink his, Sean just a swallow, so I drain 'em. My man and I laugh. He speaks no English. I can talk some shit but not much – It only smears so far. We manage though to get it done – whatever that might prove to be. He loans me his phone. I call the number. Get female anglophile French with the Bon Anglais.

We get the address.
We get an address.
So on we are and out and off.

But soon and now we lose ourselves again.
Driving driving driving.
Faster faster faster.
Quick lights flash like a lance through glass
And bounce off brick road to blind.
Sean downshifts, Grand Prix right on red.
Wham wham wham, what happens?
La Gendarmerie.
Cops!

Guy cuts around the corner, no flashing lights, no horn, no noise, no nothing. Pulls out a little card and holds it out his window in front of us at the intersection. We get the point, pull over, get out the car. But cool we be; been through this before. Though don't know that Daddy has.

Backup arrives. Three cars, five cops. Just us there, old man in the back. Brace. Amateur frisk. Some kind of jive. There is the problem of language. What we do? Why it is?

“Traffic jam, traffic jam,"say one.

"Traffic jam," say another.

“Je ne comprends pas,” say I.

Maybe mean the semaphore. I lose a knife. Brother lose a knife. There is the matter of the illegality, I think. Be bit bold – ask direction. Not so bold – don't challenge loss of blade. I fear for what might be done to Daddy, not so much to us – we three louts. They give us a break, I guess: neither ticket nor jail nor club us. But they didn't help much either. Though they didn't bother Daddy. I been rougher rousted before. And what a lucky thing that it was I, not Sean, who drank up all the drinks.

But God save Daddy.

Then on the road again.

Driving driving, taste of touring.

Roundy-roun cobblestone.

Picturesque but pain in the ass.

Back to edge of town.

Back to edge of darkness.

It's late and after hours but seems fairly early still. The Faltering French with The Local Citizens. Just cain't get there. Back to city center. So, find a phone. After-hours phone. Well, the phones all need cards. We have none. Got a pocket full o’ euros:

Undone 'n' Un-fun.

And OK, we finally find the place – a series of quaint huts within a complex, all numbered. We somehow have a number but we can't find ours. Dismount. Scatter in the unfathomable night to hunt. Daddy holds his ground, which is to say – he slumps and sleeps. You know what comes next: Minor Adventure. I search and walk here and there in the dark. Cannot find the flop but do run up on a gaggle of goofing gals. I don't normally approach young girls on the street – Don't want to scare 'em. Help me out – They speak no English; I speak slightFrench; they twitter and giggle a lot. Some fine fillies, I will say. I play the gentleman; they sneaky uproarious laugh, give each other looks and make bigeyes. They think the whole thing funny and a game. I think that too. But I be desperate. But they don't know. I try to act right and so what.

Walk around, dick around. Fifteen minutes later I find the right spot. Hi ho! Now I don't know how I'm going to get back to the car. So I'm walking lost again again. Now I hear a voice. Find the guys. Get on back. Here we are!

But oh my God, we can't get in.

The rigmarole:

You got the place – we found by chance.

You got the number – we stumbled into.

You got the code – somehow we broke it.

And now you need the key – but we cain't find it.

It's like a Sherlock Holmes thing –

The key is hidden somewhere here:

Motion and commotion,

More bursting and busting about.

More phone. But this one works. Punch the code, enter like a burglar, steal admittance. Take a right. Look left. It's in the brown cupboard. Look down. In the drawer. And there's a brown envelope. That's us.

The Holmesian play, as I say.

But we get on in. The Fellas hunger for the food but I gotta have some action. Off they drive again to hunt for vittles. I'm down for the kung fu fun and the quick and copious laying on of the drink.

So much mandatory sitting
Makes me moan to move.
Enforced grim taut nervous tension
Force need the strong spirit.

Now I'm writing and thinking and drinking, and then the squad is back, and they got us sumpin' to eat. And what? (here in France) but burgers and fries to go!

Chow down. Out for a smoke. Hushed, still, prodigious night of darkness. Willy and I chat quietly, fraternally.

The little adventure. Now ensconced. Tomorrow? The plan is to check Daddy's Places. The signal Locations. Look forward of course to that. Hope for no hard feelings from the hard pressed back and forth of today's long day.

Only one thing wrong – I lost my pocket knife, illegal though it might be. Belonged to my dead brother, Nick. That's what I get for being scofflaw, I suppose. But, do you know? Now I'm pissed off. Fuck them too. Although they gave us a bit of a break of sorts – no arrest, no ticket, and didn't bother Daddy; they could have simply and saintly saved and spared us the whole Megillah. No?

So, what's to be up?
We say we will see.
Be up early.
We'll give 'em a flight or the fight.

Daddy

Chapter Three

Thursday, October 11, 2007
Dover, Calais and Dives-sur-Mer

We took the ferry from Dover to Calais after a big English breakfast at the hotel, including toast, orange juice, coffee, corn flakes, bacon and eggs (sounds American).

After much delay (I can't recall why) we got our car from Hertz in Calais and left with Sean driving.

Since this was our first day in a car, we forgot to take the precaution before leaving Calais of emptying our bladders.

I wish I could say that all four of us (Chris, Sean, Willy, and Father) asked for a bathroom stop at the same time. But since the boys will be reading this, I must admit that after an hour or two of driving, the father was the first to raise his hand.

We happened to be on a narrow country road (one lane in each direction). Sean pulled off onto the shoulder of the lightly traveled road. We all got out to use the facilities, which were the two roadside ditches. I walked across the road to the opposite ditch which had more shrubbery giving added privacy. I can almost hear the chuckling of some military veteran when he reads that I, having four and a half years of army active service, had not adopted the practice of men in the military of no longer seeking privacy or showing modesty while urinating. I think my thinking (if any) on the topic of modesty is, "When in Rome, do as the Romans do."

The ditch was about six feet deep with bushes and a few inches of water at the bottom. The down-grade was steep. I started to take a step and began to slide down on the grass. So I dropped my right shoulder to the ground and lay on my right side.

I called to Chris who was nearby on the road. He called Willy who jumped down into the water and pushed me up.

Chris grabbed my left arm and pulled. I was up and O.K. in no time.

Willy especially must be given credit for his immediate and selfless action. Without hesitation he leaped down into the deep ditch, not knowing whether or not the water was six inches or six feet deep. Although he was not injured, he spent the rest of the day traveling with water and mud soaked shoes, socks, pants and underwear. If Willy had been in the army when he performed his rescue mission, he might well have been awarded the Soldier's Medal.

Sean, who had been busy using the facilities on the other side of the road, heard the commotion, came across as I was reaching my feet, and asked with concern, "What happened?"

We arrived at Dives-sur-Mer (not far from Omaha Beach) at about 8 p.m. While driving through the dark streets, we were stopped by the police in a squad car. I'm not sure why, but I think it was for a minor traffic offense such as making a right turn (after a stop) on a red light— a lawful turn back in the U.S.

The boys got out of the car. I stayed in my place next to the driver's seat. Two more squad cars joined the mix. The police talked at length to each of the boys. Although the gendarmes shone a flashlight in my direction, they did not question me. They took and kept the pocket knives that Chris and Sean had with them. No tickets were issued, and after 10 or 15 minutes we were back on our way.

The police incident has led me to invent and to tell this fictional story, the story of the infamous four-member "Devitt Gang" which had received nationwide notoriety back in the U.S.A.

The leader of the gang was an older fellow called Big Bill Devitt who was known for his craftiness in dealing with the law. In his numerous run-ins he always found the best lawyer in town to get him off the charge. There was even talk that years ago he had spent a few weeks in law school until he was expelled for copying the answer to test questions from a fellow classmate.

The other three were said to be brothers, CD, Speed, and Soup Crust. They didn't seem to have a last name, but there was speculation that Big Bill was their father.

CD was the oldest of the three. He was the language expert of the gang. Knowing French and German while in Europe could be very useful while the gang was there pursuing its usual less than respectable transactions. The story goes that while still in high school, his family sent him to Germany one summer to get him out of the house.

In the middle was Speed who had an aptitude for driving, especially fast driving. He saved the gang's neck numerous times in avoiding the law by virtue of his driving skills. There are also hints that on occasions, while being pursued by the cops, he found it necessary to exceed the speed limit. Undoubtedly Speed would argue that there is no irrefutable evidence of his speeding— namely that he never received a speeding ticket. An answer might be that he never got a ticket because the police were never able to catch him.

Speed, when not driving a car, spent his time reading. He seemed to like history. If a passenger happened to mention a name such as Jackson, he might have been welcomed by Speed with 50 miles of discussion of Thomas "Stonewall" Jackson, the famed Civil War general, and Andrew Jackson, the seventh president of the United States. Included might have been details that would have put most listeners to sleep, such as analysis of the names of the Jackson's great grandmothers.

Napoleon Bonaparte said that an army travels on its stomach. Napoleon must have known Soup Crust. He happened to procure his name because of his dexterity as a cook. Some of his beneficiaries called him "Soup" as in "tomato." Others knew him as "Crust" as in "bread." Time produced "Soup Crust" — not his favorite name.

Although not peculiar to gangs, men like and need to eat. And Soup Crust was the experienced cook of the gang. Considering the frequent irregular hours they kept, first-class cooking was often an indispensable skill necessary for the gang's successful if uncommendable endeavors.

Cooking was just a sideline for Soup Crust. As a steady reader, he had an interest in numerous topics, one of which was war. If someone was talking with him and uttered the word "war," followed shortly by "Napoleon" or "Waterloo," Soup Crust would have treated the listener to somewhat more than a brief discussion of the 1815 Battle of Waterloo. The British, under Wellington, and the Prussians under Blucher, defeated Napoleon and his French army. Surely Soup Crust would have enlightened the listener with names of generals, the tactics of both Napoleon and Wellington, the importance of the battle, and why and how it was fought.

The listener, if he was short of time, might have become more cautious in choosing another topic for discussion.

Regrettably nothing further is known of the Devitt Gang. End of story.

Sean wanted to call the hotel from which we were to rent the rooms, but we couldn't find a phone booth. After two hours of looking, Sean found someone who had a phone. He called the hotel which was actually a kind of condominium which rented apartments of owners who were not occupying them. The call was answered with a voice message addressed to Sean, who booked the apartment, telling him where the key to the apartment was hidden. Sean and Chris found the key, but it was not near the apartment. Each apartment had its separate entrance to a street with a barely discernible address in the dark. How does one find in a black night a single apartment out of hundreds? I don't know, but the boys found the apartment and we moved in.

We had not had dinner, so Sean and I went searching for a restaurant, which sold us pizza and soda pop. We ate, brought back food to Chris and Willy, and went to bed.

I would not have been surprised if Chris and Willy, after consuming their pop and pizza, had voiced their dissatisfaction with such an ordinary American-like meal in a French countryside filled with memorable carefully prepared and tastefully delicious dinners.

Willy

Aboard the big boat. Out on deck. White cliffs slowly recede. How many down the ages witnessed this same and wondered what lay ahead. The Hundred Years War. Bonaparte. Ye noble English. Ferocious Scots and steady Welsh, my courageous Irish forefathers too. The War to End All Wars. Twenty one years later so much worse. American soldiers, sailors, Marines and fliers. Many their first voyage over the ocean. Many their last. To die in foreign fields. The mud and squalor of Flanders. Hedgerows of Normandy and the thick pine forests of the Ardennes and Huertgenwald. Crossed this water.

Come see.

Sit in the lounge with Daddy, chatting about his memories of crossing this English Channel. And now again. Me with my little tape recorder. I listen and take it in.

Now approach the bar. A drink, I think. Been practicing me French.

"Bonjour. Parlez vous Anglais?"

The barman stares.

"Oui."

Splendid. And what now? I would like a drink, thanks.

"Je voudrais...uhm...la boisson, s'il vous plaît. I think."

More staring. Will he speak? Will it be English? Or Greek to me and my fluent gibberish.

I suppress the urge to sneeze.

"erm...pardon, monsieur."

I walk away. Lacking drink. The Channel calm this day, balmy yet lively sea breeze blows back the hair and invigorates the senses. Alas, I'm a sailor! Ha!

Pull into port. Do the customary Customs dance. To the terminal in search of telephone, Sean trying to contact the rental car person. Who is not here. At the Hertz Rental counter. In fact it's closed and locked. For business.

A woman finally shows. Business transacted. The woman corrects Daddy on his pronunciation of Caen. Sean finds her distasteful and I find her lazy. Not being at her post during business hours. So we can give her a bunch of money.

A motorcar. Black BMW. Tiny. Will it seat four big men from America? Barely.

Sean deft at the wheel, the rest of us to navigate. As best we are able. Maps many. Signs too. In French. As this be France. Onwards always. We are looking for a place called Dives-sur-Mer. Where have they put it? Let's see.

We drive and look at maps. Daddy riding shotgun, Chris and I in the back hard on the maps. It is soon revealed that we must needs phone the proprietor of our booked-in-advance lodgings to say we are indeed arriving, as said proprietor will not be there to meet us. This seems to be a common way of conducting business. In these parts.

We lack the au current cellular telephone, as ours from back home will not function overseas. Telephoning in France seems a tad difficult. So we drive. And observe. Many things. Signs. Roundabout traffic emplacements, which have oh so many more signs for us to look at. And maps. Always maps.

It grows dark. These medieval towns. Where we are. And where?

Stop-signs set back from the intersection a good 15 feet. Visibility limited. As is our comprehension of nearly anything.

We run a stop-sign. Ooops. We do it again. Sorry about that.

By now thoroughly confused and slightly annoyed. Just stop here at this lil' bar. No other patrons inside. The barman reserved but sympathetic. No phone– imagine that. But Chris allowed the use of his cell phone. Speaking the French while few here speak the English. Ah, merci, merci. Some information gleaned, maybe of the useful sort. And now a drink, a toast. To luck! God granting. Stella Artois in large goblets and wine for Daddy. Could we just sit for a bit. Say for three hours? Regain one's composure, bearings, courage.

Sean fortuitously gives his drink to Chris after a swig or two. "I gotta drive, man."

It's "bonsoir" and "merci" and back into the night. And soon we are again. Lost.

Streets deserted. Suddenly a car. Right in front of us. Middle of an intersection. Oh, the nice man wishes to assist us. Has something for us. A badge. La gendarmerie. Pull over.

Scrawny chap with scruffy goatee and ill-fitting black battle-dress. I resist the urge to laugh. Aggressively addressing Sean in French.

Sean: "Bonsoir, monsieur l'agent. Americans... good-guys... lost... Je ne parle pas Francais..."

Policeman: "le Blah blah blah."

Policeman walks back to his little unmarked squad. Soon two more little cars arrive, these looking more like proper police vehicles.

Four more cops. Shoulder patches say National Police. Torches in windows, Sean out first. Hands on the hood, the whole bit.

Many consider the French language to be quite beautiful. Always sounded slightly insolent to me.

I'm next, along with Chris. Daddy, the eldest of these big men from America, allowed to sit.

One cop with hand on holstered weapon. Visibly nervous, these blokes. Chris explaining – "we are lost"– and cops chatter on excitedly. A big deal for Dives-sur-Mer law enforcement, this, no doubt. Amateurish frisk, very poor tactical positioning of these black-clad constables.

Shaved heads. .40 or. 45 caliber service autos on belts. Dude to my left, not paying attention. No defensive posture.

Holstered pistol three inches from my hand. What'd they teach these chumps at the Academy? Could have been in deep shit. If we were really mean guys. Which we ain't.

They take a couple pocket knives but don't give us a ticket. Can't help us find our hotel – even though, as it turns out, it's just a mile or so away. Not bad sorts, I reckon. Not very impressive policemen either. Or tourist guides.

We find the place. Maybe.

Out walking around in the dark, trying to find an entrance, a mailbox, a key.

A telephone miraculously found, communication achieved. Equally miraculously.

The riddle solved. Sherlock Holmes had nothin' on us.

We stow our bags and argue about rooms, and Sean and Daddy set out to find food.

CD and yours take a drink. Or nine. Too exhausted for any more action. This night.

Food is discovered, and burgers and fries are kindly brought, gratefully consumed, and it's lights out.

To do it all over again tomorrow.

CD

Dives-sur-Mer, 'bout 9:10 in the AM 12 Oct

All up, scuffling, shaving.
Daddy with a song in his heart.
Quaint and quiet like long gone time.
The seaweed smelling seaside town.
Grey and foggy in monochrome frame.
Seabirds screaming their presence known.
Espy the harbor and the lonely unattended boats
Waiting for Godot.

Salutation To The Sun and rubber stretch-band play. Daddy talks of going out to breakfast. Sean and Daddy then off to take care of business, whatever that might mean. Willy seems a bit subdued. But I'm up and brisk, and so's the air. Think I'll take a walk. Grab the fleece and go. Dogs bark.

Walk down to the small boat harbor.
The off season quiet and ghostly still,
But bits of stagy activity stir.
Small craft now brave out to sea.
Gulls cry, (are they in pain?),
Couple solitary walkers.
"Port Guillaume" I spy on an official looking building.
A boat sails past with dignity.

Back to the little bungalow. No more sleep; the cleaning crew comes. Russian, I think. So grab our grip, load the car and go. Sean drives, Daddy shotgun, Willy and I to the rear. Which we falteringly share with what surely must be excessive baggage – suitcase tightly wedged between us and various crap on our laps. We won't move much.

Drive.

To and into Cabourg on the coast at the mouth of the Dives river. Drive around and wander around and look for breakfast, coffee, sit-down. Find none of those. Little shop with quiche – exquisite smell and "bonne journée." Eat that in the car – American style. God help us!

Now our maps are somehow insufficient but we luckily find another, which may or maynot guide us. We, Willy and I, pass a magnifying glass back and forth. And off we go to look for the Normandy beaches.

Wend our way down the coastal highway, except the coastal highway is not always on the coast. It's often offset and sometimes we don't see the sea. But then, round a curve, and it jumps back into view to shock and awe with its power and splendor.

"How ya doin', Daddy?"

Roundy-rounds aplenty. Crane the neck, watch the signs. Through small towns, they happen fast, then back on highway.

Daddy starts to have foot problems, the bad circulation. We stop a couple times so he can walk and move.

Juno Beach. There are children playing. Daddy walks up to people and talks – joyful and jolly, somewhat in his element.

It's grey. There are gulls. There are the tourists. Daddy chats with some women, tells them of Minnesota, and laughs. The Great Lakes, local interest and whatnot.

There are signs indicating we know not what. Something official and wordy and beyond my meager French. Perhaps that we ought not proceed further. Is there still unexploded ordnance that remains? There is a concrete edifice that looks to be the remains of a gun emplacement.

The children fall silent, grow quiet.

Now bated breath serene.

We martial and break for the next beach,

Our next battle.

We drive inexorably on.

Stop in tiny provincial town. There's an old church. Its steeple stabs into the sea-blue sky. Daddy and I go in. Daddy signs the book. I bend a knee. Just he and I, we together. But maybe Mama's here too.

The precious prayer in concert together

For which all living would die together.

Is it that this moment is noble but for signal past failure, for lack of down paid attention and soul? Or is there something true and luminous here in this close, doubting, miraculous Catholic dim?

We're on the road again.

Omaha Beach Memorial. There's the imposing cemetery/visitor center. How to say? – Decorous, majestic, august, solemn as a funeral church. Daddy looks for a friend of a friend who is involved in the running of the operation, and it has been(I hope and think) arranged afore with whom to meet.

Quiet, cool, gray, peaceful.

How many men lost life here?

How many men carry that day with them?

This a big day for Daddy. Hope we can support him well.

The people are quiet, composed, dignified. I am insignificant, a fake. Though the people are present, there is a solitude. Even the birds are still.

Alas, a bit of confusion unfortunate: Daddy into the visitor's center to meet the someone who knows a someone who knows somebody else. We all stand round and wait. But he doesn't reappear. Daddy is lost. Or maybe we. Willy searches at the beach. Sean somewhere. I waiting. Sean back. Willy back. Somewhere else. Daddy still long and gone.

At length walk into the visitor's center. No Daddy. It is thought that he's gone on. So we walk out, listen to the beach, look at a guide's presentation, take some pictures.

Alas, Daddy shows up somewhat saddened. He thought we'd gone on without him. We have been saddened; thought Daddy had gone on without us.

Unfortunate. Hope the blood's not too bad.

Stout hearts. We press on.

We be driving driving driving.
Stone cold cry hallucinating.
It's cutting cold and I'm disoriented, addled and baffled.
The fingertips lose feeling, tongue tingle;
Undies in a bunch, socks slack in bundle.
Like Brother Pig in Orwell's Animal Farm:
Must try harder.

And on to the next point of interest: Pointe du Hoc, site of the celebrated Ranger attack. And how did those mere men, of so recent late of merely peace-time civilian sweet insouciant boyhood, so abruptly scale the precipitous craggy heights and rush dug-in and fortified enemy positions in fucking face of withering pre-sited rifle and machine-gun fire, and emplaced Goddamned artillery hell and ever tumbling exploding grenades; with failing grapnels, falling earth, bodies and hamburger body parts of buddies bodies crashing on your head, in your face, about your spirit and soul, and to your sudden pornographic dirty death, and no one will ever even know your bitter name?

The jaded bold spirits some higher now.
Inquire after une magasin de spiritueux.
We grand and great the drinkin' men,
We like some ‘at to drink.
So good to get our good drink on.
We who are about to die salute you.
Salud!
You see.
We'll see.

For to walk among the old craters and gun emplacement ruins. Willy boldly climbs down into what must be a shell hole. And it's a long way down.

Accosted by a party of oldsters (not so ancient as Daddy but surpassing my meager callow years). Daddy telling stories and stories. Photo op. They want to take our picture and do. Chat amiably for a while on this hallowed ground. And they hale from California. Imagine that! A jolly time. Is that what this is all about?

Great good luck au supermarché. Get some vodka, get some vitals.

Daddy with the trouble with the feet. We roll inexorably on and now we're lost. We're in the soup now.

Drive the coast road back to the digs.
French road rolls away from the sea,
Then through fine towns with poor markings.
Endless startling wheel-abouts.
Oh, we have a tough time.
But do we weakly really?

Driving, driving; whirly gigs.
Brute blinking, searching for a sign.
On and on.
The maps and magnifying glass.
And on and on.
Now forage for the French café.
Sandwiched together, squished and squinched,
Jam up and jelly tight.
Come on, come on!
Allons, allons!
And on and on and on and on.

Finally call a halt. Park on the sidewalk as they do. Jump out. Fall down. No feeling in the legs which just won't hold. Willy pries himself out and staggers about. Sean helps Daddy with the foot difficulties – to free himself and stand.

The inviting French café. Cosy lights now gleam against the gloam and gloom. They all go in but me. Daddy, Sean and Willy sniff about for something to eat.

But I just can't do it.
I've had enough.
I've had enough of crowds,
I've had enough of cars,
I've had enough of maps,
And much too much too much mental,
And signs that I just can't quite see.

Pursue the walk.
Stretch the legs.
Expand the lungs.
Focus the eyes.
Search the soul.
Get yourself together.

Pull down the hat, turn up the collar against the crepuscular cool.

I don't feel well;

I won't be good.

They meet me in an hour, they say. Then back to somewhere where I can stretch and drink and eat something stark and simple and then sleep. And then, Good Lord, do it all again tomorrow once again.

So walk and walk and walk some more.
Swing shoulders, hips, and life itself.
Cross-eyed, half-cocked I go.
Find a cross street, dark, to sneak.
Tap tap tap, my stick.
A couple overtakes me of a sudden.
Oh, my own misanthropic God,
I'm sick and tired of populace.
And maybe even everything.

Pedestrian feet crunch crackly leaves.
I want to make, I would, make no noise.
Hope not to get lost,
To forlorn lose myself.
No no, not lost;
Not me, myself, not I.

Alone again. Dark. But hard street lamp. Hard shadow. Hard life. But it is as it should be. No? Didn't I ask for it, request it, invite it, agree to it, allow it?

Algid gelid cold. But could be worse or worser yet.

Avenue Clemenceau. Duck to avoid a tree.

And keep on ducking.

And ducking.

My leg is leaden.
My heart is too.
My eyes don't focus
And neither do I
And neither I do.

Walk, walk;
Tap, tap.
Grand Hotel perched high atop hill –
Elegant Fin de Siecle,
Bathed in luminous light.
Shadow people dine behind glass.

Take a left. Chance being lost. Cars parked Euro style, two wheels on sidewalk. Quiet here and crooked. Hear human noise, take another left. Dark side street, no left possible. Steep hill – descend. Silver euros clink in pocket as I walk.

High hedges, ornate wooden fence. Sidewalk shrinks to shoulder width. Car approaches from rear. Run away, run away, but where? No where to turn. Turn left. Upwards. Up to the Grand Hotel. Smoke. Keep on moving. Try a right.

Idle cars, construction on medieval building, scaffolding, old brick walls, more green plasticine hedges, brown and white Alpine-looking chalet.

Can I take the journey's hardship?
Oh, can I, will I, may I last?
Oh Pretty Goddy, please help me.
Give me strength of soul and snot.
Humiliate me not.

Sidewalk disintegrates. Turn right.
It's black – black like no tomorrow.
Hugh vanity-like lights – light the way to then.
Center square, deserted. Thank all form of Allah.
Am I lost yet? – Lost in this raging Vale of Tears.
Avenue De Valle. Circle 'round; the roads aren't straight.
Careful now. Careful.

More white fence staged on stone embankment.
Monumental buildings join together.
Hands chill and go numb.
Avenue Aristides Mourion. Go right. Hope to find your way.
Bearings lost, roll the hill.
Hope for hope; wish for wishes.
But I've always said and say: "I gave up hope years ago as a bad habit."

Whilst at that, assume another, brother.
Don't let the sun set on your ass.
Don't be eaten screaming alive.
Damaged legs still work (to degree).
Ace in the hole.
Hope against hope.
It's not a lowball game.

Terror strikes – I may be wrong.
You've done it now.
You've done it all along.
Can I find the car?
Can I find my core?

I was lost, Alleluia,

But now I'm found, Hallelujah.
There's the car, our own special rented voiture.
Now wait? (Internal chess.) Or walk some more?
To take a chance or play it safe?

Smoke'em if you got'em.
When will mine be back?
When will I get back?
When will mine be mine?

Daddy

Chapter Four
Friday, October 12, 2007
Dives-sur-Mer, Omaha Beach, American Cemetery and Pointe du Hoc

As I have said, prior to the trip I urged the boys to take notes each day as to what happened. My own note taking lasted two days. The following is the sum total of the truly sparse collection of my notes for the entire trip.

"October 12, Friday. We drove to Omaha Beach and Cemetery—Sean always driving. Time delays. Wrong turns. Roads not marked. Met Dan Neese, Supt. of the cemetery."

The plan was first to visit the cemetery itself, look down at the beach from the high ground, walk down to the beach (for those who wished to do so) and then drive westerly to Pointe du Hoc. I had no curiosity or desire to walk down to Omaha Beach.

I still remember quite clearly early August of 1944 and being deposited on the sandy beach courtesy of the US Navy. The fighting there had ended two months earlier (D-Day, June 6 1944). I, and everyone else, was lugging a full field pack – about 75 pounds. After 200 yards of soft, sandy beach came an abrupt change in the terrain. Out of the beach arose what seemed to be steep cliffs, with two or three pathways winding to the top.

I'd turned 21 on May 25, 1944 (old enough to vote) and made it to the top (near where the cemetery is now located) but only after much, much huffing and puffing. I remember wondering how the American boys in the first wave on Omaha Beach on D-Day made it to the top that morning. Most did not. My good and old friend (we were grade school, high school, and college classmates), Bob Hutch, was a section leader in the first wave on D-Day. A section was a landing craft of men – about 20. They were part of E

Company, 16th Infantry Regiment, 1st Infantry Division. Of the 183 men in E Company, 112 died (were killed) on D-Day. Most of the survivors were wounded. While on the beach that morning, a German mortar shell landed near Bob and the concussion knocked him out for a few seconds. Three days later he found a small piece of shrapnel in his leg.

In '07 I did not go down to the beach and back. The boys did. I'm 64 years older than I was in '44, and I've slowed down a bit. Even without a full field pack, I wouldn't have been able to walk back up to the high ground. Even if I were physically able to walk back up, my memories of Omaha Beach, those of August '44, but especially of D-Day, kept me off the beach.

The cemetery's parking lot is a block (100 yards) from the main entrance of a new building, a museum of artifacts covering World War II. We parked at the lot, and I walked ahead while the boys assembled the stuff (cameras, recorders, etc.) to bring on our walk. I stood outside the entrance while waiting for one of the boys to meet me. (There's some dispute about this. I don't think that any of the three boys remember this.) So, my recollection is that I told that nameless son that I was going inside to meet Dan Neese, the Superintendent of the American cemetery, a friend of Jim Begg.

Jim is president of the American Overseas Memorial Day Association, Belgium. It is a non-profit association formed to perpetuate the remembrance of American soldiers from World War I and World War II who lie buried in the American cemeteries throughout Europe. Jim discovered me through my book, "Shavetail," and we have known each other since 2005. Jim is an Edina, Minnesota boy whose career led him to Belgium and he ended up living in Brussels.

I intended to tell Neese that my three sons were waiting outside. I expected he would invite them in. I went into the building and after a short wait he came out of his office to greet me. Seeing a World War II veteran was apparently a big deal, and Neese and I talked for 10 or 15 minutes. He gave me a package of souvenirs which they give to us old geezers. He told me he'd like to meet my sons, so I went out the door I came in, but not one son was there. I looked around the entrance to no avail and then went through the front door and asked the four French uniformed attendants if any of them had seen the boys. Their English was no better than my French. My recollection is that someone (or more) indicated that my sons had not gone through the entrance to the museum, but rather had walked past the museum down a walkway toward the top of the high ground on which the cemetery is located overlooking, Omaha Beach itself. I went back into the museum and searched through both its floors. No boys.

I then hurried down the walkway which continues, probably for miles, with the rows of identical headstones of the grave sites on the left, and to the right the faraway sand beach with the English Channel even further out. The walkway is beautifully manicured with numerous trees, grassy knolls, and lovely gardens. Every few hundred yards the walkway widens to provide overlooks with benches and telescopes with which to see more clearly the landing beaches which, on June 6, 1944, gathered in the bodies of those dear young American boys who now lie buried above the beaches.

I continued walking westward along the walkway hoping to find the boys looking for me. I'd stop now and then to rest on one of the walkway benches. I had not anticipated such a rigorous outing. After about an hour of walking the walkway, made a 90 degree turn to the south (my left). I had come to a heavily wooded area which the walkway circled around. So I headed south and somewhat up a hill. The walking became quite tiring. I stopped and sat down and thought "What if the boys don't show up? Might I have somehow got by them? Perhaps I've gone too far."

I couldn't stop thinking and wondering how the boys and I could lose each other. I thought that I made it clear to the one who was with me outside the entrance to the museum, that he should wait there for me until I called him in after I met the superintendent. Since all three of them said they were not with me at the entrance and I can't recall which one it was, I began to wonder at the accuracy of my memory.

I kept hoping and thinking how I could find the boys. If I didn't find them near the first overlook, I told myself, as a last resort, I'd walk back to the car and wait there for them.

I was never angry over our mix-up, but surely I was befuddled (confused – per two dictionaries). I couldn't recall which son met me at the museum's entrance because no one was there. I was confused (befuddled).

It didn't take much self-persuading to decide to turn back. And I did. After an hour or so of retracing my steps, I came in sight of the first overlook on the pathway. It was crowded with people listening to a young man explaining the happenings on D-Day on Omaha Beach lying within the sight of the fascinated listeners. But still, no boys! If they weren't there, where could they be?

I walked slowly closer to the crowd. In the midst I noticed a hat which seemed familiar. Under the hat was a face I knew. It was Chris. And next to him was Willy. Sean showed up soon. He had been across the walkway exploring the cemetery. Knowing Sean (a voracious reader—much like his brothers and sisters) he probably knew, or at least thought he knew, as much about Omaha Beach as did the young man addressing the crowd.

How could the three boys and I manage to have completely lost ourselves? Despite the numerous claims and counterclaims of both sides of the discussion (the all-wise father and the three irresponsible sons) I have not yet been able to answer the question of the lost boys—how and why! The boys might make a correction and say the "lost father."

In 1988 Mary and I visited Omaha Beach by driving to the reconstructed German concrete gun emplacement overlooking the beach. The reconstruction included a parking lot as well as a path down to the beach and the beautifully furnished gift and snack shop. Mary, who knew antiques, brought home a handsome square ancient seashell taken from the waters of the nearby English Channel. Mary loved the place, as did I.

On the 2007 trip I resolved to visit there again. Sadly, after our visiting the American cemetery near Omaha Beach and the boys trudging down to the beach and back, we spent at least an hour trying, unsuccessfully, to find my charming spot.

A major disappointment.

Our final stop of the day was a cliff-like area lying west of and overlooking Omaha Beach called Pointe du Hoc. It was there, on D-Day, that a battalion of brave and skillful U.S. Army Rangers approached by boat in the English Channel facing a sheer stone cliff, at the top of which was the German fortified area, Pointe du Hoc. The only way up the cliff was for the Rangers to shoot grapnels (a long rope with a hook on one end) to the top of the cliffs and climb hand over hand, scaling up the face of the stone cliff to the top.

If D-Day had been a training exercise, the spectators watching would have cheered those getting to the top and ending the exercise. D-Day was different.

On D-Day, the German soldiers at the top of the cliff fought hard to push back the Rangers. Prior to the attack American planes had bombed the area at the top of the cliff (Pointe du Hoc). But the Germans were dug in so deeply that most survived the bombing. So, when the Rangers scaled up the cliffs, the Germans fired down at them. They were also able to release some of the claws so that some of the grapnels fell back down to the base of the cliff. Yet despite the German efforts, many Rangers got to the top. Then came a tough infantry firefight, which the Rangers won. Pointe du Hoc was theirs.

When the boys and I arrived at the Pointe, it seemed to me that it probably still looked the same as it did right after the fighting in 1944. It was the size of two football fields (probably 100 yards square). It was treeless, barren, windswept and dotted with huge, deep round holes, the aftermath of the American bombing which preceded the ground attack. Here and there were outcroppings of decaying cement and steel, evidence of German fortifications dug deep into the ground.

This lonely place was almost deserted. I recall only one other group there besides ourselves. I sat down for a rest on my little portable stool. Soon after, the other group (two couples) walked up to me. One of the boys introduced me as a veteran of World War II. I'm sure that they thought or hoped that I had been a Ranger at Pointe du Hoc on D-Day. I had to confess that I was not, but that I had landed on nearby Omaha Beach. The story became much less interesting when I told them I had landed on D-Day plus sixty – 60 days after the fighting took place.

Not incidentally, the portable stool was Willy's, which he brought solely for my use. It was precisely what I needed. Throughout the trip Willy would often come through for me with some useful item which added much to my comfort. I'm now adding a long overdue "Thank you, Willy".

Although our conversation was in English, I don't recall whether or not those in the group were American. The only thing I recall for sure is that if they were not Americans, they were something else.

It was gratifying for me to see, some 60 years after the event, a group of civilians spending their time exploring a remote, hard to get to location which was the scene, similar to all of Omaha Beach, of the death, dying, and mutilation of young American boys, in the brilliant winning of one of history's great battles—the battle for Omaha Beach.

Willy

Omaha & Pointe du Hoc

Early in the morning when the mockingbird sings. A pleasant stroll along the canal outside our hotel. Nod to a woman and her dog. Misty morning. The boats in the harbor. The crunch of pebbles underfoot.

Back to base, and Chris and Sean returned from their respective constitutionals. Daddy looking over maps, a favorite pastime for all.

Ready to do some driving?

Neat!

Let's go find some stuff!

Out the door. Driving, driving, driving. To St. Malo and Dinard. France blurs. Where I was, what I was doing coalesces.

Squeezed into the little car. Tempers flare, tension and confusion. Getting to be a habit. Maps, magnifying glass, all attention focused on one's surroundings always. The Lost Patrol.

Motoring dead along the coast, smell the unmistakable sea air.

First stop: Omaha Beach. Not too difficult to find, just a straight shot west.

We approach. Large car park, small tourism building. Daddy is to meet a man. A friend of his mate, Jim Begg, whom we'll all meet up with later in our travels.

Out of the car, stretch, assemble various effects, while Daddy somewhat too hurriedly hustles to the tourism facility. We follow, smoke and consider where we are. This place. Normandy Beach. Pausing at the entrance of the path to the American cemetery, which winds all along the cliffs above the bluffs.

Wait for Daddy's return and further instructions. I walk on to the cemetery, Sean and Chris still waiting for Daddy.

So green and peaceful. This place. Where dead American soldiers lie buried 'neath Norman soil.

I enter the cemetery.

Maintenance crew lowering American flag. Not for these nor for those being killed and maimed this very hour in Iraq and Afghanistan. Merely working on the flag pole.

All quiet, all still.

Approach a tombstone. The first of thousands:

"...1st Infantry Division...KIA June 6, 1944...Minnesota."

Startled. The person physically closest to me is 100 feet away. Might I have told that person, in any language I could—I too am from Minnesota? And here another. Down there.

I walk back to the path. Return to my living Minnesotan kinsmen. A large group of school children in their teens presses down the path towards me. Jabbering away in French. Laughing and behaving as young people do everywhere.

The signs posted:

This is a place to honor the dead.

Please show proper respect.

Back to the tourism building. Greet Chris, Sean gone to do the needful. No Daddy. Have a smoke.

Sean returns and Chris goes to do same. Sean heads off to cemetery. Chris returns. Still no Daddy.

Chris and I enter the building. Blue uniformed staff, friendly and quite young. Have you seen an old man? Here to meet the director, Dan Neese?

Oh yes, they went thataway a while ago.

We peruse the small museum. Equipment, memorials. See here. A captain of the 116th Infantry, 29th Division. Led a rifle company up a track from the beach. I read on. Men hit everywhere...cut off...no weapons. These made it by sheer luck. Others follow, the whole area mined. "Stick to the track we came up!" they screamed to those below. "Stick to the track!"

We leave the museum and move on down the path. A young Brit is giving a guided tour, speaking now to a gathering at an overlook memorial spot. We nod to Sean and listen to this chap's presentation.

And here comes Daddy, up the path, a bit weary. I walk over to meet him. He's nonplussed. Can't imagine where we've been. As we couldn't about you, I explain.

Tour guide moves on with his group. The who's, how's, when's and where's of being lost are considered with Daddy still unappeased.

Shall we down the beach? Daddy can't or won't. Chris staying on with him. Sean and I will go down. There.

A long winding track now studded with timber to form steps. The same track that captain of the 116th led his men up 63 years ago, now leads us down.

Quite a haul. We get to the sandy beach, the Channel out there. Waits.

Sean and I consider. As we stroll about, picking up smooth round stones to be deposited in my backpack. Some sand scooped into an old cigarette pack.

"Can you imagine? Down here and trying to get up there?"

"Motherfuckers trying to kill you. *Really* trying to kill you. Like it was personal..."

"Probably was... Who would be in any mood to give quarter after going through that?..."

"...a good thing all those Polish and Ukrainian conscripts up there...all those Panzer SS units pulled back to Pas de Calais..."

"...MG-42's, Kar98's...a 7.92 round will kill a full-grown buck at 800 yards..."

"...mortars, huge naval guns..."

"...how to defend? Where to assault?"

"...weapons jammed with sand or no weapon at all..."

"...no cover..."

"...fear."

We stare up at the bluffs. I feel ever so slightly—sick. Sean snaps some photos.

Ambling lazily on the beach.

"I gotta take a piss. Or, rather, leave one. Here."

I do the needful. Our eyes train on something, out there in the surf. A small hack, drawn by a horse, fine and black. At the canter. I'm mesmerized.

Me: "What is it about a horse running by the sea? All the images down the ages..."

Sean: "Simple—it's beautiful."

Back up the bluffs now. Good God, Daddy was right – hard enough going without people trying to kill you. From above.

Pile into our motor and it's off down the coast—destination: Pointe du Hoc.

Late the afternoon, we arrive at Pointe du Hoc. A few visitors at the entry area. Barbed-wire down at the cliff's edge. Sign says "Danger! Keep out!" Four Brits wandering where they oughtn't. Uniformed French tourism man admonishes them. They ignoring and laughing at him. Surely not expecting to step on unexploded ordnance. Which still litters the area.

The landscape green, wild and windswept. The sun descending. We walk.

Massive shell-holes still in evidence. Courtesy of the US and British Navies, no doubt. I leap down into one, CD snaps a photo. Slabs of concrete gun emplacements, which American Rangers scaled these cliffs to destroy.

Carrying backpack and small folding camp-chair for to seat Daddy when weary, we pause and do that very thing. Atop abandoned gun emplacement.

Here a friendly group approaches. Two American women from California, two men, one a Brit. We chat, Daddy tells stories with humorous anecdotes. Awarded the Bronze Star for having diarrhea. Ha ha. All have a good chuckle. Of course it's funny now, sort of. Always thought diarrhea was pretty awful in itself. But to have people firing small arms at you as you suffered? That's simply not on. But what further could be said about having to fight the German Army of 1939-45?

Sometimes an old trooper must needs, as the man said, laugh like hell. And so we did. But I'm sure glad it wasn't me scaling those cliffs.

I hand out some of Daddy's business cards for our friends to buy his war memoir, *"Shavetail."* Then trek back to the car to return to our place in Dives-sur-Mer. And tomorrow move inland. As one does. The game's afoot.

CD

10-13 10:35

Tossing and turning and squirming,
And hang-dog yearning and churning.
All the long dark lonely night.
Anticipate with taste the drive.
Even the fear, so sorry to say.
How can one be so cowardly?

Up and at'em. All things, everything congenial – copacetic even. The cleaning people arrive, inform us that we've got to go. Well, all right then. We're gone in half an hour. Under way for Dinard.

Nuthin' to it but to do it!

Stop for a breath in Cabourg.
Sniffin' for breakfast.
Lookin' for phone.
Findin' no breakfast.
Sumpin' on the fly.

Exquisite dainty quiche, the best I ever had. And canned juice, which occasioned opportunity to say my favorite thing to say in French: "Je voudrais un juice d'annanna." Found a phone and a phone card but alas, we couldn't make anything advantageous occur.

Eat by the car like to tailgate at a football game. Get up and go. Find the department of tourism.

Oddly perhaps for the tourist tune, no English is played.
There is but my poor fractured French.
And anemic and sad at that.

But, against all odds, we somehow and some way figure it out and manfully make it happen. Special thanks to St Jude, patron saint of lost causes. And, in theory, we now (modern men) know how to make the post-modern telephone call.

So, we're on the road – beautiful day – under way.

Allons, allons, mes enfants.

Let's go!

On the road to Cannes.

Then on to Rennes.

More rotary.

More fuckery.

The beautiful day to die for.

And sooner or later we will.

Cramped – You need a can opener to pry your ass in and out.

You need atropine to stab your thigh to counteract the numb.

Shitty driving but what the hell.

Tightness, tautness, tension to make your teeth ache.

We be lost.

Stop for gas. Major clown show. First time putting petrol in the rig. No concept how to do it. No idea which side the port is. Can't get the plug out. The French explanatory text refers to the nozzle as "le pistol" which takes me time to fathom.

Can't make the card work. Ask questions in faltering French. Pretty girl laughingly tries to help but to no avail. Finally figure it out. The French citizenry are amused but we're good to go.

And on into Dinard and not too terribly lost, just the proper degree. Dinard looks pretty.

Lookin' good.

And gold sun streaks strong through green trees.

We get there.
But where there?
Cain't find the place;
What is this place?
Back and forth,
To and fro.

We make continual loop – small town, fields of France, small town, same farmyard again. We stop and pause and take our ease at the terminus of a cul-de-sac that sports an old-time rural inn. Nobody there, deserted, this fine warm burnished gold fall day in the French Provincial Absurd.

Thrice we bite the bight.
Still daylight.
I'm cramped and sore and tight.

Third shout's a crime, a charm.
Deux gendarmes discreet,
Standing talking sweet.

He: shouty shades, trim mustache, after the French manner.

She: flat black eyes, slightly olive skin, trim, after the French manner.

Both wear Euro blue golf shirts, strap stylish baby nines.

I shout, dismount, engage:
"Where am I?"
"Where would one wish to be?"
No English,
But my French.

I can talk a little shit but suffer misunderstanding of the said.

Dude cell phone ring; lacking cop radio, he. He fast French talks; she fast French stares his every move. I fidget and pose. Call done. He tells me something. What? I report to the posse. I tell them something. What?

Great gig if you can get it, I say.

Then on to More Adventure.

Imagine that.

Then into the little town – St. Lunaire, just out of Dinard. Can't find the place. Stop at Hotel for information. Pretty blond French girl (delectable woman, no less) with the exquisite English, most kind, helps us with phone but we can't get through. We'll try again. She say she can book us rooms. Will have a drink somewhere and mull it over.

If we can't get ahold of the first guy,
Baby, maybe get her.

Tired of the tourism and the incessant driving around and can't make our match and our reservations aren't and the gal what helped us with the help what happens to have a hotel room, her own sweet self, and so here we are – a little room, 'bout ten foot by ten foot. Sweet little nautical looking building, dead in town center.

Which calls for the celebratory swig. Gonna get the drink on. Step round the corner to find emporium of same.

And try to find
The civilized
Dinner.
Oh Yeah!

There is an old stone church across the way with crucifix on high in the waning luminance, and people devoutly gather for worship. This must be the France of old.

Daddy and Willy consider morning mass. The sudden attack of piety.

I stand aside, sip from silver flask, and consider The Absurd.

And then ensues the beautiful poetic evening in the small town of wonder by the sea.

Set to step on out – Sean and Daddy scram fast. Willy and yours savor a civilized hotel drink and consider life, luck and love.

Brother with new-found interest in photography. At length we discuss the medium and shoot up the hotel, the environs, the surroundings.

And then we four together again.
We lordly walk the town.
Out for the eminent adventure,
Daddy and Brothers and Me.

And Good God, great it is it is.

Glimpse the sea from slanted road through crooked houses as we walk together imbued with wonder, esprit de corps and bonhomie; and it must be that the happiness I always mock as myth abounds in our brave little band.

It's gray on gray in the gloaming,
But bright as noble metal within.
Chance on seaside seafood bistro –
Lit up like motion picture set.

Two American Midwesterners gobble le bifteck, Sean some soufflé, Daddy eats fish as one should. We drink dry wine. Daddy with a stunt I've never before nor since seen – adds additional sugar. (Yuck!) But the waitress is pretty, the faire not dear, and a persistent tabby cat breaks in and wanders about over and over, again and again. Might there not be the odd salute here and there.

The great, grande evening out for all.
In fictive civilized fashion.
For which we always hope and long –

But mostly never ever meet.

Then somehow suddenly alone,
Wandering cobbled street and lost.
Startled and frightened to be almost out of town
And on the road to somewhere else.
Or maybe even nowhere.

Peer into amorphous shadows and quaint quiet premises.
Deserted, abandoned public space;
The harbored, guarded private place.
Dark on dark within and without.

But at length and at last, and all of a sudden –
Bright lights, a bar, and raucous laughing fellows.
Euro rugby in Paris on TV.
Vodka and beer make the world go round.
There is blood and men are carted off.
And then: The stark white faces in the pale moonlight
through the shimmering glass of the window. My Brothers.
Come on! Come on! Come on in! Reunited again.
Bright lights, a bar, and raucous laughing fellows!

Daddy

Chapter Five
Saturday, October 13, 2007
Mont St. Michel, Dinard and St.Lunaire

The next morning we left Dives-sur-Mer and piled into the car headed for Dinard (in Brittany) with a stop at Mont St. Michel, about 50 miles from Dinard. The Mont is a spectacular, one-of-a-kind, island-like landmark lying in the waters of the English Channel, joined to the mainland by a narrow strip of land. For centuries, the incoming tides would daily cover the strip, so that the Mont was an island once each day. In recent years the strip has been raised above the tide, providing easy access for crowds of visiting sightseers.

Until the French Revolution in the 1790's the Mont for centuries had been a religious monastery. Since then, it has been largely a tourist site, but with a small chapel with a large cross at the very top. From a distance it appears to be a tiny round island starting at its base and then in narrowing concentric circles filled with ancient buildings until there is no more room at the top. I guess that by today's standards, its height is 10 stories and without elevators—only steps.

I somehow got the idea into my head that I should walk to the top of the Mont. The lack of elevators did not surprise me, nor did it change my decision to hike to the top. I think the boys suggested that it would be a tough walk, but I said I'd give it a try. The first set of stairs were of a well-worn stone variety, probably more than five centuries in age and leading to a landing half way up to the second floor. It's time to say again that I am 84 years old with some knee and other health problems. As I continued to drag one foot upward after the other, I felt that my breathing was getting a little heavy and that both legs were losing strength and signaling me to stop. The landing was clearly in sight, so why stop now? I have always considered myself a reasonable man, one who acted according to reason. Reason told me to continue to the landing and there to stop and rest. Suddenly, some ten steps short of the landing, I stopped and told the boys that I was going back down to the ground floor and that they should continue to the top. They agreed, and so we did. I waited near the foot of the stairs in the long walkway which leads from the ground floor entrance past the tiny shops and even smaller merchandise and refreshment booths which crowded both sides of the ground floor.

Fortunately, I was able to find a tiny cubbyhole near the stairs in which to sit. The walls of the ground floor were lined with those one-person niches dug into the sturdy stone walls, thereby accommodating a single weary traveler such as myself. The ground floor was at all times filled with customers seemingly eager to satisfy the needs of the purveyors by purchasing any and all items offered for sale.

I especially remember what seemed to be the large number of Oriental people who were visitors. I think they were largely Japanese. I've just looked at my globe of the world. Japan and Mont St. Michel are fairly close to the same distance north of the equator and south of the north pole. But they are over 6,000 miles apart, at opposite ends of the world's largest land mass, Eurasia—the single area of land consisting of Europe to the west and Asia to the east. Today the trip from Japan to the Mont by plane takes only a day or so. But before the modern airplane, the trip by boat was months and by land well nigh impossible.

Since the time of the trip I've wondered why the Japanese seem to have such a great desire to visit the Mont. Wonder remains.

For the reader, the question might be asked, "What does your discussion of the globe have to do with the story of 'the trip'?"

Answer: not much!

What moved me to retreat to the ground floor? I don't

think I used a reasoning process by which to carefully consider the pros and cons of continuing the climb and reached the reasoned conclusion to head back down. Somehow, suddenly, without wading through the reasoning process, I realized that continuing the attempt to climb another 10 flights of stone steps while still short of halfway up the first flight was pure folly and probable disaster. I don't call it reason which directed me down the stairs, but rather a sometimes element known as common sense.

As we were leaving the Mont, I fell into a conversation with an English man and his wife. They were not my age but seemed old enough to have lived through World War II. They were interested in the war.

I told them that I had written a book ("Shavetail") about my experiences in the war as an infantry platoon leader in Europe. They said they would like to get a copy. I had several copies in my luggage back in the car, but I didn't think to mention that. Willy, who was wearing his backpack, forgot that in it was a copy of "Shavetail". We missed a sale!

I think that I, as well as Willy, might study up on the subject of how to sell a book, especially when the book is near at hand.

I had almost been to the Mont before, in 1988, when Mary and I planned to visit the famous Le Mont St. Michel. This required our parking several hundred yards from the Mont and walking from there, over a path that was rocky, irregular and somewhat uphill.

Mary for several years had trouble walking, trouble in both her knees. That day, both knees were giving her steady pain. We sat in the car trying to decide if she should try to make the walk. What would we do if one knee gave out? Or both knees? Or if the pain increased?

It was not worth the risk. We drove away.

Some months after we had returned home the doctors advised Mary that she should have surgery to have both knees replaced. The usual process was to have two separate procedures—one operation followed by a second at a later date. Both operations at the same time could be done and would cost less. But most patients chose two separate procedures.

Mary chose the two operations at the same time. She said she wanted to get the knee business out of the way as soon as possible. So she did—one operation immediately followed by the second. She was tough! She gave birth to eight babies. No complaints. Two new knees in one day. No complaints.

Tough. And then some!

I think that most women—surely Mary—are tougher than men when suffering through pain. Thank heavens!

We left Mont St. Michel at about 2 p.m. for the short drive to Dinard. We had reservations for the night at a bed and breakfast in St. Lunaire, a small town just west of Dinard.

Although the distance to Dinard and St.Lunaire was short, the drive to get there was not. Instead of the one hour drive we planned, we did not arrive at our final destination in St.Lunaire until 6 p.m., after four hours of driving and searching.

What caused the delay? There were clearly two causes. The first is that on at least two occasions where there was an intersection and a choice of two or more directions to take, we took the wrong one. The result was that after a few miles and quite a few minutes we realized our mistake and returned. On one of the occasions we saw we were running low on gas and stopped at a gas station for a refill. After visits to the bathroom and ordering and consuming coffee and doughnuts and filling up on gasoline, together with some extended discussions about the correct direction in which to proceed, we managed to use up close to an entire hour of travel time.

The second cause of our delay was worse. We couldn't

find the bed and breakfast in St.Lunaire. We had its address on Rue de St.Lunaire and had been told that after driving through the center of town, it was on the outskirts where the farm country began. We drove back and forth three or four times. No luck. We stopped and asked a couple passersby. No luck. A police officer. No luck. After an hour of searching we decided to look for a telephone in the center of town. So we drove back. We stopped at a small (very small) hotel and asked to use their phone. I don't recall which of the boys called the bed and breakfast. But we did not make contact. Fortunately, we had not prepaid our rooms. Someone (I thought it was me; Chris thought it was he; and if I had asked Sean or Willy, he would have thought it was himself) suggested that we get rooms at the hotel from which we were calling. We did, and spent two delightful evenings and the next day there.

That evening we had our first sit-down dinner of the trip. We found the restaurant a block up the street from our hotel, filled with families and friends delighted with their fine French dinners. This was no place nor time for any inappropriate antics from foreign visitors. We entered the crowded room, fearing a long wait. Happily, however, they soon found us a table, covered, as were all the tables, with a scrubbed clean white tablecloth. I can't recall what each of us had for dinner, but I can say that we all agreed that our French food was scrumptious.

The low-light of the evening, for the boys, occurred when their father, after tasting the wine, found it too dry, and thereupon added to his glass a heaping teaspoonful of sugar. The three sons, Chris, Sean, and Willy, probably for the first and only time in their lives agreed on precisely the same subject matter. To them, their father's performance was disgraceful, uncalled for, shameful, ignorant, embarrassing, etc., etc.

In defense of the father, whom I have known all my life,

he likes sweet wine.

The highlight was the pussycat. Unlike in an American restaurant, the cat had free rein. It would go from table to table, look up to the diners, and perhaps add a "meow," and then move on. The waiters and guests treated this as a usual thing and made no attempt to hush it up or to put it out. After a while pussycat went to the front door, and after a meow or two was let out. I wish I could witness such a performance back home.

Willy

Further inland today. To Chartres. We drive like hell. All I can see are maps and indecipherable road signs. Stopping at large suburban supermarket. I walk around looking for rations. Similar to American super stores. All the pictures on boxes and bags of food look so tasty, though what are they? Where will I cook these articles?

Buy some chips, nuts, peculiar juice concoctions.

Trying now to fill up gas tank. Can't figure out how. Two friendly French girls trying to tell us how, the ubiquitous language barrier. Finally succeed. "Le pistol," that's not a pistol. It's a gas pump.

God, how I hate driving — cars, motorways, suburbs, ugliness. Where one would prefer beauty. Same as in USA, probably everywhere. Civilized. Ha!

Daddy took this same trip by car back in '88. With Mama, who was no use on the maps, didn't even attempt. They had no troubles, considering.

Why so lost, confused, befuddled now?

Stop here. I jump out, run into a hotel lobby. No French, no English. Woman points to a spot on my map. Nods her head. Thoroughly bamboozled, I thank her and back to the car. Thinking I may know what road to take. Five minutes later, find I'm wrong. Again.

Ask this bloke. Alighting from a café. Does he know where we want to be? Dutchman, perfect English, makes disparaging remark about France. Sympathetic, but can't help.

On your way, son.

Looking for a St. Maxime. I think.

The driving tour continues. We are finding it increasingly difficult to procure those things which tend to put a bit of zest back into one's life, a bit of lead in the old pencil.

Such as food.

We are four big men from America, and we are accustomed to a certain caloric intake. We hear tell of many yummy comestibles to be had in the land called France.

Where is this stuff?

Quite difficult to find a wee bite. Restaurants abound, but we are men on the go, with places to circumnavigate and people to quiz as they stare blankly and uncomprehendingly. We must never slow nor falter. We require nutrition whilst we perambulate. Where be the grocer? Thanks. And a spot of coffee would be nice. But, alas, we cannot take the coffee with us. It's not done here to do that thing. We are expected to be seated and relaxed as we sip and contemplate.

But there is no time.

We must go further, faster.

Hunger is general.

Heading to St. Maxime. Small towns, the streets absent of people. Where are they? Sean proclaims that they are all watching the "Oprah Winfrey Show" on television, a big woman from America who is apparently quite popular here. Shops all closed at 2 o'clock p.m. Very civilized to be sure. Unless one is a big man from America soon to be a medium sized man from America. In search of sandwiches.

One thing we will not be denied: potable libation of the sturdiest variety. Chris and I will dedicate ourselves tirelessly to the task of finding said grog in any and all addresses, and we are always successful, being well trained in the manly art of foraging in strange climes for the needful elixirs, nectars and poteens. We shall have, when the hour arrives, a few stiff ones.

Driving cross-country. We stop to do the needful of the urinary sort. At the side of the road, as one does. Daddy across the highway hollers to Chris, who in turn hollers to me. Sprint across the road, Daddy's taken a tumble in a ditch. I leap in, Chris pulling, me pushing. He gets up and out, none the worse for the proverbial wear. I, however, have become soaked in muddy water, and more unpleasantly, have a nasty reaction to some nettles or nasty plants or other. As we drive on I feel dazed and out of it. More so than is my usual custom. No fun. No use on the maps as I can't focus my eyes. The road seems endless. Not enjoying this part of life awfully much.

Arrive in St. Maxime. Old farmhouse set up in a quadrilateral, still in operation. Sean and I engage in the now traditional argument about who gets what room and other minutiae. And then embark on more general lines of disagreement. I wash me trousers and socks in the bathtub and take a stroll around the yard. Where I see a massive dog in a pen. Which growls and barks threateningly when I approach with my customary canine greetings. Fine. Be that way. I curse it. In English, so as to confuse and enrage it further. The day not going well. Now the animals, usually my staunchest of allies, are being disagreeable.

Daddy and Sean want to find some food. Good luck, gents. I take a drink with Chris, too wound up for sleep and too tired for hunger. Tomorrow we'll be off to find Mont-Saint-Michel. I couldn't care less right now. I want to go home. Woe is me and all that.

Daddy and Sean strike out on the food front. None to be found. How do these folk survive? No wonder they're all so fit and trim, les bastardes.

We share our meager rations with each other—some trail mix, a bit of bread and cheese, and some nuts and crackers left over from the airplane. Western France had bloody well better cough up some goddamn food here pretty quick. This is stupid.

Morning arrives, and we breakfast downstairs with the proprietress and a wee bairn grandchild. Friendly folk.

Languages not mutual, though Chris does yeoman's work keeping the convo cheery.

"On the road again, I just can't wait to get back on the road again..."

Shut up.

We find Mont-St.-Michel, out there in the ocean. Tide is out and there it is. Gosh, that's one big parish church. St. Michael the Archangel way at the top. Legend has it that in the 10th century, St. Michael paid a visit to the bishop of these environs, and told him God wanted him to build a *really* big church. The bish said nope. Michael comes again. Ya better build, boyo. Iffen youse know what's good for ya's. Uh uh, Mike. No way. Not gonna do it. Next day God zaps the bish in the bean with a bolt of ye olde lightening, burning a hole in his skull. The bish got right to work. Job went a bit over, though. Took a few centuries to finish.

In a few days I'll send a postcard to a friend describing it thus: "It's really big. It's really old. It's made of stone."

And so it is.

Long road leads out to the surf, now at low-tide. Huge car park, hundreds of vehicles. Quite a long walk to get to the Mount, Sean unfortunately ruining his pictures from Omaha Beach along the way. Warm sea breeze and foul smell from somewhere waft inland. The base of the church/fortress jammed with tourism vendors. A bit tawdry, this. Selling all manner of crap. Just like we do in good old USA.

Start up the steps that wind their way to the summit. Several small graveyards along the way. Monks down the ages buried here.

To gain entrance to the church-proper at the top of this gargantuan structure, they want 10 Euros. Which I won't pay. To visit a holy place. Simply not on.

Leave Chris and head down, soon find Daddy resting after he gave up the ghost as well. Quite the haul it is.

Daddy wandering off to do this and that, have a chat with

some Brits.

I feel like a dope. The tourist scene not my bag. Too many people, often behaving in an unbecoming manner. Too much expensive junk about, the temptation to buy always present...

Quickly losing interest in the Mount itself. Walk around a bit. Consider buying a sword, but a bit too expensive and no doubt difficult to get on an airplane.

A French woman says to a Japanese woman, in perfect English, and with a distinctly grave air:

"This is not France. This is Brittany."

I espy a young woman working one of the stalls. Helping her mother or grandmother perhaps.

Absolutely gorgeous. Short cropped blonde hair, très chic black blouse and pants, not a touch of makeup. Smiles when she sees me gawking, not nervous, annoyed or haughty as so many American women would be. I lean against centuries old rock and strike a pose, a match, have a soigné smoke. Think now of something brilliant to say.

"Bonjour. Je suis un grand homme de l'Amerique et j'ai beaucoup d'argent."

Can't take me eyes off her. Oh dear. She's looking again. I pretending to be not looking. The "Eye Dance," I call this.

She adjusting a stack of tee shirts or some such. Has a word with the older woman. Trying not to stare so, really I am. She looking back again. Such an open and confident face. Does she know her own beauty? How could she not? One just says "hi". How it's done. French women seeming so much braver.

She has a brief chat with the elder. Turns directly towards me and gives a slight laugh. Which I do not hear through the hubbub of the marketplace. But would have loved to. She yawns, stretches a bit, runs a hand through her hair. Oh boy. Turns her back and disappears. Merde. Blew it. Not many like that back home. And worth the price alone. Of admission. To this beautiful land.

All meet up and repair to the car. Whatever shall we do now?

I know...

Let's do some driving!

On to St. Malo and Dinard. Seems we have lodging booked somewhere. On and on we go. Lost, naturally. Driving in circles. Shouting out various names and addresses. Oaths too. Stop to ask a cop. Chris and I being most polite and sincere. Cop with brusque aspect but good natured. But, of course, no English. Long handlebar mustache makes him resemble Inspector Clouseau. Using cell phone to enquire of the address we give him. His partner approaches. Young girl of maybe 19 or 20. Looks like a young Juliette Binoche. Shoulder patch says "Cadet", but armed. She silent and coquettish as CD tries to bring clarity to the proceedings.

Mustachioed cop chuckling, trying to help. She with eyes downcast, slightly pigeon-toed. Jet-black hair and almond skin. Really must stay focused here.

No luck and back to the car.

Round and round and back and forth we go.

Stop here, ask directions, maybe the use of a telephone. Which may even work properly.

This town christened St. Lunaire. This small Hotel Kan Avel, with sky-blue trim on windows and doors.

Sean and Chris in to seek assistance. A few minutes later returning. Good news. To hell with the original joint, not yet paid for anyway. Why not stay here?

Capital idea, all concur.

Parking right outside. Carry in the luggage. Big church right next door. Might need that.

Our proprietress kind and helpful, speaking the English marvelously.

Very quaint digs. The blue motif continues inside. Our rooms separated by an outside balcony overlooking an excellent garden. So civilized. This is lovely. Appears they even have food in this town.

Barely settled, Daddy and Sean decide it's time to eat. Reluctantly I join them, as does Chris.

I don't like restaurants. Worked too many of them in me youth. Expensive and bloody filthy, most are. But I acquiesce and up the road we stroll. Selecting an eatery. Then... eating.

After dinner. Out on the street. Dark now. Dinard Bay right there.

I leave the others, take a stroll down a steep hill to the shore. The ubiquitous smoke. Young couple make love on the beach. I can dig it. This soft night.

Back to our hotel. This time Chris and Sean share a room, Daddy and I in the other.

Daddy down for a bit of a nap, but it seems there are places to go in this burg. Public houses. I'll have some of that.

On my way out our proprietress, Isabelle, intercepts me. This fine, elegant woman of anywhere from 30 to 50 years vintage. Straight brownish blonde hair cut to her jaw-line. Fine boned and svelte.

"So you are here to see where your father was during the war?"

"Oui. Sorry—yes. Yes we are. Tomorrow on to Benelux then Germany."

"This must be quite the experience for you and your brothers, no?"

"Oui, oui. Yes it is."

Out with Sean now to find a pub. CD already on the case. We check windows, many already closed up for the night or the tourist off-season. But we are tourists. See us tour!

Aha!

Lights bright, this one, this night.

Oh look. There's Chris!

Tip on in. Hale fellows, well met.

Large-screen TV. World Rugby Tournaments happening just now in Paris. The joint empty, apart from the owner and wife and young nephew at a table intently watching the sport.

Stand to the bar. Much ordering of drinks, smoking allowed, maybe even encouraged. The owner does same. The crack loud and general.

We tipping with coins various, a bit lavishly considering the homely circumstance.

CD bringing the French, our man behind the bar with slight English but better humor. It is explained that, though we realize tipping is not often done here, and indeed if done overly much could be construed as insulting, we are Big Men From America and we like your pub, your service, easy fellowship, and you. Therefore, please have this money. 'Cause that's how we say thanks in the USA.

Barman understanding, laughing, thinks Americans goofy with all their tipping. But we're okay by him. Merci, monsieurs.

Great fun, just watching the television. A few more patrons now, very involved with the rugger. Sean and I say bye-bye to Chris who stays on for a bit.

Sauntering back to our rooms. Keep an eye peeled for the church, that'd be us. Much laughter and witticism.

Later I'll see, while standing out on the balcony having a late night smoke, CD walking streets below, stick in hand, looking just the tiniest bit lost. As is the order of the day.

I hustle on out, give the lad a shout. Show him the way.

Back home.

To sleep and dream in bedroom blue.

Our first welcome night in France.

lunar lit,
lucky light
St. Lunaire
bid you
good night.

Next day. Down the road apiece to see the Ile de Cezembre, located offshore in Dinard/St. Malo Bay.

Daddy's unit, 330th Infantry of the 83rd Division, would have assaulted this island in 1944, had US Army Air Force and divisional artillery not bombed the German occupants into submission.

It was a close-run affair, Daddy says.

Might not be here today had the German garrison not surrendered. Nor, of course, would I or my brothers and sisters.

We laze about on benches overlooking the sea wall. I walk down a path for a ways, down to the sea. Not much to see. But sea.

Hard to get an impression of the potential danger involved in sea-borne assaults from standing on the shore of the point of advance.

But I do have a respectful fear of water. Especially when combined with heavy weapons being fired at me whilst on that water. Which the German Army proved quite adept at on June 6, '44.

Sean wants to see the Psycho House – the house used in Hitchcock's filum "Psycho," which is visible from our vantage point.

I'm not terribly interested, nor are Daddy and Chris.

Out for dinner tonight, Daddy, Sean and I. Chris otherwise engaged.

Find a café, take a table in back.

Bit of unpleasantness ensues.

Daddy gesticulating a tad aggressively to the waiter. As he waits other tables. I comment that this may not be the most effective way of getting prompter service, as he does seem busy and anyway it might be seen as a bit rude. Just a bit. Maybe.

Daddy takes umbrage at this suggestion and tells me off.

Sean delicately states that he's heard tell from friends who've lived in France that, you know, French waiters and all that. Ha ha.

Daddy not liking this notion either. Tells Sean off.

"...the hell with them."

Sean rising.

"I'll meet you by the car in an hour or so."

Daddy pleading with Sean not to go, sit and eat with us. Sean well peeved. Leaves.

Unfortunate. Misunderstanding. My theory, after working in restaurants for several years in my youth, and dating many a waitress—always be extra nice to people who handle your food. Lest they spit in it. Or worse.

We manage to order. Excellent crepes and earthenware jug of local hard cider.

Table behind us. Unmistakable Australian accents. Much bawdy laughter. At the waiter's expense. Taking the piss. True stereotypes, these Aussies. The older one even wearing bush hat. Inside, at that.

Poor waiter. Not sure if he's aware of their boorishness. Very patient and helpful chap he is. Dummies who can't figure out enough foreign tongue to get some food. So they don't starve to death. The paperwork from the Australian embassy most time-consuming and annoying, I reckon.

We finish up, Daddy paying the bill and kindly seeking out our waiter for to present him with gratuity. "Remember, now, Daddy—not *too* much. Ha ha."

Outside, walking to the car. See the two Australians ahead, still laughing their heads off about whatever.

Brief notion to have a word with them.

"I say, diggers. You cunts were a tad unparliamentary to that waiter. Young chappie was working his ass off. Back to the penal colony with ya's."

But I relent. Been enough nonsense tonight.

Meet Sean, no mention of the troubles. And back to Kan Avel.

In pursuit of further and more comfortable habits.

CD

10-14-07 10AM

Wonderful restorative night's sleep in small cozy, exciting yet soothing apartment berth, imaginatively suggestive of the sea. Can barely stand for tapering of the ceiling. Stretchy band exercise, nice bath.

Recall and savor the fine chat with Sean before retiring last night – mellow, reflective and friendly. We flip for the better bed but it occurs to me to present it to him in repayment for all his magnificent driving, some of which I should be shouldering. Also that there might be sufficient room for the early morning sport.

Seek to find to find Daddy in the sweet mid-morn. Pause to look, smoke and meditate on the upper veranda overlooking the lush garden plaza below. Colorful flowers, black iron-work, brown wooden benches; half in shadow, half in shade. Daddy and Willy materialize. We talk warmly in this bright beautiful spot while clutching the antique rail like straphangers over the French ordered Eden, whisper distance near below.

And hence down to breakfast, the first in some time it seems, and I can but hardly wait.

The folk are friendly.

Pretty and peaceful here.

Look for good day.

Daddy and I,

Spirits run high.

Early up to attend mass across the street. Beautiful centuries-old church – You can see it from my chamber window.

Sadly, it isn't Sunday.

We missed it.

Full-on French breakfast attended by the beautiful French proprietress: Yogurt, granola, dried apricots, dried prunes, a fine fresh apple of a type unfamiliar, French bread, saucy homemade jam, excellent black coffee. (Would this be French roast?) The solicitous, subtle woman quietly puts music on for us – soft jazz, Ella maybe. Kindly offers to move our rooms adjacent so as to form a suite.

So noble, so kind, so sweet.

Not what you usually meet.

Rich and glorious, proud sunny day.

Saddle up for Mont St Michel.

God help me – I may have to fucking drive.

Me bad leg twitches, shakes and quakes.

On the road to Mont St Michel.

Stout and True Sean at the wheel.

Doing half-a-way well, I say.

Not lost yet.
The glorious grand sunny day.
Fun with maps, (ironically intoned).
And run-on sappy snappy banter,
But no, not just yet disaster.

Le Mont St Michel:
The approach is magnificent in aspect.
Warm and warmer, almost hot. Shed clothes as we go. Athletes in training today.
March foreword, maybe to the top.
Capital view. Airy soaring spirits.

At the foot of the Mont we pause to look about and lean. Sean has the unfortunate with his camera – lost all his film from Omaha Beach. He takes it manfully and well. I try to help but fail.
We press on.
Commence to climb.
God help Our Daddy.

To the foot of the edifice. Daddy talking the endless talk, tells stories to the passersby. We can't seem to get started. But he's having a good time, I think. And is happy, I hope. And that's what it's all about.

Sean in swell spirits but now in the shit. There's an attendant in the public toilette who must be paid, forty cents, say. Sean bereft of coin with but a five euro note with which he pays. The woman smilingly hands him a pocket full of metal and now he be-laden with weighty small change coin. But stoutly takes it well once again.

Et moi? I'm warm. I'm happy.

I say:
Not only may we not achieve the top,
We may not even get started.
As we anticipate
Ascent.
Ha ha!

Unearth small graveyard as we ascend in the rarified air. Hadn't expected that. And yet maybe it makes a certain sense.

Why not?
We all end up there.
Why shouldn't it be here?
But they must have had some serious coin there, these.
The statuary, stupendous;
The monuments, monumental.

Part way up, what foolishness – must buy tickets, eight euros. I think about it, damnit. OK, give it a shot. Just a bit surprised and shocked by the venal crassness of the enterprise.

Fuck'em anyway.

I find Sean.
Or he doth me.
Here we are.
Nous sommes ici.

Pay our way but the path ends 50 feet hence. Hrumph!

Apparently we have crested the summit, achieved the pinnacle. The vistas from here are spectacular – Heavenly, might one say. Trees shrouded in fog off to the distance. Sand and water mix to form Rorschach virtuosity. Futz with camera to make Deathless Art. So do everyone else. You just can't lose with the subjects so strong. That's why pretty girls sell you toothpaste and beer.

There are the Japanese tourists, of which there are many, enjoying themselves or whatever it is that they do.

And alas, we hear the bells toll in the background, foreground really.

We take our time,
Make our peace,
Have our smoke,
And descendre.

Sean says that one day he will bring his children here, that they might behold what faith can build. "Well founded or ill," say I. Says Sean, "And look what 9-11 did. You can build with faith or you can unbuild with faith, and destroy."

Un-Catholic, un-full-of-faith Sean walks about. I think it's a spiritual thing of some sort or something he seeks. Out of curiosity or something else. I'll meet and greet him presently.

I stand in the sun and look and think and smoke.

Japanese tourists abound.

I pray to Dead Mama,
I pray to Dead Nick;
For myself,
For us all.
God help us.
God help us every one.

The sand flats extend and render, reach and dazzle so far as you can see. There are people who vigorously and leisurely traverse this briny expanse. They look like so many moving colorful dots against the blue-gray-beige monochrome background.

It must be ebb tide.
So go with the flow.
This is the beginning
Of the sea.
You can walk right into it.

We enter the church, Sean and I, we do. It's vast and old as history itself. Not so Rococo ornate – the architecture, the glasswork, the appointments and furnishings – as some salons of God; but sure does something to the soul, and is grand and magnificent beyond all mere earthly human understanding.

Do the tourist thing –
Shoot some shots.
Service still held here?
Do they still say Mass?
I bend the knee.
Time to go.

5:11 on the road to Dinard.
Not too lost,
Snacks in stash.
Spirits run flow-tide high.
Into Dinard,
Drive round- roun,
Looking for things,
I'm not sure which or what.
I think maybe maps,
Or banks,
Or information of some sort,
Or something.

Crunch to point of pain in the back.
Look for signs

Or sign.
Can't understand
The plan.
Hope for food or some sweet release.
But one never knows,
Now does one?
Now that's that.
And we drive back to St Lunaire.

And suddenly among us a bit of the spirited and sprightly political discourse springs forth, mildly uninhibited and wildly unabated.

And then we're there.

Daddy, Sean and Willy step out, or rather, drive out for Dinard for dinner – some touring, they say.

I stick and stay.

Willy has commissioned me to photograph this beautiful building, these rooms, the environs. Sean had similarly appointed me earlier at the church. Flattered on both counts, I'm sure.

Hope to do well – never to fail.
Always and ever shoot true.

Sun gone down like a plan gone wrong.
Now dark as sin, as they say.
I trip the trigger,
Cross the line;
Drink the vodka,
Think on wine.

Hope not to hurt the feelings by not tag along too. But I like and love and maybe even need the solitude; want the work; finish up and down the drink. And then perhaps step out for a walk and then perhaps find a funky café.

Booming party nearby. I try to pay no mind. Whole lot o' livin' goin' on. Hey – talk and drink and laugh – have fun. It is grand, great and good, is it not? And what's it like to be they?

Stout maintain and fast remain.

Party people flee their rooms.

They heartily party hearty.

They are jolly sons-of-bitches, aren't they?

I a solitary man in the dark.

Solitude – recognized, respected, perfected here in France. The man walks down the busy street or sits in a crowded park. He projects the aura of alone – no hard feelings, but I'm by and with myself. It seems to be countenanced and no big deal. One can even assume a certain attitude, strike the ineluctable lordly air.

It's commences to cool now out here on this balcony of beauty. Cooler yet, no doubt, (or hot?) in the wild and wooly on the town.

And cooler yet – what ho! – within.
Lights flicker off and on in rhythm –
Copy the movie set light cue.
Bourgeoisie scurry quietly
Like rats on their way in the night.
The courtyard I can but feel below
Be dark and lush as a jungle –
Oh yes, but a macedoine kempt.
After my silly and foolish and eminent art endeavor,
To sally forth in the street and on the town for yet another sortie into the land of potential pleasure at the cunning café.

Back to ma chambre.
All the liquor here down the hatch.
Shot all the shots to be shot.
Contemplate all that I could or I would,

Maybe more than is good for me.
My drink is diminished.
My … is diminished.
Drink it up, pack it up;
Get down and get off.
I finish my drink – I'm finished.
Time to step out and step off.
Timely time to play.
Sey Hey!

The kindly concierge gave both Willy and me ashtrays, replete and complete with a small placard placed within. A beautiful hand-done painting of a sailboat. At first I thought it was a poem writ on back but now see it only explains the smoking rules. At the end it says, "Merci de votre comprehension."

But maybe I don't.
Don't be that way.
OK.

9PM, step out, cool and dark.
Sunday night, nobody on the street.
Step 'n' stride.
Pace the promenade.
In search of the tender sweet swig.
And always and ever
Lookin' fer adventure.

Walkin', talkin', tappin', tonkin'.
It's cool but not too cool.
It's dark but not too dark.
Deserted but not too deserted.
A magical mystic night, I say.
Noble photo ops everywhere.

The Sea swirls and sings its dangerous symphony –
Poseidon, Cyclopean presence.
Narrow funky age-old sidewalk,
Tree of good and evil to elbow,
Long-gone stonemason wall to left.
Great light lit, like when you're knocked out and come to.
The great raging looming living sea sounds to starboard.

The surf breaks hard like a bomb on the beach.
Walk on down to see The Sea.
And, Bless My Soul, I can taste it.
Past Office du Tourisme, I see.
It's lonely, dark and deserted.
Sunday night,
Nobody there.
Take a left and find a bar.
Hard and soft, the sounds.
"La Potiniere," says neon sign.
“L'Ambiance,” says I to meself.
Jazz within.
Boire le vin.
Think I'll stop on in and visit.
Hard and soft the sounds.

So, swing through door, me own bad self.
Open stance; got a chance.
What ho! – a rugby bar. Double shot and a beer. A few folks watch the game on TV. Mostly guys, of course. But by no means all. I don't know the game, the rules; but what the hey, at least I know the conventions and even some of the ceremonies. Argentina against South Africa, it is. Crowd cheers. I too. I think it's a goal. O look, there's a scrum and then a penalty. I sit at the bar but all clear out to gather and sit around a table. What does this mean? There's a kicking goal. Of some sort. What does this mean? Instant replay.

Swim-through-the-muck surreal to me.
Or finally wrongly really unreal.

Another scrum. And there's a whistle. Signals another vodka to cheer my beer. Long kick like a field goal. Fumble. A punt and a fumble. I can see that. There's a bloody face. "E's coming off!" Amid and amongst rousing music. Touchdown scored. Looks like point after attempt. Another trick at the bar. There's more rugby. More and more.

And what face do I see that suddenly ghostly peers through the window? But brother Sean. And there's Willy too. Bang on glass, rush outside, wave 'em down; they follow me in. The profusion of salutary toasts. Somehow at somebody else's expense. Get on down. Hail fellows well met. I thought I heard the TV announcer say, "son of a bitch." No doubt, not the case. He is, after all, speaking French.

Game over. Can't tell who won or lost. So what.

Funny – Sean and Willy strolling by. Small town though, don't ya know.

But then they're gone.
I'm all alone.
I drink with strangers again.

At late long last it's time to go.
So out the door and off.
Much colder now; it's really cold.
Wind whips hard – slaps like a bad bitch
Hear the sea – wonder if I'll live.
Hey, take a right.
But in just a short stumble I'm lost.
Oh shit.
To be lost.

Another foolish fine-feathered night,

Another rocky road,
Another harrowing nightmarish thing.
Dead-assed lost, wander round and round.
Circle the wagons, circle the self.
Must find my way, lest I run out of strength.
Hungry, cold, no idea where I am.
Search for the great church that I remember.
Seek God, or at least where He hangs His hat.
God help me; where the fuck am I?

Cornered in a circular something. Town square. Up against the wall. Nobody here. Nobody there. Cobblestone street. It all runs together. No idea where to go or what to do. Hell 'n' High Water – I'm lost.

Look up high. Try to look tall. Where's the church? Find a false horizon. Where's the spire? It should crowd the picture, dominate the scene.

Shit. I might be miles from miles from where I want to be.

Walk,
Walk,
Walk.
O, save my soul.
Oh God, won't You deign to help me?
Please help a guy out, if You please.
Way the fuck am I?
Do those street signs indicate that I'm heading out of town?
Where am I?
Won't some one or body kindly lend the assist?
Who in hell is playing the point?
There ain't nobody there to help.
I may have walked to another world.
Have no golly-gee ideaer.

Recognize none of this shit.
Not now and maybe not ever.

Then suddenly, all of a sudden I'm here.
My God, Sweet Jesus. Delivered out of Egypt, first born all intact.
There it is. On the left: Hotel Carnival.
I once was lost but now I'm found.
Hey baby, how you like me now?
Slick dude after all.
Thank you, Jesus.

It is that I have arrived. Here's the hotel, the crib, my destination, my final resting place.
Come on, come on. Have a smoke, long and deep; savor the salvation.
Negotiate the thick front door, walk in, past the desk; I'm home.
Find and devour the Goddamned peanuts and pretzels from the airline.
Ooo, my God.
Thank You.
Mon Dieu.

Daddy

Chapter Six
Sunday, October 14, 2007
St. Lunaire and Dinard

Our hotel in St. Lunaire was across the street from the town's Catholic church. Soon after we arrived at the hotel the day before, I saw a large number of people leaving the church. It was about 7:00 p.m. I didn't pay much attention to them. It didn't occur to me that they had just attended the Saturday evening mass which, in the Catholic Church, fulfills the Sunday mass obligation. At 8:00 a.m. Sunday morning I walked across the street to check the Sunday mass times. No Sunday mass! With the current shortage of priests in France, not unlike the shortage in the US, priests from one parish must also say mass at other, priest-less parishes. Hence, no Sunday mass in St. Lunaire.

My only reason for visiting Dinard was that in August, 1944, I had my first combat experience, which involved the Ile de Cézembre, in Dinard Bay. Combat infantrymen who might read this would surely say that my experience was not combat. No one was shooting at us. I agree. So here is my first *near*-combat experience.

This is from my book "Shavetail: The Odyssey of an Infantry Lieutenant in World War II". I was a lieutenant in E Company, 330th Infantry Regiment, 83rd Infantry Division. The book tells of our proposed attack in August, 1944 against the German-held Ile de Cézembre outside of Dinard, France.

From "Shavetail":

"...Before we left Dinard, E Company had one further task. Although the city of Dinard had been taken from the

Germans, they continued to hold an island, Ile de Cézembre, in Dinard Bay, and this prevented the Americans from using the port. In August 1944, there were no ports open for supplying the American forces, so the landing beaches in Normandy were still being used. Therefore, it was vital that the Ile de Cézembre be taken from the Germans so that the ports of Dinard and Saint-Malo, which adjoined Dinard, could be opened. The Second Battalion of the 330th Infantry, which included E Company, was ordered to assault the island.

The Island was about 1,000 yards from shore and stood out of the water like the top of a hill. It was fairly round in shape and was probably 500 feet across. The Germans had fortified it very heavily. There were big guns dug into rocks, and tunnels and living quarters were burrowed deep into the ground, making it difficult to knock them out.

A few days after I joined E Company, we started preparations for attacking the island. The company was assigned an area of the beach to assault, and my platoon was assigned a portion of it. We spent the next week practicing landing from assault boats.

Each platoon would get into an assault boat and go into a part of the bay that was out of sight from Ile de Cézembre. We would circle around in the water for a while and then land on a designated beach similar to the island's beach...

At the same time we were practicing landings, another method was tried to make the Germans surrender the island. Each day it was bombed by B-24 Liberator bombers and P-38 Lightning fighters. The B-24 was a large, four-engine bomber that was bombing Germany in great numbers almost daily. The island was so small that the B-24s had to fly over it one at a time to drop their bombs. They couldn't fly in V formations as they normally did, for if they did, most of the bombs would have landed in the water. The P-38s bombed and strafed the island, and our artillery also shelled it regularly. At the end of each day, we would check with headquarters to see if the Germans had surrendered. The answer was always, "No".

Finally on the morning we were to assault the island, the Germans thankfully surrendered.

In 1988 Mary and I were in the coastal town of St. Malo. I looked out over the water and saw the Ile de Cézembre for the first time since the war, the island which in 1944 we had planned to attack and where we avoided numerous bloody casualties when the Germans surrendered just before we were to commence attacking.

In over 50 years of marriage Mary had heard, listened to all my war stories more than once. Yet she never reminded me that she had heard the same story before or even that she had something else to do at the time. She understood that those stories were an unforgettable part of my life.

I was excited. I wanted to tell someone the story. Mary and I were in a small shop overlooking the water. I turned to the proprietor, a grey haired Frenchman about my age.

As I started to relate the story, I of course referred to "World War II". Upon mention of the word "war" the man turned and walked away, saying that he didn't want to hear about it.

I was angered by his reaction and started to walk towards him. Mary put her hand on my shoulder and told me to "calm down." I didn't want to calm down, but I knew she was right, so I stopped. I'm no fighter, so I don't know what might have happened. He might have had a war story more compelling than mine.

Mary did not try to scold me. Instead she acted with wisdom, and possibly, love.

I was thinking of her when, early in the afternoon, the

boys and I got in the car and headed for the nearby coastline to find a good site from which to observe the Ile de Cézembre. We found one complete with telescope and seating benches. The boys had read my book and had heard me recite my story of the Ile often enough to know it was an important event in my life. Yet when I saw that island again, I had a feeling which I cannot convey to others. In August 1944, the day we were to assault Cézembre, I was the leader of a platoon of 40 men, almost all of whom had just finished fighting German soldiers in Dinard. I was barely 21 years old, probably the average age of the men in the platoon. Only a few months earlier, we might have been described as a platoon of *boys*.

Since this was to be my first time in combat, I was concerned that I should have the courage to lead my men (or boys) well when the bullets started to fly. Nevertheless my concern did not overcome my confidence that I could do the job when the test came. Weeks later my confidence was justified. When we got into the tough combat of the Hurtgen Forest, I did all right.

I did not, however, do so well in keeping a good supply of the useful euros. I know very little about the European Union, but one fact of the Union which I like is that they adopted one currency (the euro) for almost all of its countries. It is comparable to our dollar. The current rate of exchange is about one euro to one and a half dollars.

I say "almost all" because I know that in one country, the United Kingdom, the British have retained their currency, the pound, and the penny. I haven't checked whether or not any other member of the European Union has failed to adopt the euro. Britain might be all of the "almost all."

On the trip we visited England, France, Luxembourg, Germany, and Belgium. On several days we visited two countries. Imagine the time and turmoil if we had to exchange our money every time we crossed into a different country. The euro solves the problem.

For travelers such as myself, cash machines are very helpful. I've only traveled overseas four times in my life: first – to Europe in 1944-45, courtesy of the US Army; second – to Japan and Korea in 1951, again courtesy of the US Army; third – to western Europe in 1988 with my dear wife, Mary; and fourth – to western Europe in 2007 with three of my sons on "the trip." I don't remember cash machines in 1988, but I remember them well in 2007.

European cities are replete with cash machines which are often found in niches just off the sidewalk. You insert a credit card or debit card and 'voila,' there from the machine comes crisp local currency, namely the useful euro.

A reader should understand when reading of my experiences that I am an old geezer who was 84 on the trip and has added years since. I've used credit cards for years but the debit card was new to me. Sometime before the trip one of the boys suggested that I get a debit card and bring it on the trip as a backup to my credit card. I got the debit card and the advice proved to be fortuitous.

I don't recall where or how I got the first of my euros on the trip. It was probably on the ferry from Dover to Calais. Some days later in Dinard or St. Lunaire I was running low on euros and asked Willy where we could get some. He replied that there was a cash machine nearby and that he too was running low. So I gave him my credit card to get $200 in euros.

Willy thereupon became my cash machine expert.

To put it mildly, Willy and I found the cash machines erratic. Thereafter I gave Willy both my credit card (to try first) and my debit card if the other failed.

Our next try was in Chartres, where Willy found a place which had two machines. The first refused his debit card, but the second gave him his euros. Both machines refused my credit card, and the first also refused my debit card, yet the second accepted it.

Of the four or five cash machines that Willy and I visited

on the trip, Willy's debit card was refused twice, my debit card was refused once, and my credit card was <u>accepted</u> once. Since I don't know which of the boys suggested that I bring a debit card, I now thank Chris, Sean, and Willy for seeing that I avoided the debacle of trying to procure cash without a debit card.

Incidentally, after returning home, I inquired of my credit card company why my card was not accepted on the trip. The unsatisfactory answer was, that because of some problem relating to their credit cards outside of the United States, they put a "hold" on credit card use in Europe <u>unless</u> the holder of the card advised my credit card company <u>in advance</u>.

I think it would have been nice if they had advised me of this <u>before</u> the trip. Not surprisingly, I was not so sanguine as this during the trip while in pursuit of the elusive euro.

Today, in pondering the Ile de Cézembre experience during the war, my thinking (and possibly my confidence) has changed. What would have happened if the Germans had not surrendered, and we assaulted the Ile? Chances are that I would have been hit (wounded and out of action) soon after leaving the assault boat – either while still in the water or on the Iles' sand beach. The Germans surely had mortars dug deeply into the reverse slope of the Ile with their sights set exactly on the beaches where we would land. The result might well have been a miniature Omaha Beach on D-Day, with the slaughter on the Ile of over half the attacking force of American boys. Unlike Omaha Beach, the Germans might have counterattacked and pushed us off the Ile. War is hell, but it might be even worse if one's imagination gets out of control.

Willy

Chartres.

Pull into Chartres. This beautiful sunshiny day. The city center. Park in underground garage. Which will prove difficult to get out of.

There's the Cathedral. But first a bit of the inane. Attempt to get funds from ATM machines. Which seem to work no better than the telephones. Which require a special phone card. Which we purchase. With the result that we are still unable to make the phones work.

Walking around. Beats driving around.

Looking for a place to buy a cell phone. Can't manage to accomplish that either.

Okay. We'll try to get something to eat. Maybe we can succeed in that.

Daddy and Sean want a café or restaurant where you sit and have people wait on you. I do not. I want to sit in the sun, in the courtyard outside the Cathedral. CD agrees with me.

I spot a kebob shop which seems inviting. We trudge on over.

Delicious smells. Smokey from the cooking and the large Turkish owner puffing away on a cigarette. Two girls chatting with another dark-complexioned chap. On the game? Too pretty. Chic Euro get-ups. Big Turk says he lived in New York City for a while. Sean thinks he may be involved in gangsterism.

We take our fare back to the courtyard. Pigeons flock, children frolic. Just settle on these benches.

Beef and vegetables slathered in yummy sauce, on long thin baguette. Pommes frites. Absolutely delicious, best meal for days. So simple yet fine.

Children playing in the park. Different, somehow, from those in America. These actually seem like children, rather than ill-mannered and miserable miniature adults. Plenty of time for that later. The misery. Play now. And laugh. Without video game or other electronic device. Here in the shadow of Chartres Cathedral.

Finishing our lunch, now over to the church. A guided tour by a Brit named Miller. Charming chap of 70 or so.

Sitting in pews for his introductory presentation. Me, right up front, my over-stuffed backpack still on. Squirming in my seat, not enough room for me arse to sit comfortably. Miller speaking, all 30 or so folk attentive. Me wriggling, trying to get positioned. Not wanting to unharness my pack and distract the proceedings. Bad leg going numb. Hmmm. This won't do. Hell with it. Up and down the aisle, un-ass me burden. There. Wasn't so bad.

Now walking. Miller explaining the majestic stained glass windows. How they depicted and explained stories from the Bible. To illiterate peasants of yore. Maybe use similarly stained glass. To explain beauty. To illiterate peasants of now. Back in my country.

The tour over with. Explore the big church. Solemn and hushed atmosphere. As is proper. And here. A shrine. The Black Madonna. A young man. Down on one knee. Ubiquitous backpack. Face buried in one hand. Deep in contemplation.

I'm struck.

A votive candle he's lit. For loved one? Dead or still amongst the quick. Or just guidance, wisdom. Or grace.

This darkly-hued pilgrim. Of West African extraction it would seem.

Godspeed you, my man.

May you find. Here. This house of God.

That which you seek.

Wandering these hallowed halls. Chris and Sean taking pictures, Daddy nowhere to be seen. I make it my task to find him. To paraphrase British General Leslie J. Morshead, of the battle for Tobruk:

"There will be no Omaha Beach here."

We now exit the Cathedral. Two beggars on the doorstep. Selling plastic flowers. Rough men in shabby clothes. They still have these? Pilgrims and beggars. Down – in supplication. Asking for money or mercy.

I pretend I don't see them. Which is what one does. In America.

Within minutes I'm ashamed of myself.

Sitting on concrete bench, outside the wrought-iron fence in front of the Cathedral. Smoking. Others doing other, elsewhere.

A vast mob moves towards me. Not to worry but wonder. These young blokes. In ecclesiastical garb. Some with backpacks, one with earphones on. I almost laugh. Young seminarians, judging by looks and languages various, from all over the world. Chattering and shoving, usual horseplay of young guys. Could be a platoon of soldiers or footy squad. All lining up in rank for a photo. The monsignor in charge with unmistakable American accent, probably Midwestern.

This being all highly amusing to me, these future priests, all messing about. I nearly proffer a smoke to the one in charge, think better of it. Appears he could use one. A drink too.

They all hustle on into the Cathedral, suddenly quiet again outside.

Daddy and the lads appear, and it's decided to, once again, look for telephones.

Perhaps we could just entreat St. Michael the Archangel to deliver our various communiqués. Might be easier.

That or carrier pigeons.

Or smoke signals.

We set up camp at yet another park, here in the city center. Sun going down, the denizens heading home from work or out for the evening.

Tall black girl with veritable lion's mane of curly golden hair doing the double-take at Sean. Which he's well pleased about. Ought to be in movies, that one.

Daddy and I repose on a bench while Chris and Sean wander off in search of the all important cell phone. Bonne chance, chaps.

Daddy and I looking at maps. Probably. Dude on bench next to us. Dirty clothes, tell-tale paint splatters and dry-wall dust on boots. One of my tribe. Drinking from tall can. Keeps looking at us. I don't like him. In dog language I let him know it will not be easy. Two big men from America, though one be old. Yankee dollars. Soft tourists, easy marks. Or maybe just not like the B. M. from A.

I stand and walk over to his bench, watching his hands. Position myself between benches and carry on chatting with Daddy, facing front. The yob soon ups and leaves.

I will later advise Daddy to be less conspicuous in his public displays of cash, he being in the frequent habit of pulling out a thick roll of notes and slowly counting them.

He doesn't seem convinced nor concerned.

Chris and Sean returning now. Bought a cell phone. 150 euros or so. Can't make it work. No surprise there.

Trying now to exit the parking garage. Weird blue fluorescent lighting. Can't figure out how to pay the toll, make the bloody traffic arm go upwards. We want out. Several cars backed up behind us. Wondering, no doubt, what new strain of stupidity they are witnessing. Guy tries to help. Can't understand him. As we are four big clowns from America. Chris and I offer up all our coins, Sean offering up all his credit cards... somehow we convince the machine to allow us to leave.

Whew! That place was giving me the creeps.

Back to the farmhouse. I imagine. Did we get lost on the way? I imagine.

Tomorrow we'll drive to another country entirely, Luxembourg. This should be a riot.

Lock up your daughters, batten the hatches. On your churches.

Disconnect all telephones.

Hide all street signs.

Let loose the dogs –

Here we come.

Watch out.

CD

10- 15- 07

Up'n' movin'. Kung fu exercises this morning. It's fun to fight. Plenty of room to move since we now have the grand suite, so kindly provided by the concierge – no – our lovely hostess – no – this dauntless adventuress who had knocked about Alaska in her youth, as I had been knocked about in mine.

So sad to leave this beautiful picturesque spot.
But it's down to hungry breakfast
And then with dispatch on to Chartres.

It would be with the certain sadness
That we depart this pretty place
And our fine fetching artiste hôtesse.
But we have the sumptuous breakfast before us.
Then hence, no doubt, the bonne journée.
Onward – Chartres, that ancient city.

Glorious sunny day here in Dinard. After driving driving, squinting at maps, squished together, damn near holding the bated breath. But somehow manage to avoid shouldering my share of the driving driving.

Yea, shittily shirk the duty.
Better for all; best indeed.
Thank you, Jesus; thank you, Lord.

Takin' care of business, lookin' for phones. Failing that, find shades for Willy. Meet success there. Several banks and money changing stations, one after the other. Daddy finally scores the ready, maybe Willy too. Now we look for Pointe de Moline and Ile de Cézembre for the old man's memories and the younger man's photo op. Following that, where's the scary Hitchcock Psycho House that Sean says is somewhere near? And then, I suspect we'll be on our way.

Under way, I say.

Here we are – voici.

Nous sommes ici.

Pointe du Moline. And a quick-opening place close to park for the proximity. It's tough for Daddy to traverse, but he's quick out and up and on the move and moving fast. (Well, sort of.)

The promontory from which we can view Ile de Cézembre. Here is where the green second lieutenant was almost introduced to combat. The amphibious assault was planned and practiced; the apprehension was. They were saddled up and ready to go but the Germans at the last minute of the eleventh hour surrendered.

There is memory and meaning here for my father. That little piece of worn rock there signifies something to him. For true – beyond anything I have ever known.

Viewing the Ile de Cézembre companionably all together. I think we like each other today. Shoot some shots. Daddy, uninvited, approaches a French couple and chats with them and explains and explains some more. They are very kind and courteous to him. They even speak his native tongue. (Well, sort of.)

Willy climbs over a sea wall and down to the beach, to the craggy strand. It's not so much beach as ragged slate rock and shining obsidian gravel.

It strikes me ... I feel like a tourist. Which I've rarely been or felt. And it's oddly not bad but good.

There is a small sign which we squint to see on the Ile de Cézembre out to sea. Sean says the sign may say you can't go beyond that certain point because, to this day, there is unexploded ordnance and danger of death.

So sad for such a splendid spot –

Now civilized, sightly, serene.

Beautiful day in the warm and warming sun.

Beautiful day not to be on the attack.

Beautiful day what with no bombing and shelling and shooting.

We converse, confer, marshal our selves and our stuff, and move out and move on.

Off for Chartres. On the road. Au revoir to Dinard. Through St Malo.

Kinda' clubby in the crushed little car and we get on each other's nerves.

Must need stop to piss. "Better pull over quick." Park on the side of the road. Nothing but cow pies and grass. Now, back home it's Minnesota Nice and such – We have the WC for the privacy on the side of the road. But not so much in France – no offense. Truckers pull off, park and pee; just pull it out and piss.

Daddy considers the modesty and spies a stand of trees across the road, sets his jaw and sets forth. Cars wiz by but he makes it and climbs over the embankment. Then, of a sudden and with a shout, into the ditch.

Man Down! We rush to help. I run and dodge and dive for the ditch. Willy moving quickly, slides down the slippery slope, plants his feet and picks the father up. "You push! I pull!" And huffing and puffing, he's up and OK. Catastrophe narrowly averted.

Unfortunately, Willy soggy soaked and got some prickles on the hand from nasty nettles in the rescue rush. He'd be thereby dogged with rash the rest of the day. Heroic and stout lad he.

Sean saunters back zipping up.

We laugh and tease and laugh some more.

But now we're hard back on the road

And hope to gain Chartres before long.

Pass Armentières of World War One fame – the famous fun ditty that everyone knows – and we all commence as though on cue to sing together with great glee and in full voice though sadly not to stellar musical effect:

"Mademoiselle from Armentières,
Parlez-vous.
Mademoiselle from Armentières,
Parlez-vous.
Mademoiselle from Armentières
Hasn't been kissed in fifty years.
Inky-dinky Parlez-vous
Vous vous vous."

There it is.

There it was.

By and gone.

I make the photograph but we've passed it. Must have the population of twelve souls.Where are all the people? Where are they? Is it possible that the French countryside has never recovered from the guns of August?

To this very day?

Can it really be?

Sean says they're all indoors watching Oprah.

A beautiful town just the same.

And now we pass the village St Christoph.

That would be my own namesake town.

They would welcome me with open arms and the brimming bouteille of …

Wouldn't they?

Flyin' toward the next little burg. Good tactics call for reconnoitre for something to drink. But Willy must stop to take a little leak and then he has to take (or rather, leave) another and then he's OK and then less OK and then he's sick – must jumpout now. Now!

The man at the wheel can feel it and deal it.

He jerks the wheels over the shoulder into a pasture. Willy out fast. Me too – Maybe I can help my brother.

We crouch, doubled over; he retches; I pat his shoulder.

And ...

This cup shall pass.

No soiling of the garments

Nor anything else,

Of the car

Or us

Or one's squeaky reputation.

So on and on we go.

Roll on.

Ill effect of poisonous bog of Daddy's fall and Willy's fine brave show.

The next crisis will be mine:

Do we secure the Swig or do we not?

And now at last arrived. Here we are at an honest-to-God picturesque farm house in the countryside middle o' nowhere and the name escapes me but I will recall and recount it later, he said.

"St Maxine," says Willy.

Sean and Daddy in to check out les chambres, and all seems friendly, jake and copacetic.

Willy and I idle in the courtyard and regard the old ivied walls and get wind of a dog that barks – no, growls – no, beastly grunts. I tighten my grip on my stick and wish I had my pistol.

Smell good earth. Spirits up. Chins up. Soak up sun. We had stopped at a little magasin to pick up some supplies.

So, something later to savor; something on of a substance here – by and by, and bye the bye.

As we pace in picture postcard precinct
And the Beemer engine idles
And we wait to move and move on,
And to grab our rough hewn room.
Yeah!

Load in the luggage.
It's good to move.
Stake out quarters.
Waves and currents –
Sean and I not compatible.

Not only does he eschew morning exercise himself, but he can't stand it of others, even if he himself still sleeps. Noisy in the morn, is it now?

We switch.

Daddy now stretched out in the bed, on his back, head to chest;
Takes his ease softly and is of angelic aspect.
I look to my father – old and at rest.
And am quietly happy
But almost cry.

The Great Northern Cool now,
Old world drafty.
Dig big sweaters from bags and don.
Lots and lots and lots o' talk
But I'm out and off for the walk.

French provincial countryside. But quickly here's a little cluster-clump of age-old small structures, and the street becomes thick cobble, but lights are off in the eventide and there's nobody there.

But none-the-less and all-of-a-sudden:
ZOOM.
Norman cars careen on funky surface.
Four feet from my death.
Voila.
Come on,
Come on;
Can it be?

Daddy

Chapter Seven

Monday, October 15, 2007

Chartres

Sean had made a reservation for us to stay for two nights in an interesting farmhouse a ways out from Chartres. We somehow managed to get a late start from St. Lunaire, so the 200-mile drive made us arrive after the dinner hour.

Sean and I drove out into the countryside to find food. No luck. Unlike the roadways in Minnesota's farming areas, there were no drive-ins or small towns. It appeared as though there had been no change in the countryside for years. All we saw were farmland, farm houses, farm buildings and farm animals. The only non-farm buildings were several tiny churches which arose from the landscape. I don't know their denominations, but I might make a guess and call them "farm churches."

Since Sean and I returned empty handed, we survived the night on our meager supply of cheese and crackers. However, our gracious proprietress assuaged our hunger the next two mornings with man-sized, all-you-can-eat breakfasts.

Our farmhouse was a sturdy stucco building of, I'm sure, many years of age, in which the second floor had been brought up to date with modern plumbing and windows to attract travelers.

When I hear "farmhouse," I think of my grandfather's farm in sandy-soiled northern Minnesota. It was a small single story house with the biffy outdoors and a well for water outside away from things. Nothing fancy.

Quite a contrast from our large, beautifully redone second floor bedrooms with beamed ceilings and private baths, undoubtedly designed to satisfy the needs of the less penurious modern day travelers.

Chartres. That ancient city with its ancient cathedral (dating back to 1260) was not a destination where I had any combat or near-combat experience. I chose Chartres in order to visit for a second time Chartres Cathedral, also known as the Cathedral of Our Lady of Chartres. I had visited the cathedral once before (with Mary) and resolved that the boys (and their father) must not drive across France from Dinard to Luxembourg without a visit to it. We could, and did, skip Paris, but could not, would not, and did not skip the Cathedral of Our Lady of Chartres.

Chartres is a tourist site with crowds of people in, out, and around the cathedral, reminding me of the shoulder to shoulder lines in and around Mont St. Michel.

Before going into the cathedral we had to park the car, so Sean drove to the cathedral looking for a vacant parking spot or a parking ramp. No luck. After a half hour of driving around, we came upon the entrance to an underground parking ramp only two blocks from the cathedral. We had driven by it two or three times without realizing what it was. How could we have been so dumb? But dumb is not quite the correct word. It should be "illiterate." The sign near the entrance was clear – but in French. We thought that the entrance was for private rather than public parking. My high school French did not help. After two or three drive-bys Sean decided to try to enter and was successful.

If we had trouble getting into the underground ramp, we had double trouble getting out. At the end of the day we walked back to the ramp, got into the car, and drove to the exit. Then came the trouble.

A single line of fifteen to twenty cars faced the only machine leading to the outside. The driver had to put some sort of card into the machine, which would raise the gate, allowing the car to leave. Sean inserted a card, possibly a credit card, into the machine. The gate refused to rise. He tried two other cards. No luck. Sean, our constant driver except for one fairly short jaunt with Chris at the wheel, then displayed the most skillful driving of the entire trip.

Since we were holding up all the other cars behind us, Sean decided to pull out of the head of the line. But how? There was no room to turn around and drive out, so he had to back out. The only way to accomplish this was to try to back down the narrow space between the left side of the cars and the far side of a narrow cement walkway which was a few inches above the garage floor. The far side of the walkway was a concrete wall. It would be a tight squeeze.

Sean pulled our car up a little so he could back along the left side of the cars behind us and then try to navigate backwards between the line of cars and the concrete wall to an open space. He called to the back seats, "Willy, look out your side. Chris, look out yours".

We started to back down – very slowly. Although I knew that Sean was an excellent driver, I feared that the car could not squeeze its way through the narrow space. Adding to the difficulty was the fact that the way back was not a straight line, but curved a bit from time to time. Not only did Sean need to find and follow the curves while twisted in the front seat facing backwards trying to avoid the cars to his left and the wall to his right, but also expecting Willy or Chris to call out at any time that we were about to hit the wall or a car. Impossible? Not quite. Sean got us down without a scratch.

To call it a miracle would be to diminish Sean's driving skills. Even if there were some help from Above, all of us would have been grateful for any little bit of help. I contributed my bit. I kept my mouth shut.

After the backdown we found a machine that dispensed the exit cards. After a hurried and successful search in our pockets for coins that would satisfy the machine, we got our card and after a brief, but seemingly long hesitation, the gate opened, and we were free – at last.

The cathedral that we visit today dates back to the year 1194 when a massive fire destroyed the earlier cathedral, leading to the construction of the current one, which was largely completed by 1260. Churches and cathedrals were located on the same site as far back as the fourth century A.D.

I won't even try to describe the cathedral. Any words of mine will fail. Pictures help. But in my view, you must be there to feel what you see. I remember standing outside near the front entrance (the Royal Portal) and looking heavenward at the two towering towers which flank the Portal. The gradually tapering towers seemed to reach the sky itself.

Upon entering the cathedral the boys and I learned of a guide who conducted tours of 10 people and spoke in English. We signed up. Not only did he speak in English, he was English. We Americans found his language quite similar to ours. He was a gold mine of information. But what I remember especially was his discussion on stained glass windows, of which there are 176 in the cathedral. I had always thought that stained glass windows were installed in churches solely because they were pretty and let in light. Wrong! In the 13th century, when most of the windows were installed, most people were illiterate. They could not read nor write.

So, besides beauty and light, the windows were designed to teach, to tell stories, largely stories from the Bible, and help people learn their faith. For example, the Incarnation window has 25 panels with the first three showing the Annunciation (the angel Gabriel telling Mary that she's to be the mother of Jesus), the Visitation (Mary visiting her cousin Elizabeth), and the Nativity (the birth of the Christ Child). I suspect that in the early centuries a priest or another biblical expert would have discussed and explained the stories in the windows much as our guide did with us. He sat us down facing the stained glass window (he only had time for two) and explained in detail each of the 25 or so panels in the window.

In order to forestall any reader's impression that I'm some sort of expert on the subject of the Chartres cathedral, read on. Soon after the boys and I left the cathedral, Willy presented me with the gift of a book entitled "Chartres Cathedral," written by Malcolm Miller, our guide. It's large (100 pages), the shape and texture of a magazine. It is filled with colored photos of the cathedral, inside and out, including flying buttresses, carved statue after carved statue of biblical figures, full-color photos of all the stained glass windows, color photos of panels (portions of windows), and more. The text covers everything connected with the cathedral, including its history, architecture, sculpture, glass, and anything I've overlooked. Whatever I've learned about the cathedral has come from Malcolm Miller's book.

Willy's gift of the book reminded me of when Mary and I visited the cathedral in 1988. I bought a small booklet for Mary containing some of the photographs and writing contained in Willy's book. I don't recall the cost of either, but the comparison would be like a fifty dollar book vis-à-vis a ten dollar booklet.

I don't believe that either Mary or I knew that there was a big book for sale. If I had known of it, I nevertheless, knowing my buying habits, would have bought the cheaper booklet. But as to Mary and her appreciation for handsome books, I think she would have prevailed on me to buy the big book. And if I had hesitated, she would have found a way to acquire it. She might have commented that she believed in top quality merchandise.

I wish now that I had known of the book and bought it for Mary. It would have given her true joy.

Before going to bed that evening, I noticed in my suitcase the booklet which I'd forgotten I had brought with me. It was the same little pocket-sized booklet which I purchased for Willy's dear Mama 20 years ago. The author is the same Malcolm Miller. I'm grateful that Willy, unlike his penurious father, is, like his mother, a more generous soul.

CD

16 Oct AM

Here on the Norman farm, and a working farm it is. Talking to the proprietress, or the farmer's wife, with her grandson over breakfast – a simple petit déjeuner. Her husband is actually and even now and since before dawn out in the field on a roaring tractor working the farm. You can hear him.

Here in the beautiful courtyard the cock crows constantly, making me reflect on yesterday. Bit of a tough journey for Willy. He had some sort of ill effect and thought himself sick. Had he had a stroke or some signal event while rescuing Daddy? Were the nettles somehow to blame? Neurological, otherwise physical, psychosomatic, psychological? Jesus! But it sure scared me, frightened us all, and indeed gave brave Willy pause.

The rooms are spacious redone old farm rooms with the big exposed beams overhead. Is this what they call French Provincial?

Sean and I had thought to room together, Daddy and Willy adjacent. Yet Sean was concerned that my morning exercises were too noisy for his unfettered beautysleep. I tried to be polite; think I fairly was; and he, one concedes, was too. So we changed rooms. So what.

I revel in the quadrangle, walk around and talk to Daddy who stands on the balcony offering the amusing remark.

Meanwhile, Willy and Sean have words of some sort – but not too terrible or awful. Though none are armed today, and hope the understanding can be reached. Sean may not shine in close quarters. But then maybe I don't ever bright the light at all.

The storybook courtyard now drenched in warm gold light, though a bit autumn of crispness to the air.

The pleasant conversation with the missus over breakfast. She with a little English, I my bit of French. We laugh a lot and make merry. Her grandson is there in tow too – bit of a party favor, he. The small child always offers entertainment and promotes understanding among the peoples. No?

Presently off, I presume, to adventure to Chartres and the famous cathedral.

Slow and relaxed after breakfast. Unhurried, unharried. Daddy down for a nap. Sean out for a walk. Willy reads. I myself will peregrinate, perambulate, maybe just go for a stroll.

Farm country here:

Rich loamy pungent dark brown soil,

Garish, gnarly, neat trimmed hedgerow.

Narrow narrow roads – Two cars can't come abreast.

Small town – You walk through it in an instant.

Looks like we'll not make Chartres just now nor maybe even ever but most likely just a bit later.

The cock caw-crows portentously.

Birds chippy-chirp in symphony.

As time goes by.

And time goes by. We're off to Chartres to check the church, Daddy drags laundry along for some reason and is eating an apple. Sean expounds on something he calls "Memory Palaces." Also, Paul Fussell and the book, "Class," which he claims might be of interest.

Thank you, sir.

Beautiful day of great glory,

Historical fine farm country.

And at last the gun goes off and we're off.

Thank You, Sir.

Here we are. Chartres. Approach underground parking. Here we come. Oops, private parking. Can't twig the sign. Back up, roundy-roun, more parking, more roundy-roun.

Gott Sei Dank, stout Sean's at the wheel –

I'd just sell the son-of-a-bitch.

Finally safely ensconced in the underground public car park. Dismount. Take to foot.

Commence to do what we do every day:

And that is:

Look for money exchange,

Look for information,

Look for phones.

And may I please addend the list?

I simply seek matches, my own bad self.

In the shadow of the cathedral we find ourselves, and as Lady Luck smiles on us, we're in the frontal courtyard full of God's glorious miraculous warming sun.

While waiting for the guided tour to begin, hunger makes its mark and we think to find something to eat. As usual, split decision, and we walk and talk. If one can be said to be both hungry and content at the same time, then that's what one would say. Willy finally says, "Let's get some kabobs and bring them back to the courtyard and eat them there." Which down and dirty we do.

Turkish takeout discovered amidst the maze as we wander like at the Minnesota State Fair, but with added Euro-tangle haze. Everybody smoking here. Barrel-belly-and-chest chap had stayed in Manhattan near Sean. “You like?” “No.”

So then there is the capital picnic on the plaza. Delicious chow, spirited scuffling pigeons and children flap wings and play. I warily eye incongruent loud talking miscreants as they strut and pose away.

But on to swing inwards; time for the guided tour.

And a marvelous and magnificent and memorable tour of the cathedral. A worldly cultured Englishman straight out of Central Casting, Mr Miller, explains the readings of the stained glass windows and some of the history too.

We had wanted to take the tour of the catacombs beneath but ended up by accident going our separate ways – Daddy talking to people and then getting lost, Willy looking for Daddy, but Sean and I unaware.

Thought to buy and light a votive candle and say a prayer for Mama. It is said that if you pray that prayer that lasts for the entire burning of the candle ...

Sean, not being a believer, asks me to pray. (And who, says I, believe in anything at all? I don't even believe in belief.) He neat lights a candle and I kneel and pray silently. With eyes clamped closed: "It has been hard, Mama, but I love you." Then Sean speaks softly from behind. Was it prayer or just talking to Mama or talking to himself or to me, or just all talk?

I contort myself on my knees
That no one should see my hot tears.

Throughout the cathedral there is something going on far beyond mere tourism, surpassing and superseding and outshining and outlasting the practice of traveling for recreation. I come upon a man leaning against the wall – eyes down, arms folded. Don't know if he be praying, sleeping, resting, or viewing like the rest. Sore urged to photograph the tableaux but feel cheap – To merely and crassly and only make the picture in front of him while he thinks, meditates, prays ... I leave, come back half an hour later. Still there. There are still pilgrims in addition to, and in the land of tourists.

Finally find Willy who has discovered Daddy, who apparently, just like at Omaha Beach, had found himself lost and had thought himself deserted, that we had gone on without him; and was in abject disarray. But as we leave the church he is again composed and in good spirit. We have a laugh.

Exeunt the high church. There are men standing on either side of the elegant baroque doors. They are beggars who hold out their hands. By way of technique, they hold small ornate boxes that the flesh might not actually press.

Out into the light – blinded.

Out of doors, disoriented, searching and fumbling for hat, stick, camera.

And I continue, march on.

They get nothing from me.

Should I be ashamed?

I think I am.

Now we explore the twisting labyrinth streets of Chartres, looking for a sodi or postcards or something. Not I. But you may bet that we discuss and deal with the phone thing.

I long lounge linger

And strike the pose.

"What you doin'? Posin'?" says a brother.

"Yeah. You know it," says I.

Shopping breaks out.

Know not for what or why.

Willy kindly buys a beautifully appointed book for Daddy by the just encountered Mr Miller of touring fame; and almost shyly, even slyly, presents me with a gold commemorative coin.

Tears must be hidden a second time today.

So once again we look for phones, information, banks.
And some victuals.
And some vitals:
That would be vodka or Pernod or even the Evil Absinthe. (Can it now be got in the civilized world?)
Mon Dieu.

And Sean and I strike out.
Step 'n' Stride at Speed – TCB.
William The Elder and William The Younger
Hold down the fort in a central square.

Well, we finally find the department of phones and then we ask questions and then we find another phone store and then we go back to the first phonery and we talk and talk and talk and look at objet d'art, and I could not do this in my indigenous land nor in my native tongue with a telephone from just down the block, and yet we muddle on.

So, ultimately and at long damned last, we have a fellow with whom we seem able to communicate and knows about the devices, and we walk out with the prize, take it out of the box. Walk briskly down the way and two young French girls giggle at us. And of course we can't make the fool thing work; we don't know how to use it. So Willy and Sean now proceed to push buttons and curse like you lost the Super Bowl over/under. I want none of any of this. But we have a shiny new mobile phone for a hundred and thirty euros and I was hoping someone, anyone, would be happy.

Perchance I would be happy too.
But sadly and badly it seems
None of those things are true.

But all the little buttons sure cause an itchiness. Daddy looks mystified. I just stare off into the distance and watch the passersby. Oh ... and I think we have either a plan or some minutes or both. And what can it all mean? But I stalwart stand to take my ease and watch the changing world – what I can see of it. What can I make of it?

The sun sets low, low as our mood.
The shadows lengthen till all is umbra
And we strike razor silhouette.
Most of the boulevardiers are indeed stylish, after the French fashion.
But we in fact are not.

While my good brothers struggle to make the unspeakable speaking apparatus work, Daddy says he has found a place to exchange more money. So, once again, we drive and get lost and drive some more. We look for phones and try to make phones work. We look for money and try to exchange money. It almost would be easier to get a job.

And I
Of course
Develop
The Great And Grimpen Thirst.
And is there anything to drink?
O no. O no, there is not. Oh, no!
This doesn't look good. Not good at all.
What does Sean call this?
The Psycho Clown Buffoon Show?
Or something similar.
Maybe even better.

How beautiful!
How picturesque!
How idyllic!

Of greatly good to body and soul
To sit in presence of Chartres cathedral,
Before God and the fine French people –
Struggle to make a fucking phone function.
Just Work!

Be nice to devote ourselves to Daddy's original intent – the spirit of old soldier returning with sons, and maybe the meditation. But we seem to be derailed by daily life duties and foibles. Put off just like in steady-rolling everyday living, where everything important is always tomorrow and tomorrow and tomorrow and tomorrow.

And all walk off;
I'll trail behind.
Try to keep my cheer.
What ho!
Good Show!
Hot Damn!
Damn Straight!
Very well so far.
So far.

Sean gone off in search of a restaurant. Daddy and Willy depart for elsewhere, sure as shit hunt for same. I think my task is to sustain the spot where we are to meet – here in the pretty as a picture French plaza.

To hold my own,
To guard my ground,
To protect my post,
Maintain defensive position.
Although I'm not really sure.

Could be in for a longing night.
('Twas a dark and stormy night …

Ha ha.)
As per always and ever usual
I'm thirsty dirsty bursty cursety
And have to piss,
And tire a bit too.
But hope that all those years of training and conditioning
And all that physical culture
Would stand me in good stead.
But if it don't,
At least I'm not yet dead.

By and by we sit and dine at a little corner café. Quite congenial, actually; 'spose not so awful bad. Might be in an ad for tourism. I've got me vodka, got me beer. Willy and Sean have a bit of a to-do. Daddy plays the raconteur.

I present for everyone's edification: my accomplishment today. While we were finally able to find a phone, vaticinate to make it work, I know I'll never use it. I don't care a fig for phones. For one hundred, two hundred, three hundred, or a thousand euros or dollars or marbles; I just don't give a damn! And that's just that.

And yet I am able to achieve something, some thing, and a fine and useful and jolly sort of thing at that. It says on the box: flamme, F-L-A-M-M-E, in garish script in red and black, which would signify: allumettes, matches. I bought a box of matches, the wooden matches for the pocket, that I might light my smoke in the wind with elegance and without displaying inept manner, and hence to really enjoy.

I think the men are impressed.

After the grand and civilized time together at the little corner café we try to retrieve the car from the circular, cold, blue-lit underground car park. Well, the problem is that we descend and then ascend, find the gate, the machine to pay, but we just can't make it work. Our money's no good, it won't take it, and we can't get out.

We put cards in – credit cards, debit cards, then driver cards and anything else that could jam in. There is nothing; nothing happens. All the while the cars back up behind us. As luck would have it and praise The Lord: the people are friendly or maybe just understanding or at least and at very worst piteous.

Jump out.

Ask dude –

Whazup?

Can't understand, of course, but there is the helpful waving of the arms. Sean forced to back up, get out the way, let other people proceed, and somehow then to manipulate the machine without alighting. Willy and I, les clowns, meanwhile on foot hustle into a little room that contains various automats that hum and blink insultingly; put in all our little euro and penny pieces. The arm is still down. Well, dammit, put more cards in the machine, bang my fist till hurt, curse desperately – and finally we are free, free at last.

But we are lost, and so we'll drive in circles until we are not lost.

Sean jumps out to look around.

Sean jumps out to look around.

We all but Daddy dismount and get out to ...

In my angst I meet a guy who speaks the lucid English, a Dutchman, who kindly tries to help us.

But he just don't know.

Chapter Eight

Tuesday, October 16, 2007
Chartres, Luxembourg City

Look at the map. Drive east out of Chartres and after a few hundred miles one reaches the city of Luxembourg. But wait! There is one obstacle on the way which we can't drive over, under, or through. The obstacle is a sort of megalopolis known as the city of Paris, the capital of France.

My answer was simple. Drive *around* the south side of the city to the east side, and from there take the highway east to Luxembourg City. Simple. Except for the traffic. Paris, like any of the sort of megalopolis (e.g. New York or London) has automobile traffic in and around it, which can best be described as slow and slower. Our going was yet slower because of the increased traffic brought on by the international rugby matches being held in Paris that week. My impression is that these were comparable (in American terms) to both the Super Bowl and the World Series going on at the same place *and* at the same time. Traffic – slower and slower.

Another problem which I had largely disregarded was maps. European maps. Before writing this I had intended to deliver a diatribe against maps made in Europe – European maps. I was the one who had picked up the map we used throughout our journey. It was clearly American. I purchased it at the American Automobile Association (AAA) facility near my home in Edina, Minnesota, USA. As a member of AAA, I bought it for $6.95, $2 under the retail price of $8.95. My penny pinching habits made me leap for the two dollar discount. The front of the folding map proclaimed "Deluxe Series (AAA) France and Benelux" It covered France, Belgium, Netherlands and Luxembourg. But our trip included a strip of far western Germany, including Aachen and the Hurtgen Forest. The "Deluxe Series" had a separate map of Germany. But before investing in another $6.95 for Germany, I took a hopeful peek into "France and Benelux" to see if my strip of western Germany was included. I knew that western Germany is contiguous with all four of the France-Benelux countries. I peeked, and my hope was fulfilled. Western Germany was on the map, and I wouldn't need a second! I had a twofer (two maps for the price of one). It would be a slight exaggeration to say that the twofer was the deciding factor in taking the trip. But it surely didn't hurt.

Fortunately our driver, Sean, did not have the bias towards maps, European or American, which I seem to have. So despite some map and other troubles, we arrived at all of our destinations safe and reasonably sound.

We arrived in Luxembourg City a couple hours before dark. It was not until a couple hours *after* dark that we discovered our destination, a youth hostel. We had its address and telephone number. After we see-sawed back and forth through the streets, we stopped to find a telephone. Chris and Sean got out to find a public telephone while I continued to sit in my spot next to the driver's seat. After what seemed like hours, but was only a half hour, the boys found a phone and got directions to the hostel. Then followed another hour of driving that included numerous heated discussions concerning the name and location of the next street to take, whether to turn right or left, and the exact address of the hostel. My contribution to the operation was to keep my mouth shut, and (to use a military term) my head and eyes straight to the front.

Street signs. To a fellow who grew up in the Twin Cities of St. Paul and Minneapolis, it was quite a shock trying to find the youth hostel with only a street address and a near useless map.

In the Twin Cities, at most street intersections is a steel pole with a metal sign showing both the street you're traveling on and the cross street. Compared to Luxembourg and other European countries, the Twin Cities were mere fledglings, being founded in the mid-eighteen hundreds.

In Luxembourg City there were no such poles with signs. In that ancient city, many, perhaps most intersections have brick buildings with one side of the building facing the street being traveled on and another side facing the intersecting street. Quite naturally street signs were placed on the sides of the building facing both streets. Probably much of this was done years before the coming of the steel pole.

Sometimes a problem arose when we stopped the car at an intersection looking for the street where our youth hostel was located. Often there was a sign showing the street upon which we were traveling, but when we looked around the corner at the side of the building there would be no sign showing the cross street.

Why should a sign showing the cross street be omitted? I don't know. My only, but far-fetched conclusion is that sign installers in ancient Luxembourg City were more interested in the driver remaining secure in the knowledge that he was still on the road on which he was traveling, than in discovering the road (and intersection) on which he wished to turn off.

Despite the sign problem, Sean, with plenty of not-sought-after advice from his passengers, somehow found our youth hostel.

The youth hostel was chosen while at home by Willy and his sister, Anne, with special emphasis by me to keep the price down. They complied by finding the cheapest place in town. After determining that the youth hostel would accept an 84 year old geezer (me), they booked it. The hostel was very nice. It was clean, well organized, with free breakfast, fresh pillowcases and blankets, and restaurant. I had never been in a youth hostel. With emphasis on "youth." Once was enough.

There was but one room for the four of us. It was small, even tiny. Two bunk beds stood on opposite sides of the narrow walls leaving only enough space in between for two average-sized men to pass each other. Beyond the ends of the beds was a tall, narrow window with a small wood table and chair sitting snugly beneath. A tiny bathroom with a narrow shower filled up the remaining space. I remember especially the water in the bathroom sink. It turned off automatically after short use, apparently to prevent overuse of the water supply. After bringing our four oversize suitcases into the room together with our smaller carry-on luggage, there was only standing room (no walking room) remaining.

Towels. Soon after arrival I washed my hands in the bathroom. I reached for a towel. No towel! I'd never before seen a hotel room without towels. But I was not in a hotel room. I was in a youth hostel in which the price was lower and the amenities are fewer than a hotel. No towels, limited water, minimal storage space, crowded room.

I went downstairs and asked about towels. I was told they were not furnished, but they had towels for sale. I bought four, one for each of us. Careful fellow that I am with the dollar, I wondered if I should ask my daughters whether or not I should make the towels my sons' Christmas presents! I had enough sense never to ask the question.

Our towel problem reminds me of my time in World War II when I was fighting in the Hurtgen Forest. The only available water had to be carried up in five gallon cans through German mortar and artillery fire. We were lucky to have water once a day to brush our teeth. Bathing or even washing hands or face were usually not possible. Towels were not needed. After three weeks in the Hurtgen, the forty men remaining alive and unwounded in the company (down from the original 190) were relieved by a fresh group of cannon-fodder (also known as infantrymen). The forty were trucked back to Aachen to be treated to hot meals, showers, and a full set of clean clothing (the first time in three weeks to remove our long winter underwear, woolen pants and shirts, cotton pants and shirts, sweaters and field jackets). The woolen cap and gloves, the stockings and shoes, and the high buckled overshoes had all been removed on occasion.

63 years ago I was 21 years of age. I was a U.S. Army infantry lieutenant in Germany's Hurtgen Forest in one of the bloodiest battles of World War II. My concerns were the 40 men in my platoon under my command. After three weeks in the Hurtgen, and after the killed and wounded had departed, the 40 had been reduced to 10. Quite a contrast, at the age of 84, with having the duty of purchasing four, not three, not five, but four unnecessary but useful towels.

Willy

Luxembourg.

So now we are for Luxembourg. Getting closer. All along the road to Paris. Which we decide to skip. World Rugby tourney and tens of thousands of yobos from the world over. More aggro than needed. Or presently experiencing in the smaller locales.

Fine with me. Not that I wouldn't want to visit, but I've nearly had enough. And not yet into Germany...

All manner of directional confusion abounds. But a bit of laxity is suggested. Is there anywhere in particular that any one of us would like to see? My hand goes up. Several places, though not directly associated with Daddy's war, present themselves.

Waterloo – just a ways south of Brussels, is a place that's always fascinated me, but it's a bit too far out of our way.

We do pass through Verdun, one of my few suggestions to bear some merit. Children on field trips abound. Try to find tourism center, with no luck.

The day of leaving for this journey, I'd met a guy at my tobacconist, while stocking up on the needful to come and chatting about what I was up to, told me I *must* visit Verdun, as he had while in the US Army stationed in Germany in the '60's. Said Fort Douaumont had a massive plexiglass window where one could view the bones of tens of thousands of French and German soldiers killed in one of the most horrific slaughters in human history.

We pass by the massive walls of a fortress – Douaumont? Fort Vaux? Can't say. Though the walls are pock-marked with every imaginable size and shape of artillery and small arms fire. We see no bones, but just the few minutes passing it are hair-raising to me.

Do these ghosts sleep?

"Known but to God".

Requiescat in pace.

My first sense of ease is stopping at a convenience store outside Luxembourg City.

Chris and I pop in to enquire about the usual circumstance: where in good God's name are we?

Plump girl at the counter. Dyed-black hair, tattoos, and – what do you know! – the German language.

This we comprehend quickly. Down past that big bridge. Somewhere there.

Into the city center. Street signs on buildings. Language a combination of Dutch, French and German. And all three spoken individually, English as well. A truly international nation, or at least city.

Very modern, Lux. City be. Rainy day, grey, concrete and lights. Looking for a hostel, not just for the youthful, this one.

Stop the car on a street – what could well be downtown Minneapolis for all I know. Or care. CD and Sean out to glean info. Phones. Clarity. Liquor, hopefully.

The usual.

Daddy and I stay with the car, myself accosting various passersby for information on – I forget what.

Mosey on down a few city blocks, stop in this bar. Inquire about... I honestly can't say. Old men sipping pints, don't speak the king's English anyway. So what difference does it make what I wanted to ask them? Forego the much needed bevy.

Back to the car. Soon Chris and Sean too. Evening on. More goddamned driving. Though the further we get to Germany, the easier life seems to become. Wonder what Daddy thinks of that notion. Now or 63 years ago.

After several hours of driving through environments that resemble a European art-house film, we find our lodgings.

Large, asymmetrical building of grey concrete. Parking quite a ways away in this small metropolis.

Man on the desk fluent in several languages. And not to be trifled with, as I learn when I complain that my electronic pass-key doesn't work, allowing me to gain the upstairs rooms from the lobby below.

"Of course it does."

"No. It doesn't."

"Yes. It does. I test all pass-keys every night."

Try it again. This time properly.

"So it does! Sorry, sir. Very sorry, forgive my ineptitude."

"No worries. Many much younger people I see far more inept than you."

Ha ha. A good laugh and he seems a stand up guy, must have to deal with all levels of intelligence. From all corners of the earth.

Up the long concrete stairway. Very clean minimalist room. Small space of 20 x 15 feet.

Two sets of bunk beds. For four. Big men from America. Who immediately develop the thirst.

Bust these bottles of wine Chris and Sean grabbed on their walkabout in Lux. City.

Forgot my Swiss Army knife, which I swear I packed, with corkscrew. Bottles popped open by less elegant means. Spills. More's the pity.

Down in the café, gorgeous but surly girl at the counter. For libation and feed. Wine, beer, the odd sandwich ordered. Must be sick of these bloody foreigners, she. I do, in fact, make that comment. She is nonplussed. Well then. Looks aren't everything are they, baby?

We settle at a long table. Talk of God-knows-what. Some emotional memories from childhood. Things getting sloppy. Some more drinks before last call, something to eat for Daddy. Without any bread, thanks. Can't have wheat, you know.

Pretty girl rolls eyes. Sorry, honey, that you have to do such difficult things for a living. Must be awful to have an interesting variety of folk to deal with every day, from all over the world. Silly ingrate.

Time for a smoke. Out on the large spacious terrace. Several groups of mostly young peoples there, high school and college and that.

Standing away from these, I do the needful. Tobacco stylee.

Such a night. And all the travails of the day – now lost, now found, bone tired, incessant worry about the most recent fuckery. I feel, now, a bit at ease.

Just watching these youth. What are their stories? Who their ancestors? From whence come you and why here now...

The sky black blue. I know this because I'm looking that way.

A muffled musical murmur. Rising up from a group of tables. Soon melding into absolutely perfect unison harmony.

Not like back home – where 20 young women might end up in shrieking or general caterwaul. While trying to sing. The same song.

And the song was unknown to me 'til a year later, a bad American pop song created mostly by machines and software.

This night, this group. Sang together in Luxembourg. And sounded like angels. And I do not mean hyperbole. They were beautiful. Together. And it seemed to me, then:

Good tidings.

In the sweet by and by.

All in for lights out. Pressure drop fall. Sean claiming Chris' bunk. CD in his cups, Sean comes the cad. Close quarters not for everybody. Daddy intercedes. Stop this, boys.

Big day tomorrow. Need all the sleep available. To us.

Day next, after breakfast in large dining room. Light out for Wormeldange, bordering Germany.

The drive rather pleasant for a change. This crisp autumn morning. Sun brilliant bright, as in greeting. Crossing the Moselle into Germany, checking with tourism woman. Little office/showroom, Abba's "Waterloo" playing on the radio. She funny and nice. This is going to be fine. "You really must see Trier. It is the oldest city in Germany." We agree we'd love to, but, as usual, we must be getting along. Back over to Luxembourg. Driving steep hilly streets. Not so very lost. We are actually in Wormeldange itself now. If you can believe it. We stop and park, high up over the banks of the Moselle River. Miles of vineyards. Where Daddy's rifle company posted 63 years ago, watching the German's movements, hoping not to be spotted. And fired on. About this time of year, too. Grape vines straight and steep down to the river's bank. Stand taking it all in, gazing across the wide river to that other nation.

CD: "What of that? We humans. Time immemorial. 'Let's go rape and kill those. Over there. On the other side.' God help us."

C'est la guerre.

God is on our side.

"Kill them all. Let God sort them out."

Arbeit macht frei.

The day is fine. The tensions of the previous now forgotten.

Crossing back into Germany, now driving north for Monschau, lodgings reserved for four nights. There to visit Strass, Untermaubach, Huertgenwald, and hopefully into Belgium to the tiny town of Bra, where Daddy was nearly killed one cold January day in 1945.

Northeastern Belgium, on the German border.
This crucible, this vortex.
This blood soaked land.
Of centuries suffering.
This is why we are here.

CD

10-17 9 O'clock

Crows the cock – He calls,
Birds chirp their morning prayers.
Morning morning meditation,
Primordial chi gung to get things rolling.
And roll the rock up hill.

We'll boldly sally set forth, we say –
After the fine breakfast laid on,
With the fresh-baked cake just for us.
Repair to the crisp half-dawn square
To smoke and meditate:
Contemplate
Yesterday's yesterday.
Yesterday, with its triumph and travail.

'Twas late last night, it was, it was:
Smoke the final cig – or so I thought.
Dark, quiet night in the quadrangle.
Suddenly – slam bang bash clang chang!

Startled and confused, I run past the caged dog to the door.

Sean shakily appears, edged in telling orange yellow light.

But it could have been a black and white scene.

It seems that someone, I-he-they-we, (but, in the words of Bart Simpson, "I didn't do it," since I never chill drink but Champagne), had set bottles of wine to cool behind the heavy shutter that Sean had sought to open and did, causing crashing in the night and the need, of course, to clean up. Which on hands and knees we did, surreptitiously, cold sold like naughty high school sophomores.

"Ironic with the work," I thought.
"Not even on the clock."
But Sean thought not to thank.
Ha ha!

And then after breakfast the touching private chat with Daddy about the church, about Sean's sweet gesture with the prayer and the votive candle, and some heartfelt reminiscences of Mama.

What's it like to lose your mate of many years?

Pack the kit and whilst at work review the remains of my erstwhile dinner that wasn't. I see that some kind soul had presented me with a box of errant granola – Dear Old Dad, I think.

Thank you.

But somehow, I never say it.

But so off for Luxembourg. Daddy thinks that this will be the toughest drive of the tour.

Good!

Au revoir to St. Maxime.
Bye bye to the quiet cloister.
We're on our way to Luxembourg,
Along the road to The City Of Light.
Paris, site of one's first love (sex),
When but smooth-skinned, and not so sweet sixteen.
Another story of another time.
For another time too.

Hard on Paris but first Versailles. Rallying from the southwest – we hope to avoid, to skirt the traffic snarl. Just like New York and London – No Drive Zones. But still, just a hint of the pang to miss.

Did we miss the fork in the road?

Despair.
Savor the despair.
But now less despair
And we think we can find our way.

Spirits run irregular high.
Uncomfortable, painfully cramped.
What's new?
Willy sings.
Sort of.
(Sorry.)
[Verily pretty well and swell.]
We may miss Paris
But we won't.

Black and white photo grey.
Roller coaster rolling hills.
Major trucking route in modern France.
Motion 'n' commotion.
Maps and maps.
Break out the magnifying glass.
Oh my.

Le Mans start and Grand Prix turn.
Make it through Parisian auto shitstorm
And on the road for Rheims.
Or is it really Rennes?
Has anybody any feeling in their feet?

Near Rennes, we stop for gas, get some supplies: bread, nuts, apples, water. The fellas get sandwiches and snacks and things.

Ah, but what a pity – No drink there, here to be had.

Hope that's not our last opportunity –
The dreaded and leadened Last Chance.
But we do like to ball that jack.
Do we not?
But could be a dry day, dammit;
Or the abstemious evening.
O my God.

Speed along to Luxembourg by way of Metz. Approach Verdun, decide to take a jaunt. Willy's thought, I think.

Directions not quite clear. But one thing is – We go through war country: The World War, The Great War, Franco-Prussian, Napoleonic, longer and longer back in history and more and more than I can contemplate.

Dwell on this.

Get real quiet

Verdun, beautiful burg on the Meuse river. We, of course, can't find any information but we sure do try.

And neither nor for what we look.

Indeed unsure of what we search.

But the sun also sets and we shiver.

But we do find a massive gravesite, row upon row of identical white markers arranged in a military manner. Also see the bullet riddled massive walls of the city. And also a lot of teenagers getting out of school.

The multiple graves cause one pause.

Roll into Luxembourg.
There is the ambiguity of the directions.
And indeed to direction itself.
Come the rain.
We're tired
And of it tired.

But almost there, we think, unless start looking for information, banks, phones.

Our directions fall short; they don't suffice. Things go smoothly and largely and for long, until we hit Luxembourg. Seems a civilized spot but we've lost our way and it is raining.

Our directions fall short; they don't suffice. Pull into city center early evening. No map. Difficult to park. Difficult to drive. High marks to Sean for his motoring.

Finally find a spot to beach the Beemer. Park the car – Euro side street and up on the curb. Cold gray rain on shiny slick cobble street.

But lucky to be here
All in one piece.

Willy and Daddy remain with the car. Sean and I rush off to raid ...

I accost people on the street. Looking for direction, instruction; where to go, what to do, how to be.

Language working well today. Real communication is actually achieved it seems (as seen on TV and portrayed in cinema). We have the English, the French, the German. Most here in this land have several. Even I too. Ha Ha!

Willy and Daddy stick and stay,
Watch the ride, study maps and rest.
Sean and yours step sprightly off to play.
Step'n' Stride and Ain't It Grand?
Look for Info, Find Bearings;
To see what there is to see.
To see what we would see.
(The Bear went over the Mountain.)

Where are we? Where are we going? Where will we stay tonight?

It's walk and talk fraternity,
Tap tap cane to cobble.
Stone cold characters fore and aft –
A gauche,
A droit.
Sean says: “Look at all the junkies. Just like New York City.”
City center cinéma vérité.
The heart of the city, of sorts.
And then there are the sorts and sorts:
There are the whores.
There are the students.
The junkies,
The lost,
The hurried,
The harried,
The harrowing,
The hurrying past,
And us.

Walk'n' talk with Sean in soft rain.
Importune the passersby.
See famous cinematic sights.
Find the city center main train station.
Pay for a piss.
Talk to a uniform.

Beat feet back to the gang.
I palpitate of possibility, vigor and youth,
(However much the humbug);
Over-brim with excitement and joie de vivre,

And yet be quietly content.

Tension between Daddy and Willy.
Nothing new, but it do get old.
Feed William The Younger a drink.
A diversionary map for William The Elder.
A shout to Sean and off again off;
Resume the search and the war.

Lord, we're trying to follow the simple map and driving driving driving. It's hard to see the street signs. Not only here but throughout artistic Europe. The signs seem not to work so well. You find them sometimes, but not always, on the sides of buildings.

And on and on we go, charge into the rainy night. Finally find the youth hostel into which I guess we're booked. This is much different now than those of my youth – newer, bigger, cleaner, far less dilapidated; and not now just for the young and indigent only.

The gentleman at the front desk has several languages. There are multiple forms and some silliness concerning deposits for keys.

No towels – My party certainly concerned. Daddy sweetly buys, not rents, inscribed towels for each and presents them with ceremony as gifts.

Thank you, then, kind Sir.
And here's to cleanliness too.
And to The Clean.

Lots of kiddies, high spirits, high voices – horsing around and having fun. That's just great. Get it while you can.

Four-square small room, four of us all to the cell – about fifteen by fifteen. Bunks. Just like jail.

I be happy to take an upper berth. But it seems as though my kin think I can't climb. And yet I climb for a living, claw for my dough, and perform they know not what daily in the course of coo li.

To down a couple bottles of wine which Sean and I had found while on our spring heel walk-about –

Looking for the right direction
In the maelstrom of the moment
In the Action Jackson teeming city center
As evening's last act curtain falls.

There is no corkscrew, so I push the corks in with my knife in the tiny over-lit bathroom, and slop-spill plenty, blood red stain my singlet, and cuss like a downtown clown.

And so the night would shape to be.

There is the thirst; we drink the wine.

We hurry scurry downstairs where there is food and drink, beer and wine. We utilize those things for fun. We chat with animation – raillery and repartee. The pleasantry and bon homme abound.

But then retire to cramped cubby cubicle room. Think my lot a bit shocked – Not used to this sort of close quarter. Spot of tetchiness develops but sleep overtakes us and Dear Old Dad just rolls inexorably on.

Daddy

Chapter Nine

Wednesday, October 17, 2007

Luxembourg City, Wormeldange and Monschau

My plan was to find and show the boys the hill in Luxembourg overlooking the Moselle River occupied by one squad of my platoon in 1944. After that we would drive north to stay in Monschau, Germany, a town within a short drive of both the Hurtgen Forest and the Ardennes Forest. I had spent my one day in the Battle of the Bulge in the Ardennes.

Early in the morning of October 17, after leaving Luxembourg City, we drove north along the Moselle to Wormeldange, the Luxembourger town below the hill on which one of my three squads was located in 1944. The town, as well as the others on the Moselle, is located on low ground with steep hills overlooking, and across the river, the German countryside (where the enemy German soldiers were hidden). For non-wine drinkers (as well as the other kind) the world-famous Moselle wines come precisely from this area, and those hills are covered, acre upon acre, with rows of large-leafed vines attached to wooden poles in the endless grape orchards.

In the fall of 1944, my platoon of three 12-man squads had the job of being the defenders (the front line of defense against a German attack) of Wormeldange and the hill, which was really a ridge that ran two or three hundred yards facing the town. The forward squad was near the top of the ridge while the other two were back in reserve. I had the forward squad dig two foxholes for observation (two men in each) on the forward slope (facing the town and river) and hidden among the grape vines. They were dug during the day we arrived, thinking that the heavy cover of grape vines would hide us from the gaze of our opponents across the river. The rest of the squad dug in on the reverse slope, just out of sight of the enemy.

When my sons and I reached Wormeldange (going north), we took the first road left (west) which led around to the rear of the ridge. There was no road up the steep forward slope. After much, much looking and backing and forthing, the boys and I agreed we could not find the spot on the ridge where my men had dug the foxholes. We ended our search at the top of the ridge with the spectacular view of Wormeldange snuggled between the Moselle River and the steep forward slope of the ridge and the German countryside across the river in the background. I knew that I was not looking from the same spot as I had in 1944. I refused to get closer than ten feet from the edge of the steep downward slope. My brave boys did better. I recalled that in 1944 the slope down to Wormeldange (hundreds of feet) was fairly gradual – enough for the grape picker to recover if he lost his balance. But from my spot in 2007, the slope was so steep that I can't imagine how a grape picker can pick grapes, keep his balance and stay alive. It's a long fall.

Digging foxholes at the forward slope of the ridge made sense. Keeping an eye on the enemy and his movements was important. But after my recent visit through the leaf-covered vineyards of Luxembourg, I can't help but wonder how and why I had the audacity (and perhaps ignorance) to dig in daylight observation posts which were clearly visible to the enemy who lay hidden only a few hundred yards across the Moselle. Although the Germans never took advantage of my stupidity by attacking our position, they might well have discovered some similarly befuddled, yet brave, American lieutenants on December 16, 1944, when the Germans thrust through the American defenses some 50 miles north of what had been my location, commencing the now famous conflict known as the Battle of the Bulge.

In 1988 Mary and I were able to find the chateau in

Luxembourg which I and my 40 man platoon had occupied for two months in the fall of 1944. Before my sons and I went to find the chateau in 2007, my recollection was that it was located in Wormeldange, Luxembourg. Although the chateau was located behind the Moselle River and Wormeldange is just a small town, and although the boys looked and looked, the chateau failed to reveal itself.

I can't help but think that if Mary had been living when we planned the trip in 2007, she might have directed us to the right place. I don't know why I think this, but she was a special person. She might have recalled something about the chateau or some unique yet hardly memorable feature of the terrain which struck her fancy, and then led us to the elusive building.

More simply, she might have recalled the name of another town in which the chateau is actually located.

After leaving the ridge near Wormeldange at about noon, we drove north to the ancient city of Monschau, Germany, where we stayed the next five nights and four days, by far the longest stay at any place on the trip. It was a delight. I think that I should award myself a prize for having chosen such a charming and interesting spot. But modesty and accuracy require that I decline. I found Monschau on the map and chose it solely because of its location, within easy driving distance to the places where I spent my combat time in World War II, namely the Hurtgen Forest, about 30 miles north of Monschau, and the Ardennes Forest, about 30 miles to the west, in Belgium.

Near the Hurtgen is the city of Aachen which Mary and I had visited in 1988. I'm not sure why we decided to see Aachen. Both Mary and I knew of Aachen as the ancient capital of Charlemagne's empire in the eighth and ninth centuries, as well as knowing of its ancient cathedral which somehow remained largely intact after the destructive battles. We decided to spend a night there since Aachen is close to the Hurtgen Forest, Strass and Untermaubach, our destinations for the next day.

Aachen was the first German city captured by the Allies in World War II. It was taken largely by the famous American First Infantry Division in September and October, 1944. The city was destroyed – flattened – by the fierce fighting. But by the time of our visit there in 1988, the beautiful city had been rebuilt, with thousand-year-old-appearing structures with less than fifty years of wear and tear.

One of the things which interested both of us was the poem, I believe by Robert Browning, entitled "How They Brought the Good News from Aix to Ghent." Aix referred to Aix-la-Chapelle, the name given to Aachen during some European war.

I haven't been able to locate the poem. I've always thought that it described how some horsemen galloped from Aix-la-Chapelle to the Belgian city of Ghent to give the good news of the defeat of Napoleon at Waterloo in 1815.

I have just looked at the map. Waterloo is a southern suburb of Brussels, whereas Ghent is north and west of Brussels and Aachen is southeast. Since Ghent is closer to Waterloo than Aachen it seems that Ghent would have heard the good news before Aachen, i.e. Aix.

I must have something wrong!

But in 1988 Mary and I did spend half a day and one night in Aachen. Aside from the splendid cathedral, my only recollection is an incident at dinner that evening, of a sort of which I have never experienced before or since.

The waitress and others in the German restaurant spoke – surprise – German. I was lost. My vocabulary in German starts and ends with "danke." Mary, however, took German in both high school and college. She chatted with our waitress and others as though theirs were her native tongue. The best I could do was a few "dankes."

The restaurant featured a homemade apple juice of which we both had a couple of glasses. Mary explained how much we enjoyed the juice. After we paid the check, our waitress gave us two large glass bottles of the delicious juice. I think it was their thanks to Mary (an American) for treating and speaking to all in her most friendly and gracious manner.

My earliest memory of the Aachen cathedral was a sign just inside the front entrance reminding that it was a "working" cathedral and that no loud noise was permitted. Quite a contrast to Mary and my experiences in 1988, in which a few European cathedrals had visitors (I suspect non-European) who behaved raucously as though they were entering their favorite hang-out back home.

In 1945 at the end of World War II, I had a grudge against the Germans, not only the soldiers, but the civilians as well. I was in the army of occupation, in which we American soldiers lived in small German towns, often in the houses of German civilians.

I remember after the war in the fall of 1945, our company, reduced by combat casualties from 190 to less than 100 men, was stationed in the small Bavarian town of Grainet. Three or four of our men would stay in each of the houses shared with the families of the homeowners. It should be noted that this was probably at least the third time that the company was brought up to full strength of 190 men after being decimated in the deadly fighting in Normandy, Brittany, Luxembourg, the Hurtgen Forest, the Ardennes Forest, the Harz Mountains, and elsewhere.

With three of my men I lived in a small house occupied by the woman who owned it and her four-year-old son. I still remember that his name was Oatmar. We fellows called him Oatmeal, but not to his face. It was good for a laugh. We did tell his mother and explained to her what oatmeal is. She smiled.

Her husband had not yet returned from his German military service. We four soldiers occupied two bedrooms and ate in our mess hall in another building.

The only other room in the house which we used was the bathroom. The house had no running water. The biffy looked similar to those found in our more modern US houses. But upon raising the seat cover, instead of the usual view of a small pool of water awaiting the reception of flowing toilet water, was a deep dark hole anticipating whatever the biffy's user was prepared to deposit. I thereby became more grateful for the more modern flushing devices.

One might think that after the war I would have had more anger at the German soldiers than I had for their civilians. On the contrary, I had some sympathy for German infantrymen who suffered the same combat experiences as I had. As to the civilians such as the woman in our house, I had a continuing anger for their having anything to do with aiding the Nazi war effort. After two or three decades my anger finally faded.

I suppose I should have been thankful that those in Supreme Allied Headquarters who ran the show from Versailles, outside Paris, miles from the battle lines, made the decision to allow us infantrymen to sleep in real houses. Perhaps I should not be surprised at the decision by my Versailles based countrymen who were near the attractions and distractions of Paris and might never have been in combat. Some of them might well have thought it unthinkable that an American soldier be slated to sleep in anything other than a comfortable bed with freshly ironed sheets, located in a weather-proof building.

My notes tell me, "describe Monschau." But how? I'm sure that a few well-placed adjectives cannot do the trick. Monschau is located in a deep, narrow valley of the Roer River, a stream no more than 30 feet wide. On either side of the river are 100-foot-high ridges which are too steep for roads. So the only way to drive in or out of the city is to follow the river. The city of Monschau is squeezed between the ridges and adjoins the river, leaving room in many places for only two narrow streets paralleling the river. How narrow? Buildings are built within five feet of the street. On that five feet is a sidewalk for pedestrians. If a car is parked heading north in a street, a car moving south must steer onto his nearest sidewalk to avoid hitting the parked car! There's an ancient building in almost every vacant space in Monschau. At least all the buildings appear to be ancient. The appearance of an American Motel 6 or Holiday Inn would be denied by anyone familiar with Monchau as a mirage. Perhaps the most attractive attribute of Monschau is the continuous and heavy foot traffic along meandering streets of the city. I remember looking out the window of my hotel room any time of day or evening, and seeing groups of people walking and chatting along the sidewalks and narrow streets.

The happiest memory of my time in Monschau was the small, fifteen room, three story Hotel Royal where the boys and I stayed in two rooms. Late in the afternoon of October 17 we pulled up in front of the hotel. I sat in the car while Chris and Sean went in to confirm that this was the right hotel. Permanent parking was blocks away. When they came out, I got out of the car to go to the front door. Before entering, I asked Chris where the hotel lobby was. To my surprise he told me that the hotel had no lobby. In order to register, I had to cross a narrow alley to a coffee shop run by the hotel's owners (a young lady and her husband). I found them there busily serving freshly baked goodies and delicious homemade chocolates and other sweets. I registered for two rooms and received keys to the rooms together with keys to the hotel's front door! Never before or since have I needed a key to enter the front door of a hotel.

Before leaving home I'd talked on the phone with my friend, Jim Begg.Jim is an old Edina, Minnesota boy who had lived in Europe since 1965. He ran a large advertising firm, was president of the American Overseas Memorial Day Association in Belgium (one of the most active military commemorative organizations in Europe), and one of the organizers of the American Club (a social organization in Brussels). I told him we would be staying in Monschau for a few days. He said he knew the town well, and he heartily approved. I told him the name of our hotel, and we agreed that he would try, if possible, to come from Brussels to see us. After the boys and I got settled in our rooms and started thinking of dinner, suddenly, out of nowhere, appeared Jim Begg. I had not been thinking about our telephone conversation, so I was surprised to see him. He had driven from Brussels and arrived shortly before us and had registered at our hotel.

I, of course, invited Jim to dinner. He, of course, accepted. And all of us, of course, had a rollicking good time at a local eatery including succulent German food and sufficient beverages of our choice (of course). Instead of behaving like the prominent person who he is, Jim treated the boys as friends with whom he could chat freely and openly. His presence was a highlight of the trip.

CD

10-18 7AM

Early to rise. The day is young in the youth hostel. Kung fu forms outside the small room in the narrow hall – Only place to play. Interrupted and surprised by some Japanese women at this hour. We have a smile and a laugh. "Morning kung fu," I say. I think they think it fine, or at least funny.

Then out for the brisk daybreak constitutional in the wending, winding streets of entranced dawning dreamscape Luxembourg City.

Remember the adventure of the last past day,
In the early morning telling half dawn gray:

Hark: a dream, or is it true?
Came Sean and I then hard to blows?
About what? I don't know.
Quartered close and disparate, desperate show.
He clocks my clock, sweet gift from Daughter Cally.
"Give it up, Sean."
"I won't."
I snatch.
He snatch back.
I snatch.
He snatch back.
"I'll break it, I'll break it, I will."
I think – to throat.
"Boys! Boys!" shouts Daddy.
We stop, no pop; we stay, no play.
Finis, we freeze; no wage to pay.
No pain, no gain; thank God.
No harm, no foul; nor rank foul play.
Or maybe just Daddy's due.

Both brothers step back, defer to Ranking Cadre. That's it, the end. That's all there is, there is no more. Catastrophe narrowly averted. Must talk to Sean anon.

Now back to Now:
I walk underneath a high angular bridge like they'd blow in an old movie.
The last night train rumble rolls over.
A jagged gorge portrays the scene
With switchback streets and twisted paths;
Up and down, up and down cobblestone.
Yellow Euro lights still glare in the gloom
Before the heartbreaking tender breaking dawn.

Pale fall light struggles to offer.
Street lights by rote gradually douse.
The still sleepy populace begin to snap, crackle and pop.
The small Euro cars start tentatively to and fro.
The air smells clean, is crisp and clear –
If I indeed am not.
March up a steep street hill,
Hard, pretty pavers under foot.
Luxembourgers stir and show themselves,
And now there the anodyne noise,
Like a just flicked on radio.
Walkabout walkabout and reminisce.
A sterling time this is for me.
Never ever thought it would be –
What with ancient youth
And in my old time anger.

A young Black European girl,
Smoking adroitly and with style,
Passes me as I ascend

(In spirit and of the body).
"Bonjour," I offer.
She smiles.
I see my breath.
I think I may even be happy.

Return to where I began. There is the tourist bus there for the Japanese and the others parked outside the hostel. A man with a cap lounges tensely in the morning sub-light cool.

Remember Now the Then
Of the gunshot-fun gallivant
In long ago and misspent youth
When destitute of all things real
But not bereft of true belief.

The others still sleep.
I'll soon to eat.
Among the young
And the beautiful
And the hopeful
At the hostel.

Break the fast back at the Luxembourg youth hostel after a wonderful dark breaking morning walk, and the contemplative and exhilarating pause for the cause to smoke and watch and think from the shadow of the spanking new white concrete and glass.

There are hordes and hordes of younglings, most of them girls, many of whom of seeming high school age or such. Sit down with a group, some gals from Syracuse, New York, USA. One girl is from Atlanta. We all, disparate and unlikely, chat pleasantly while we eat.

There's something I've never seen before, but before me on my own very plate. And I think it might be (of all things) uncooked raw tofu. Yet they had put some syrup on top. Chow it down just fine. Some bread. Some cheese. Kick the jam. Espresso from a tricky automat that, but for all heroic effort and concentrated concentration, I could hardly work.

Back up in the room, strip the bed of the sheets as is the custom and get one's self ready to roll. Think we go to see the Moselle. To what end or why, I don't know.

But Daddy may say.

Hope he's OK.

Bonne journée.

But first we must get out of Luxembourg City and so we're driving, driving, driving; searching for signs, looking at maps, and we're lost, lost, lost. Of course. But the town of Luxembourg is indeed dramatically beautiful and here comes the sun.

We're fine fresh volk today,
I say I say I sey.

At length we happen upon the Moselle on which west bank Daddy was encamped with his unit. Driving along in the sugarloaf hilliness, at times we lose sight of the river, can see but the bluffs on the other side. There are fields and pastures on each side with cows and horses, very lush and green. There is intervening heavy forest.

Through small towns like touring tourists.
The luscious bonny sunny day.
Allez en vacances!

All in high spirits.
Daddy moved in his manner to sing.
All in high spirits
But me.

I fear the suggested driving.
Must it be this way?
Must I be this way?
Ora Pro Nobis!

The Old Soldier, my Old Man, strongly recalls a lot of dead cows in this area and, oddly enough, the posture was that of the feet sticking straight up in the air. How is this possible? And to remember this awful comic oddity, lo – a lifetime later; amidst the mayhem, slaughter and offal.

Signs seem to be in Luxembourgish which is an oddish amalgam of both German and French. Cross the Moselle. I think we're in Germany now. For some reason that signals that we're lost again. U turn. Over the river and through the woods, back into Luxembourg. Cross the Moselle.

Ever watch a dog chase its tail?

We traverse the "Route Du Vin."
I take both meanings.
Wine country.
Lots of vineyards.
Lots of wine.
And here and there the beauty of both.

They dug in on the foreword slope of a hill facing across the river where the German soldiers were. The Americans would send out patrols from time to time down to the river but not across. Lieutenant Devitt sallied forth several times. And of course led the first.

Through Mandorf, a town that Daddy remembers, at least in name. On to Wormeldange. Leave the Moselle. Left.

Looking for the chateau where Daddy stayed with his unit some weeks or a month or so.

Into Wormeldange. Up a steep hill. We climb.

Daddy remembers the chateau being just outside of town on the opposite side of the river. That would be west, I believe. More vineyards.

Daddy says he and his platoon would huddle and hide in the vineyards and hope not to be observed by the Germans. (Makes me feel the terror of the hunted – as in "hide and go seek" as a child.)

Voila, could this be it? A large structure that takes up an entire block. Large, very large. So great as to be grand. Daddy thinks it might be the fabled Chateau, but then he thinks it might not.

My God, look, there's a house afire! No joke. We should get there, maybe help. How to get there? How to get?

Find the fire. Sean drives Formula fast. Here we are, here we are!

But All OK – a controlled rural burn. The people standing by tending it look pretty irritated with us as though we had intruded.

So while we didn't find somebody, some bodies, anybody, any bodies who were dead and burnt to a crisp (as they say), we did find some citizens who were kinda pissed off.

So much for Do-Right Heroics.

Back in search of Holy Grail Chateau.

Take the high ground.

Scout distant miniature houses below from precarious perch high above.

Descend. Tiny old flagstone streets. Just barely enough room for but one car to get by. Tight squeeze. Steep-steep – Put San Francisco, Duluth to shame.

Descend.

Ascend.

As we climb it feels as though we're pulled apart. Our attitude is about forty five degrees. I fear we might fall off the world. Here we go!

High, overlooking the town and the bluff and the river, stop to make photograph, to stretch and to goof. Where to park? No room in the geography. Ah, looky, there's a spot. Park. Exeunt. Frisk about like "the boys" Daddy calls us.

High on the hills among the living growing vines, we gaze across the river. It seems a strange thing to look across and decide to kill those whom we see, and those whom we see would kill us, and we lot would destroy the beautiful town down below.

"… and the falling apples. I think we walked on to the town but we didn't see any Germans. We turned and went back. We would have thanked them. Although we sent ... we sent patrols down from where we were, behind the river ... two weeks or so, I think ... about every night. I led the first three and I then had my sergeants lead the others. Our scouting ... Seems to me that we were much higher than my recollection was, not even to the crest of the hill which overlooks the river. And that's where we'd observe from ... And now we are right next to rows of grape vines and I remember sitting within the grapevines which we wanted to cover ourselves from the Germans seeing us. At least we thought that ... From where we are now the decline down the hill is much sharper than where I was ... and this is not the place where I was, I'm sure. We were right close to this but I just can't find it."

Says the Old Man,
The Old Soldier,
Erstwhile Shavetail –
O Father O' Mine.

Tolls The Bell.
Down, down into the valley.
We move on.
We'll not find The Chateau.
The sun diminishes,
Starts to die.
We drive on.

Into Germany. As usual, we look for maps and information. My goodness, we find both information and maps.

Into Trier, the oldest city in Germany with ruins dating back to Roman times. The city is two thousand years old or so.

Stop at a tourist center. Two pretty German girls – smiling, laughing and helpful. Pause to sharpen up the Deutsch.

But we can't stay; we've got to go.
On the move.
Tempus fugit.
Fuggit.
On to Monschau.

But O No – Here it comes at last.
Scheiße in der Luft.
My turn at the wheel,
My hand to the helm.

The good news: I didn't hit anybody.

The bad news: I got us lost.

Even though I was always only to go straight, immer geradeaus, take no turns, drive at all times behind a truck so as to slow go; somehow and way got lost.

Son of a bitch.

But at least the terror has passed for now.

Still on the road for Monschau.

Maybe.

As we wind our way on the two lane landstraße through the small towns in the inspiriting green green cheering countryside – the forest, the pasture, plenty of cars, plenty of cows – we seem to somehow and unaccountably find ourselves again in Belgium.

Like waitin' fer your birthday when you're young –

High spirits;

Here we come.

Roll through Belgium. Stop for gas.

Upon receiving my change I do what I've done before: Put the money into separate pockets 'cause I want to keep my Belgian francs separate from my German marks. But of course there are none. There are now only euros.

I know this true, but my reflex and sudden reaction is an old guy's ploy. Had same situation first in Germany, when about to pay, to buy maps, frantically thought, "O my God, I haven't exchanged any money. I've but French francs."

Oh Great And Living God,
Could You Please
Possibly do something about me?

So here we are now in Monschau,
A burg right out of a postcard.

And now we arch our backs and crane our necks,
And now we search high and low
For the Hotel Royal.

Willy

Monschau.

South of Aachen, into this valley, the ancient city of Monschau.

Driving slowly into the city center. Narrow streets of cobbled stone. Houses and buildings in the Old World Germanic style of asymmetric timber criss-crossing white-washed cement. From a fairytale book, Hansel and Gretel's gingerbread house. "Kinder City" toys of childhood. A sense of wonder.

Here. The Hotel Royal. Stop the car. Sean and Chris off down the street to take care of business, check in, find parking.

Daddy waits in the back seat, me up front. yawning, trying to stretch a bit in the tiny car. What's this? A girl at the trot, white service jacket, looks like kitchen staff. Up to my window, smiling broadly.

Enquires if we need lodgings, if so – come to our fine hotel. Right there!

Oh really?

Another stone beauty. What's in the water, here in Europe?

Well, ha ha, you see – we have rooms booked right here at the Royal. But thanks so much for the... invitation. Danke!

Times tough for Monschau's tourist industry? Or something more benign, more sociable. One can only hope. Oh this will do just nicely. This beautiful burg.

Chris and Sean returning. Parking not near. We haul our stuff in and up.

The usual rooming arguments to a minimum. CD and I in one, as we smoke and it be allowed here. S and D in the other. Who only smoke when on fire. Ha!

Making ourselves comfortable. Bit of unpacking. Out now to check the town...

Small market right across the strasse. Food. FOOD! Excellent bottled German lagers, Apfelkorn, Polish vodka in funny bottles. OK. What else? So much to see, so much to explore. Our temporary little hometown.

Gift shops everywhere. Cafes, restaurants, imbiss – little fast-food-type places where one strolls up to the window and orders, then eats standing at a counter, seated at patio table. Or just as you walk along. The food smelling positively gourmet. I'll damn sure not starve here!

Pause now for the cause. Outside me hotel's front door. A gent approaches. Bushy white hair. Ruddy, open face. Easy manner. speaking the English, obviously American.

"Hi! Are you one of Bill Devitt's boys?"

Somewhat surprised.

"As a matter of fact..."

"I'm Jim Begg."

"Oh! Jim! Hey, hi! Yeah, I'm Willy, the youngest of us reprobates!"

Hearty handshakes. A little chit chat and not a little chuckling. Turns out he's staying across the street at another hotel. Has to run, but to tell Daddy that he'll meet us outside here at 7:30 for dinner. Will do, Jim. Okay. In a minute. Later.

This is what might be referred to as Civilization. Right here. Right now. Meet a guy, total stranger, faraway land. A friend of me dad's. Hails from Edina, Minnesota, where Daddy currently lives. Now living in Brussels, here now for to see Daddy and take us sightseeing. This 60-ish man of some position. Runs a non-profit organization dedicated to maintaining American military cemeteries in France and Belgium from the two World Wars. Does it for the love of it. Decided this was a better life then the corporate rat-race he was previously involved in Stateside. What is commonly referred to as a "hell of a nice guy," he is.

I go upstairs to tell Daddy, who is amazed at our chance

meeting out front, no telephones, no confusion, and, God help us, no driving. Such a stroke of luck!

7:30 and we all repair downstairs for dinner. And, yup, here's Jim, chatting with our extraordinary proprietress, more of whom later.

He knows just the place. Right up here a ways.

Introductions all around.

Jim to Chris and Sean: "Yeah, he called you guys... what was it?... reprobates."

"I did not! I called them my beloved brothers."

Sun nearly down, we walk up the cobbled street. Daddy highly amused that he found us so easily. Much laughter and telling tales of our tumultuous travels.

A large table for we Big Men From America, now five strong. Drinks ordered. Much perusing of menus. Various bratens, schnitzels, pommes frites.

These last, ostensibly French fries, served in a large bowl in the center of the table. Like nothing I've ever had. How can fried potatoes be so delicious? What do they use – olive, peanut, sesame, or some other oil? It's said, "the simple things in life..." Aah!

The crack jovial and easy. Herr Begg, though distinguished and cultured, also – to coin a phrase – a regular guy. After some haggling with Daddy, insists on paying for dinner.

Gold rings on ya, Jim.

Bless you, mate.

Tomorrow he'll accompany us up to Strass and Untermaubach, scenes of serious combat for Daddy's E Co., of the 330th Infantry, fall of '44.

This is what it's all about, lads.

The past awaits us.

And as Daddy's own mama, our grandma NaNa, often

said, to this old campaigner, when still a boy, this old soldier:

"We'll see."

Chapter Ten
Thursday, October 18, 2007
Hurtgen Forest, Strass and Monschau

We awoke Thursday morning with plans to drive from Monschau, north through the Hurtgen Forest to visit the towns of Gey, Strass and Untermaubach. Gey and Strass are just outside the eastern edge of the forest. They are on the lower, flatter land lying between the forest and the Roer River. Untermaubach is on the Roer.

Soon after lunch the caravan started north along Highway 399; the boys and I in the lead and Jim Begg following in his car. Highway 399 seems to cut the Hurtgen into halves, one to the east, and the other to the west. It exits the forest at Gey and continues northeast to Duren (on the Roer) where it terminates.

From my book "Shavetail":

"In late November we received orders to move to the Hurtgen Forest. Until that time, the war hadn't seemed very real or deadly to me, but I was anxious to learn what combat was like. I wanted to be in enough combat to have the experience, probably to be able to talk about it after I got home. I wondered how I would behave and react, and I'm sure I had an underlying fear that I might turn out to be a coward...

The Hurtgen was heavily wooded with tall pine trees. They were so dense that even when the sun shone, the day seemed gray...

When the German artillery and mortar shells would hit the tops of the trees, the "tree bursts," as they were called, caused unusually heavy casualties to the American soldiers below...

Besides the trees, my first impression of the Hurtgen was the unremitting noise of the artillery. It sounded like a thunderstorm that went on and on without stopping. I had heard enemy artillery before in Luxembourg, but that was a mere spring shower compared to the deluge of the Hurtgen..."

Driving through the Hurtgen seemed similar to driving through the countryside at home. There was farmland with crops and off in the distance the trees of the forest. But there was one significant difference. Highway 399 was dotted with small towns. In the Hurtgen we would exit a small town and within a mile or two (possibly a minute or two) we would be entering another. Quite dissimilar from the countryside of my native Minnesota or its contiguous neighbors – Wisconsin, Iowa, North and South Dakota. There, the gaps between towns are much greater – probably from five to 25 miles. I think that western Europe is simply much more heavily populated than my section of the landscape, and those western Europeans must live somewhere!

As we drove north on Highway 399, with the Hurtgen on both sides of the road, I saw to our left (northeast) the area in which the men of E Company spent their first ten days in the Hurtgen Forest (December 3-12, 1944) often cringing in log-covered foxholes, hoping not to be hit by the relentless German artillery fire. I call this the <u>first location,</u> at which I had the first of seven of my most memorable combat experiences.

I pointed out the area to the boys, but we did not even stop the car. Our plan was to return to visit the place within the next few days.

I had no thought that the boys and I, in October, 2007, could find precisely the 1944 location in the heavily wooded forest, but I felt that we might find terrain similar enough so that they could get some "feel" for my experiences. Two events at that location in December '44 are most memorable to me.

The first occurred one dark night when the German artillery fire seemed to go on without letup. I lay flat on my face in my foxhole, hoping, probably praying, against a direct hit. One of my men yelled over to me from a nearby foxhole to come and help his buddy who was in trouble (combat fatigue). I ran over to their hole and crawled in. The buddy was lying face down, pounding the ground and crying like a baby. He begged me to take him out of there. I held him in my arms as though he were my child. He continued to beg, and I continued to explain that leaving the foxhole meant death or serious injury. After a half hour the shelling let up, and he settled down. As far as I know he never again experienced combat fatigue.

That event reminds me of General George Patton, who commanded the American army in Sicily in 1943. While inspecting a hospital he slapped a man who was hospitalized with combat fatigue, called “shell-shock” in World War I. The man had been in combat with the 1st Infantry Division in North Africa and Sicily. He told the general that he just couldn’t take it any longer. He was diagnosed with combat fatigue. Patton told him that he should be ashamed of himself in front of all the brave soldiers who had been wounded in combat and then slapped him in the face.

If Patton had spent a short time with us in the Hurtgen and had weathered a few hours of pounding from German artillery, he might have had some sympathy and understanding for a man with combat fatigue.

General Patton was a career army officer. War was the apex in the life of such men. Here was the opportunity to show the people, especially those influential in granting promotions, how skilled he was in carrying out any duty to which he had been assigned. War was the way to the top.

On the other hand, almost all combat infantrymen had no thought of army careers. Most of them had been drafted, not volunteered, and would not, because of the risk to life and limb, have chosen infantry. Junior officers, such as myself, although technically volunteers, would not have chosen infantry if we had fully realized the risks involved. The career officer had many incentives compelling him to excel in combat, such as advancement in his career and the desire to earn the respect of his fellow combatants. To the contrary, I suspect that for the great majority of all non-career infantrymen, their greatest incentive was simply to stay alive.

Despite Patton's remark to the man with combat fatigue, which implied that all wounded soldiers were brave, my experience has told me that bravery is not necessarily connected with being wounded. I was wounded twice. Bravery had nothing to do with my wounds. In both instances, I was standing in what I thought was a relatively safe location. A German hand grenade and at another time a German mortar shell, both unanticipated, exploded nearby, giving me two Purple Hearts. The only bravery I could have been accused of was showing up for work. I, along with the rest of the men in the company, obeyed orders and went to the dangerous place known as a battlefield.

Using Patton's logic, he would have proclaimed that every wounded soldier must be brave, and if disabled (by combat fatigue) without being wounded, he was deserving of a slap. I think that Patton had a kind of romantic conception of warfare which we infantrymen did not share nor understand. I think we privates, corporals, sergeants, and lieutenants – all infantrymen – had a different and more correct impression of infantry fighting, and could never, never have slapped a man as did General George S. Patton.

The second memorable event in 1944 occurred at the same location soon after a heavy German artillery barrage. I looked out of my foxhole and saw two wounded men from a nearby company. I ran out to help the first man who was worse off than the other. He was lying on his back with smoke or steam arising from a deep hole in his chest. His eyes were closed. He was breathing heavily, and blood was flowing from his chest. A red hot splinter of shrapnel was burning in his flesh, and the odor was sickening. I took the bandage from my first aid kit and tried to plug the hole.

I called for a litter, and we started to carry him out. The other man, who was also hit badly kept saying to me, "Lieutenant, take me. He can't make it".

After carrying the first man less than fifty yards, he shuddered and was dead. We rolled him off the litter and went back and carried the other man to safety. I never saw nor talked to him again.

I can only speculate as to what the other man might have said after I decided to take the first man before him despite his pleas to take him first. He might have said, "That dumb lieutenant. I told him Jones couldn't make it, but he took Jones first anyway. They only took him a few yards before he had it, and they came back for me. I barely made it back. If that dumb lieutenant took me first like I said, I'da been a lot better off. I guess he thought he knew best".

I was the dumb lieutenant, but I don't believe that I would have deserved the comment.

That was my first experience with a dying man in combat. I did what I could, but with one exception – I didn't think to say a prayer for my fallen comrade. I'm afraid that the good nuns at St. Mark's Grade School in St. Paul would have been disappointed to learn that I failed to say a prayer for that dear boy. (Not incidentally, I just said one now.)

On October 18, 2007, we were driving on Highway 399, down out of the Hurtgen, to the town of Gey. To our right was the heavily tree filled disastrous <u>second location</u> where, on December 14, 1944, the men of E Company probably suffered more casualties than any other day while I was in the company. I recall the day quite well. My estimate of our casualties that day, killed or wounded, is 30 out of the 130 men who started that day. Thirty casualties in one day might not seem to be very numerous. But one must understand that the company suffered similar casualties over the entire three weeks we were in or near the Hurtgen. We entered the Hurtgen with 190 men, and walked out after three weeks of battling the German Wehrmacht with a mere 40. To me it was slaughter.

From "Shavetail":

"As our leading scouts reached the edge of the woods and cautiously advanced into the open toward Strass, the Germans started to fire their fearsome 88's at us. All of us immediately scrambled back to find cover in the woods...

Fortunately, there were a few dugouts which the Germans had built and into which some of the men were able to find cover...

Those of us who did not have a dugout were obliged to find a dip in the ground or to dig a hole as quickly as possible. I was in this latter group. The shelling was especially frightening since we knew that the Germans could see where we were, and were able to fire at our positions with their 88's.

The German artillery pounded us all day as we lay there largely unprotected in that killing field.

Although not part of E Company, but wounded along with the E Company boys in the second location was Colonel Robert Foster, commander of our 330th Infantry Regiment (3,000 men). Officers of such high rank usually did not get down to the lower levels of command (such as a rifle company like E Company). My thinking is that Colonel Foster decided to see for himself why E Company was not moving faster (or at all) toward the enemy. He had nine rifle companies under his command, E Company being one of the nine. He did not have to search out for one of the junior officers to learn the cause of E Company's failure to advance against the enemy. As he approached my CP (Command Post – also known as a hole in the ground), he received a satisfactory explanation. A careless piece of German shrapnel from a nearby explosion found its way into the Colonel's throat beneath his chin sending him to the hospital – and undoubtedly reminding him why the men of E Company did not advance more rapidly.

My interest in the area was its being the location of the most memorable and most sad event in my combat experience, namely the death of one of my most faithful men, Ellis Futch.

He was a young, round-faced Southern boy who was very religious. Unlike most soldiers, he did not smoke or drink. If one of the men would let fly an obscenity, Futch would mildly remonstrate the man by saying something like, "That's no way to talk. What would your mother say if she heard ya?" I admired the way he held true to his beliefs.

He and his buddy, Kurek, were running, following me, to a forward position when I heard an artillery shell coming in. As the shell exploded I hit the ground uninjured. I then walked back into the smoke-filled spot where Futch lay dead. I looked down. The top of his head had been torn off, leaving his brains in plain sight. I cannot forget it. Kurek, although wounded severely, survived.

I might have second guessed myself and questioned whether I should have left my forward position and run back during the intermittent enemy artillery fire to bring Futch and Kurek to the front. I've never second guessed. I did what seemed appropriate at the time. They might have been killed or wounded if they had stayed where they were.

The army gave me the duty to make life and death decisions for my men. I was a 21 year old lad, with a year and a half of college, ROTC (Reserve Officers Training Corps) training in high school, and some weeks at the Infantry School at Ft. Benning, Georgia. What more could I have learned to have prevented those two dear boys from death and mutilation? Not enough! Not enough!

Jim Begg in his car, and the boys and I in ours, started to look for the brick house in Strass, the third location. I told them that I had seen the house in 1988 when the boys' mother and I were on my only other trip to my former battle sites. I recalled that it was on the edge of town without any other houses close by, and that it was brick.

After driving up and down streets for a while, Willy asked to stop and let him out. He walked away and we drove on. After a half hour we drove back to where we left Willy. We soon found him. He said he found a house which might be the brick house we'd been looking for.

From "Shavetail":

"Early in the morning following our entry in Strass, we received orders to attack the Germans who were in a woods about 600 yards east of the town...

East of Strass was a two-story brick house which stood alone, 200 yards from the nearest building in town. Near the house were two American Sherman tanks. 400 yards further to the east, beyond the brick house, was the edge of the woods, where the Germans were located...

Our plan was to pass to the left of the house and proceed straight east into the woods. Even though the night was dark, we could see the outline of the brick house and the American tanks. After we had advanced about halfway to the house, small arms fire started to come at us from in and around the house. There was also machine gun fire from the tanks. We all hit the ground. To say that we were surprised would be a major understatement. American tanks should have American soldiers in them. The Germans had somehow captured the tanks and had turned our machine guns against us.

Upon hitting the ground from the incoming German fire, we fired back. After much shooting back and forth and the resulting wounding and dying of both German and American boys, we Americans prevailed. We took the house.

If this had been a demonstration at the Infantry School at Ft. Benning, which I attended in 1943, the attack would have gone like this. Upon being pinned down by German fire, the platoon leader would have collected his three squad leaders and ordered them to have their men to lay down a base of fire (shoot at the Germans) until the German fire let up. Then the platoon leader would signal the men to get up and charge the brick house. At Benning this was called the "school solution".

In real life something like the following happened. After the Germans opened fire and the Americans hit the ground, some of the Americans returned fire. As a result, the German fire diminished. With the let-up of the German fire, a skinny boy from a farm near Fargo, North Dakota, with his bayonet stuck on his M-1 rifle, got up and ran forward. A few of his buddies looked and seemed to think that was a good idea, so they too got up and ran toward the brick house. The remainder of the company followed.

What about the platoon leader? No school solution. He gave no orders and followed with the remainder of the company. I can smile at the story now. I was the platoon leader.

We walked to the house which Willy had found. I had last seen my brick house 19 years earlier. My first impression was that Willy's brick house was not mine. My memory was that mine was on the edge of town, away from any other houses. Willy said that his house had what appeared to be bullet holes. Thinking of the firefight of December 15, 1944 in which we attacked the brick house causing bullet holes from our small arms fire, it occurred to me that <u>Willy's</u> brick house might be, in fact, <u>my</u> brick house.

We did not stay any longer because we planned to return the next day. So we drove out of town on the road to

Untermaubach. As we made the short drive to the edge of the town of Strass, I saw, standing without any near neighbors, my brick house, the building near which my company (E Company, 330th Infantry Regiment) on December 15, 1944, suffered 20 men killed or wounded.

We stopped in the street in front of the house. Since we were coming back the next day, we didn't try to go in. The house was the same, but around it was a wire fence heavily covered with vines. I think now that we were fortunate that the wire fence was not there in 1944 while we attacked the house. Having to straddle a damaged wire fence while under the death inducing German automatic weapons fire might have been one too many obstacles to overcome that day.

Back in the car, we drove east to Untermaubach. I was beginning to feel ill, but wanted to press on to the <u>sixth location</u>. In December 1944, E Co. attacked the German Army in Untermaubach for three tough days, the 21st, 22nd and 23rd. Our company of nearly 50 men, decreasing daily from battle casualties, fought in bloody house-to-house fighting against determined German soldiers defending their homeland.

From "Shavetail":

"On the edge of the town were stucco houses with yards and gardens. All the civilians had fled. Toward the center of town the buildings were built up to the street and usually attached to each other. Several streets ran to the Roer River, while others ran parallel to it. It was a small town through which it would take no more than five minutes to walk. It took us three days. The going is slow while under fire by a hostile force..."

In "Shavetail" I describe one of the buildings from which the German soldiers were firing at us as a church. Later in the book I corrected myself and described it as a small monastery with a chapel. Both descriptions were mistaken! Believe me. I'm seldom mistaken in such matters! Perhaps "seldom" should be replaced by "frequently".

The building is and has been for many years the ancient home of the German Von Spee family, and is in fact a castle. The boys and I learned this on our first full day in Monschau when we drove for the first time to Untermaubach.

It might well have been a seventeenth (or earlier) century castle built to withstand predatory attacks. It is of massive stone construction, two or three stories high, and running 150 feet parallel to and within fifty feet of the Roer River. At the south end is a garage and storage shed, which I'm sure was a large horse stable in earlier days. To complete the picture of a fortified castle is a handsome wall of similar stone emerging from both ends and circling outwards to meet 100 feet west of the castle, forming a spectacular courtyard enclosed by the building and three walls. In the far wall opposite the castle is a generous front entrance built through the wall. Undoubtedly in earlier years it had a gate or some other fortification. But now it is open to all.

How did I learn the story of the castle?

Willy

Monschau day 2

Up and at 'em. Must meet Jim for the tour up to the Huertgen Forest. First breakfasting downstairs, a splendid spread of cold cuts, cheeses, breads, juices and cereals, coffee and tea.

Meeting up with Begg. Rolling north on 399. Not lost yet. Jim in his motor, we in ours, in possession of Jim's superior map of the area.

Achieve Strass.

Daddy's Easy Company assaulted a German held house in this town, all those years ago. Earning his first Purple Heart. Not an easy thing, that. Captured Sherman tanks, were the 75mm main guns firing on the American infantry? .50 caliber Browning heavy machine guns bad enough. Close quarters fight. Rifles, machine guns. Machine pistols and grenades – fragments from one of these hitting Daddy in the temple, fortunately a minor wound. "Minor" – easy for me to say. A brick house the objective. Daddy sure he saw it in '88 with Mama. Less certain now. Looking for telltale bullet holes, that kind of thing.

Here's one. Looks a bit beat up. Let me out of the car to do some reconnaissance.

The two cars slowly moving off. I step up the road at a brisk clip. Houses of stucco and concrete, average looking suburban dwellings, but some of stone and brick. Many, no doubt, rebuilt since the war.

No people about. Up this hill. Where is it? Was just here five minutes ago...

No time for getting lost. Here. Reddish brown stone. Looks like pock marks in the walls. Could well be from gunfire. Wonder why it hasn't been repaired...

A little lost now. This the main road? OK, there are the cars. Daddy, Sean, CD and JB out talking and pointing.

Daddy tells me, no, that wasn't the right one. Saddle up and scout around some more.

One more pass down this street. There it is. Daddy's sure of it. A brick house. Set apart from the others. In a bare and fallow field, the forest over there. This is it. The place. A garden round back, a shed. Daddy's man Red shot a surrendering German soldier as Daddy was about to accept his surrender. In front of that shed. Point blank. Might have hit Daddy as well.

Driving slowly. That field – no cover, not knowing the house was occupied. Must have been a nasty shock. Germans open up, Americans go down. Some stay down. Forever.

These days we'd probably call in an airstrike. No more brick house. A better way of warring? Certainly. If no civilians are present. And one has no desire to ever again see what you struggled and bled for, and perhaps, one day, show your sons.

The old lie:

"Dulce et decorum est pro patria mori."

For a brick house.

Back on the road, heading east to Untermaubach. A castle, Daddy says. On the Ruhr.

Stopping now. Have a look-see. Check the maps. Large fortress-like house. A church or chapel attached, maybe... We spot a man, entering a large workshop, obviously a former stable. Chris and I out to meet him.

"Guten tag. Wie komme ich nach Untermaubach?"

"Das ist Burg Maubach. Die stadt... Untermaubach... Obermaubach...."

Gesturing to indicate this place.

"Das ist Burg Maubach."

The Castle Maubach.

Large man of 70 or so. Workingman's hands. Very friendly. His German infused with some other accent, some other tongue.

We chat a bit. Daddy, Sean and Jim entering the stable.

Seems our man is Latvian or Belarusian, it's unclear. His people relocated by Stalin to Germany after the war. Explains that this is the ancestral home of the Von Spee family, of the pocket battleship "Graff Spee" fame.

Chris negotiating his heavily accented German. We tell him who we are and why we've come. Here.

Calling to a middle aged woman:

"Frau Spee – kommen sie sehen den alten Mann. Ein Amerikaner."

The woman, taking bags from her car, nods and disappears inside, returning a few minutes later with an older woman. Her mother in law.

We walk out to the courtyard, this majestic castle of beige stone. The sun warming us this chilly October afternoon.

"Dies ist die Gräfin von Spee."

The Countess von Spee.

And so she is.

"Guten Tag, Frau von Spee."

"Ja. Hello."

Slightly broken English. Daddy's age, perhaps a couple years his junior.

Daddy tells his tale:

"I was here during the war. My platoon was in this castle. There was a church of some sort here then, I'm sure I remember that..."

Indeed, there was a church here then, outside these walls.

"We battled the German soldiers... there was a fire fight... they were cut off, down by the river, had nowhere to go... we called down to them to surrender... they did."

Chris translating for Daddy, the Countess mixing English and German. I think understanding. As in comprehension. Whether understanding in the empathetic sense, who could say?

"Yes. The police told us. 'Stay here, hide.' In the church... our neighbors, yes? We hid from the American soldiers...

behind – how do you say it? – the altar. The altar of the church...”

Looking from face to face. Chris and Sean. Jim. The Countess’ daughter-in-law. Daddy.

We younger Americans grasp this. Viscerally. Does Daddy? The Countess – even and dignified. The daughter-in-law, sharp featured and stolid.

Daddy and his troopers attacked this woman’s house. Occupied it. Surely damaged it.

Did death occur here?

American, German?

Neighbors, friends. Family?

This gracious woman. Elegant and kind, white haired and with the ready laugh.

Jim: “...yes, ma’am. I, too, have the white hair!”

Now these children, two. Nine or ten years. The boy hugging his mother’s leg, seems he’s taken a fall from his bicycle. Daddy tousles his hair and beams down at him.

The younger Frau von Spee. Stating that her husband is quite interested in history and will be home from work in Cologne later this evening. Going inside and returning with postcards of Burg Maubach for all.

Daddy not feeling so swell just now. Must use the head. And right quick. The young boy instructed to show Daddy inside for to use the W.C. Returning several minutes later after doing the needful. Of the crappy sort.

Saying now our goodbyes. Our sincerest thanks. How wonderful to meet you. What incredible fortune.

God bless you.

Countess von Spee.

Walking to the car.

CD: “Do you understand, fully, what has just transpired here?”

Sean: “Yeah. Yeah. An amazing thing. Not of the ordinary.

"Me: "A bit magical. Miraculous even."

Jim too must take his leave. And it's "have a safe drive, thanks for everything, and we'll see you in Brussels at journey's end."

Back to Monschau, our rooms we now call home.

Daddy not feeling great. It's decided we'll get him some take-out food for dinner, something light and easy on the stomach.

First things first. Over to the market, stock up on rations. Woman at the counter, oh so nice, but no English. Myself a bit confused about me monies. A woman behind me helps. From Nebraska, no less. "Aw geez, thanks." "Oh, you betcha!"

After a wee bump or two, out on the town to procure dinner. Daddy in bed taking his ease. After this monumentally big day. And the shits, too. Something about the Eiffel region seems to have that effect on him. You just take it easy, Daddy...

Out now. Sundown. Popping our heads into various pubs to see if they serve food, most restaurants closing up early due to the off season. For touring men such as we.

Crossing the little bridge in the town square, Chris, Sean and me. The Roer River. Flowing here through the town. Not much more than a stream at this point. Still, its flow a constant background music. In its progress.

To where rivers go.

Stopping in here. This pub, smokey and noisy. Crowded with citizens of all ages.

Pushing our way through the throng. Up to the bar. Squeeze between patrons, belly up. I grab the last stool. Order up, loud and clear and – "mein Herr – could we get something to eat? Our old father, sick with tummy problems. Something light – an omelette and salad perhaps?"

Our request conveyed to the kitchen. But hold the order for a bit, bitte.

Enjoying ourselves greatly. Smiles all around. Seated next to this bloke here. "Wie geht's?" "Ja, wie geht's."

Chap named Garrett. 30-ish, has the general demeanor of having been born and raised in this public house. English not strong, but neither my German. We get on famously, naturally. Only when peoples speak the same language fluently, it seems, does the acrimony arise.

The crack loud and lively here, as needs be due to the general atmosphere. Made more so by gesticulations and much repetition of what one means to convey, due to language barriers. And general drunkenness.

Sean heads back to check on Daddy. CD and I still awaiting the food order.

The convo all over the place: World War II, the current wars in Iraq and Afghanistan, polytricks, Monschau itself.

Garrett tells of how Monschau was spared being leveled by Allied forces in 1944. Seems a captain, lieutenant, or even a ranking NCO surrendered the town to the Americans, with the assurance that it would not be assaulted and the garrison not taken prisoner. The commander was, however, later executed. As they say nowadays – haul ass and bypass.

Says, too, that he'd be glad to take us through the Huertgen tomorrow, knowing the area well. He'd done his two years national service in the German Army, maybe they'd trained or been on maneuvers in the Eiffel. In any case, he appears well informed of the murderous campaign of '44 – Daddy's war.

All the while this friendly chap buying Chris and me drinks. Beer and shots of a thing called "Ells" – a heavy but florid liqueur made here in Monschau, a sort of cognac resembling Benedictine, though of the stouter 100-proof variety. Lovely stuff, that.

Everyone so friendly here. The owner with a bit of a twitch in his eye. The woman on the bar a fine and playful brunette. Think she's his wife. And here a blonde beauty bar-back. Garrett says she's our hostess's daughter. Oh my. Well then.

"Guten Abend, Fräulein. Schoene Nacht ist es."

"Abend."

Laughing while washing glasses. Putting on a bit of a show. For the benefit of this American Goodwill Ambassador. With coin aplenty. And only the very best of intentions. I assure you.

Our food arrives, Garrett gives us his card, saying call tomorrow. It's "tschuss, mate!" and out into the night, wobbling just the merest bit on the cobblestones. Back to the Royal to have a wee take-away feast with Daddy.

But Daddy not doing well. The GI's in full effect. Barely touching his omelette and salad. Which CD will soon make short work of in addition to his own schnitzel.

Telling our tale of the young German who has offered to show us around the forest tomorrow.

See first what the morning brings.

Another Bronze Star, at this stage of the game, wouldn't do.

Daddy

Chapter Eleven
Thursday, October 18, 2007
Untermaubach

Our first view of the castle was from a narrow road (on which we were driving) next to the river. I looked up to what appeared to be a tall, sturdy stone wall with a few small windows near the top facing the river. A light went on in my head! During the war I had never seen the castle from the side facing the river. Could this be the outer wall of the castle from which, in December, 1944, I shouted from a high window for the surrender of the German soldiers who gathered on the narrow road? It was.

I immediately told Sean to drive to the front. Jim Begg followed in his car. We circled around and drove through the front entrance into the courtyard. December,1944 was in front of me! In 1944, my men and I had been attacking through Untermaubach for three days. We hoped (correctly) that if we could take the building (and the defending German soldiers within) the battle would be won. The castle was the last remaining building in Untermaubach that we American infantrymen had not yet conquered. By then I think they were tired of disagreeing with us and were ready to give up. That was 63 years ago, and all I remember is calling down from an upstairs window in the castle for the German soldiers in the narrow street on the river to surrender. And they did.

When we got out of the cars in the courtyard, there was no one in sight. At the far south end of the castle is the garage. From the garage came garage noises, and we soon saw a man walking out. We (Chris, Sean, Willy, Jim Begg and I) walked over to greet him.

How did we handle the language barrier? Chris was my designated linguist. He had spent time in western Europe while serving his tour of duty in the U.S. Army in the 1970's. He had also spent a summer in Germany with his high school German class. He chatted easily with the French and Germans (especially the Germans) as though theirs were his native tongue. Sean and Willy did something sneaky. Before leaving home they had purchased booklets to help visitors with the French and German languages. I, who had been to both countries three times before, thought it unnecessary, or at least unsporting, to buy books. But they helped. Unlike their father, both boys, probably with booklets close by, participated in the conversations dominated by the usage of a (to me) foreign tongue.

As to Jim Begg, although he is a Minnesota boy, he has lived in Belgium the last 30 years. I consider him similar to a sophisticated western European who handles with ease any language or languages he may encounter.

But in language dexterity, I was at the foot of the class. I had been to France and Germany before and had got along okay. I knew a few German phrases i.e. "Danke schon" – I can't recall another one. I might have thought I'd leave languages to the boys while I handled the important questions such as the correct spelling of the last syllable of the word Luxembourg (or Luxemburg, or Luxemberg). Or more importantly, determining the correct pronunciation of many French words or phrases, considering the French penchant of including a few letters in a word or phrase which have no bearing on its pronunciation (such as parlez vous Francais; phonetically – parlay voo Fronsay).

Back to the man in the garage. The five of us walked up to the man and met him in the courtyard just outside the garage. He was not German and explained that he was from a country near Russia, such as Bellarus or Ukraine. I think there was some misunderstanding among my translators (Jim and the boys) as to his precise land of origin. He explained to us in some detail that this was the home of the Von Spee family. He was an employee. The German pocket battleship, the Graf Spee, was named after a famous member of the family. I still remember the publicity and accompanying joy of hearing in December, 1939 that the Graf Spee had been sunk off the South Atlantic coast of Uruguay after a battle with three British cruisers. This was a rare bright spot for the British as, prior to the entry of Russia and the United States, they stood alone against the seemingly unstoppable German Wehrmacht.

After 10 minutes of talk with the garage man, joining the group were a young mother and her 10-year-old son. Her husband is a Von Spee, and they live in the castle – "be it ever so humble, there's no place like home."

Only minutes later we were joined by the person whose presence became the highlight of the entire trip. She is Countess Von Spee, who was present the day in December, 1944, when a platoon of American soldiers battled and overcame the German defenders, thereby entering and holding her magnificent family home, the castle. Bill Devitt led the platoon.

I was stunned! Here was a person who, 63 years earlier, at this same spot, with me and others, was in the middle of a bloody soldiers' firefight. We had some things in common – including the desire to stay alive. She had to find a place safe from the gunfire and to stay there until the fighting stopped. But the rules were different for me. Even if I should find a safe place, as an infantryman I was obliged to leave the safe place and advance against enemy fire. I assume she made it through that day as did I. But a week later, the Germans got me. 50 miles to the south, while in Belgium's Ardennes Forest during the Battle of the Bulge, shrapnel from a German mortar shell found it's way into my belly. I'm still here, but it was close.

After being introduced to the Countess, I noticed that she was wearing a handsome pearl necklace. I told her that I noticed the pearls and that they were lovely. While writing this I wondered why she should be wearing her dressy pearls when called out of the house to meet some strangers. In my imagination, she did a very womanly thing. Not having time to don dressy clothing, she did the next best thing, or even the best thing. She went to her jewelry and chose an impressive string of matching pearls.

While speaking to the Countess, we spoke largely in English, and whenever she had trouble understanding me, Chris would help her out with his German.

I told her who I was, and that in December, 1944 I had led the attack on the castle. I told her that I ended the battle in a room on the top floor of the castle which overlooked the Ruhr River. I told her that I first thought that I was in a church and later thought a chapel or a monastery. The Countess replied that I was mistaken and that the town's Catholic church is just outside the walls of the castle.

She said that on the day of the American attack many of the town's people, including herself, fled into the church outside the castle wall. They all lay flat on the floor fearing the arrival of the American soldiers (of whom I was one). I didn't think to ask her what happened after that. Since she didn't say anything further about the church, I assume that she and her neighbors made it through without mishap. I have no recollection of the church that day, but I guess that if we did look into the church and saw it occupied by defenseless civilians, we left them alone and continued our attack into the castle.

Late in the conversation I complimented her on her use of the English language. I asked how she became so adept at it. She looked at me squarely, with a twinkle in her eyes and a gentle smile on her lips, and said, as if to make some profound revelation, "I learned in school." This brought a roar of laughter from us all as well as a bit of applause in recognition of the patience and good humor she showed during the entire visit. She alone made the entire trip worthwhile.

We did not get into the castle and spent all our time outside in the courtyard. Just as we were leaving, I felt the immediate need to visit a bathroom. The Countess's 10-year-old grandson kindly led me to a toilet in the castle. I might have thought, but did not think, something like, "This town has a way of bringing on the GI's." After 63 years, I had it again, and it lasted until we left Monschau three days later.

We drove back to our hotel in Monschau. I had a bite to eat and spent the rest of the night quite equally between my bed and the bathroom. Sean found some tablets for me to take. They helped, but not enough.

After my meeting with Countess von Spee and after seeing and praising her matching pearls, I am reminded of my dear deceased wife, Mary, and how the two ladies were in some ways similar.

Pearls. Before Mary and I were married, as a single fellow my interest in and knowledge about pearls was zero. And as a newly married man I began to be instructed by my bride in the importance of certain things in life – such as jewelry, and more specifically, pearls. I learned early in the pearl game that matching pearls are preferable to non-matching. So I called the Countess's pearls "matching" although as a non-expert, to me most pearls seem pretty much alike.

Housing. Both ladies seemed to like roomy houses. The Countess might object to the word "house" to describe her castle, but surely she would agree that it is useful to have plenty of bedrooms and bathrooms, a library or two, and at least one oversized room large enough to entertain for dinner and dancing no fewer than five hundred of one's closest friends.

Mary had somewhat more modest expectations for housing. But with eight children we ended up living 28 years in a big old house in south Minneapolis, which was said to have been a copy of the Elizabeth Barrett Browning house in Italy, with five bedrooms and three baths. And we never missed a mortgage payment.

The drive back to Monschau was only about 30 minutes, but it was one of the longest half hours of my life. The GI's! (diarrhea in civilian parlance).

All the time I kept thinking to tell Sean to stop the car. But what to do if we stopped? I'll never know. We reached the hotel, found our room, and I entered the biffy with its useful device for rescuing a person afflicted with the GI's. No further details are necessary except to say that for the next few hours, my biffy was the most occupied room in the house. That night I did more walking than sleeping.

Meeting Countess von Spee was easily the highlight of the entire trip. Her presence was, for Chris, Sean, Willy, Jim Begg, and me clearly the most memorable experience of the trip – possibly of any trip. I would have been surprised and pleased to learn that one of the 40 of our men who walked out of Untermaubach at the end of the battle, was alive and well. But to meet and talk to the Countess, was something which, in my wildest imagination, could never happen.

Sixty-three years ago, in December of '44, a few days before our attack into Untermaubach, we were attacking the Germans in the nearby town of Strass. It was early morning and they were dug in around a brick house. The air was filled with rifle and automatic weapons fire from both sides. As I walked forward with my M1 rifle tucked into my shoulder, a German soldier pulled himself out of his foxhole with his back to me. Before I had time to react, bullets from one of my men hit him, and he fell dead at my feet. What was my reaction? I don't know. I was in the middle of a firefight and was trying to stay alive. He was the enemy, and I moved on to the next one.

Our attack in Untermaubach against the castle was another firefight similar to that in Strass. American and enemy German soldiers were killed and wounded in both towns. But in Untermaubach, the young Countess lay hiding nearby in the village church. Was she also the enemy? When

I met her in October ‘07, her attractiveness, patience, good humor, and ready smile reminded me of my mother, my sister, my daughters and even my dear departed wife. Could the Countess, 63 years ago in the middle of a deadly firefight, have been considered by me, the leader of the attacking Americans, to be one of the enemy? I don’t know. But today, 63 years later, the answer is indisputable – the Countess could now easily be my friend.

CD

10-19-07 8:10AM

Stand in front of the Hotel Royal. Take my ease and have the smoke. I encounter our proprietress who says there is a message for Mr Devitt. Of course the ambiguity. She lets me listen to the phone recording.

Message from Dolly that Daddy call home.

Urgent.

Damn.

Can only mean death or disaster.

Daddy's brother has been ill and I fear that Uncle Bob is dead.

Recall and ponder the fog of the night before:

We pull into town, find the hotel without great difficulty but then must drive in circles for a long time to try to park the car in front to unload our luggage.

The streets are tiny. Never can two cars come abreast. There are some roads that ascend, ascend ever upwards, always and often precipitously.

Sean drives splendidly.

But we never could get the car in front of the hotel so we parked several blocks away and hustled to tote things in.

Stout lads!

The phone call from Daddy's friend, Jim Begg.

Meet outside hotel at seven.

Well met like a long lost brother.

We all, a mob, throng the street to dinner – my earliest ever.

Our teeming spirits roar and soar,

Together rollick and frolic like kids –

As the sun sets with sweet panache
On the too cute movie set street
Of the tiny antique German burg
That made it through the war.
"Stop in," says Jim.

Jägerschnitzel and heaping mounds of potatoes, both boiled and fried, in huge help-yourself bowls in the middle of the table. We make a party of it, and talk and tell tales a long time. Most jolly.

Thereafter Sean and I go to check on some business concerning the car, something about putting a placard on the windshield so as not to be ticketed nor towed.

Stop for drink on way back at little club for the young. Plenty of sound. Jukebox blares. Drinks real cheap. Vodka and beer for me, spot of whisky and beer for Sean.

I fall to talking to the volk. There is a chap who had studied as an exchange student in Tulsa, Oklahoma and had actually visited Minneapolis – knows Summit Avenue, knows of Prince, our hometown hero.

Bonhomous girl behind the bar. There is the slight language difficulty, not a problem really but merely lack of clarity, when I order double vodkas. Not the custom here, that.

But then, and alas and O Lord, there is the karaoke, which we watch as the young make fools of their silly selves. And now, O no, they notice me and seek to fête the brothers – uns, ourselves – to stand and give together voice, which Sean summarily and surely and wisely declines, and shortly thereafter leaves. I, unfortunately and improvidently, allow myself to be recruited.

Of the music that is offered, I know but one tune. And that would be: "Kung Fu Fighting." And yes, I'm sorry and somewhat chagrined to humbly report that after singing the song I do give a brief but vigorous kung fu demonstration to enthusiastic applause throughout the bar.

More drinking, more carousing. Dark-eyed Turkish-German beauty – slinky foxy show-and-go. There is the décolletage and hot hand on my shoulder, sweet breath on the cheek. Giggling girl behind the bar – curiouser and curiouser. My new-found friend, whose name is Chris, in jukebox-hero high spirits. Much clapping on the back, shaking of the hand, the odd high five.

There is an old guy, hah – old! – shy my age by half, who drinks the quiet beer. We chat. Years ago he had made a long road trip throughout the United States and we discuss that in circles. The grand good time and oh so jolly.

Sean suddenly reappears like a providential ghost. Is it really he? Very sweetly, he wants to check on me that I might be OK and not to lose myself (mich verloren).

Drink up, shout and wave to all, and take leave. Walk and walk. Straight shot, I thought, if the winding road could ever be said to be straight. So by way of exercise and game, seek to go unguided un-lost. But unfortunately I was.

But My Good Brother there to help.

So Sean and I stroll –
Alone together / together alone
In awed or un-awed silence
Along the bubbling Rur.
Sound of rushing flushing water;
Feel of slippery solid cobble.

We linger and look at the river that runs everywhere like a web, under the age-old streets and even under some of the stolid buildings as well.

"Wha' Yo, Sean. Had we then the beef last night? Or was it the night before?"

"Yeah, you were drunk."

"And why might that night be any different from any other? Came we as it were almost to blows?"

We walk, no talk.

"Sean, I want to apologize for my transgression, for my outré way," I say.

Walk, no talk.

"Sey hey, Sean. Wanna say something?"

"What do you mean?"

"By way of the apologetic, I mean."

Walk.

"Yes. I will. But with reservation."

Ha ha!

Meet Willy lurking outside the hotel, looking into shop windows.

Sean bids adieu and retires. Willy and I smoke and chat as though till dawn, but we don't as a matter of fact last so long as all that.

At length head in and upstairs to polish off the last of the beer, the last of the vodka. And then like naughty seventh graders surreptitiously smoke, conspiratorially huddled in the bathroom, heads hung out open window to see again the narrow historic picturesque Euro streets that make you know you're here and now.

And enjoy ourselves immensely.

And now I make my walk in the morning.
The music of the babbling brook.
The tap tap beat on the cobble.
Blood runs hot in the night;
Cool head and heart at break of day.
Breakfast awaits in the hotel at nine.
Then off for the featured field trip.
Yeah yeah!

The big meaty, cheesy German breakfast with slew of bread and a boiled egg in a funny little dedicated cup.

Hit the road, head out of Monschau and on to the Hürtgen Forest where Daddy once fought and hopefully we won't. Jim Begg in tow, and in fact leading the way in his fine Peugeot.

Yup.

On to Untermaubach – two clicks.

Easily achieved.

Not lost.

How odd.

Hi Ho!

We drive around and see the sites, but really and seriously look for "The Brick House," featured in the saga of the fire-fight fought.

The old feller in fine fettle and in sprightly good form.

"That might well be it. Doesn't feel exactly like it. Maybe when we get down to it. We can get down to Untermaubach. We might see something." (D)

Willy jumps out to scout. Thinks he's got a candidate for the brick house where Our Dad desperately fought over a half century ago. The old lieutenant (Is there such a thing?) is determined to find it, and we want to see it too. Willy on foot. We drive to find him. We lose him. Round and round, back and forth.

We give it a shot.

No luck.

"… came down so it was open ground, back up there. I don't remember all the trees being there. Close to the river … which I thought was a church, but overlooked the river. And there was a chapel." (D)

Hunt for the church.
God help us.
May have maybe found it.
We approach like on maneuvers.
Dismount to reconnoitre.

"Do you think this is the church where the …?"(S)

"Oh, I think so. I think so." (D)

"It's the church of Saint Brigitte. I'm wondering how they got an Irish saint right here in a small town in …" (S)

"Well, I describe this as a church and then I remember that the church is here. And this is some kind of a seminary or a monastery or something. Uh, I don't think we did any … Well, we got here. Yah, I guess we had a firefight and then we … From inside, over from that side you could see … The Germans all fled down toward the river. And they had no place to go so they raised their hands and that ended it. And I don't remember all this beautiful fancy stuff. But you know, there weren't any vacations or anything, so…" (D)

[Laughter]

"You gettin' paid. They're paying you what, thirty dollars a month?" (W)

"One twenty five." (D)

"Oh, that's right. You were an officer." (W)

"Enlisted men got combat infantry pay. I think it was ten dollars a month, you see. And then …" (D)

"Can you imagine, to be given that to risk your life?" (CD)

"But I didn't get it. See, I was a high ranking officer." (D)

"You didn't peel potatoes." (S)

"I was a second lieutenant. Patton and I didn't get an extra ten bucks. Because we were in combat, see. Patton stood somewhat behind where people …" (D)

"He directed traffic, he directed call. Sure." (W)

"I guess he was very forceful." (D)

" '44, '45 …" (W)

"He was in World War One, I guess, and he was very, he was very …" (D)

"Look, by the river. I'm guessing, that's got to be it. I'm guessing, down there." (CD)

"Too small. It's not very big. There's a little bridge there. I don't know if it's just a walking bridge. Maybe there's another older …" (S)

"The big reservoir down there." (CD)

"Yeah." (D)

"And you didn't even know it was there? When you were fighting?" (CD)

"That's right." (D)

"He wasn't kept informed of higher structure." (S)

"He was busy." (W)

"… who was General Gavin who was corps commander. Collins. Lightning Joe Collins, or something. Anyway, Lightning Collins, yeah. See, a lot of these fellas ... It's not on the map … [Look at the map.] Well see, we were … That's Strass?" (D)

"Yes." (CD)

"That's Strass." (D)

"That's – what do you call that S?" (S)

"Sharp S. Eszett. (CD)

"Wie sagt man auf Deutsch, that actual letter?" (S)

"Das heißt Eszett. But not used here. Only after long vowels." (CD)

"Ja, das stimmt." (S)

"So, wait a minute. Where is Gabe?" (D)

"Gabe is here. You've got your finger on it." [On the map.] (S)

"Ya. Ya, I see it. But we must have been… " (D)

"This is a forest up here. That was where there was a big open area." (JB)

"Is this a road?" (D)

"That's 399." (JB)

"OK. So the forest came… We were just… This is probably forest, maybe." (D)

"Yes." (JB)

"Yeah." (S)

"Oh yeah." (CD)

"And we were either here or here. [Pointing.] But we could see it. We walked out. And the Germans were there and they had 88's then. And we walked out in daylight. We lost about half the company. And we went back in the forest. And what do you do? Paulie Bard said, 'Why didn't you just go away?' Where the hell do you go? You wanted to stay on the ground. There were the tree bursts … but at least on the ground you were safer." (D)

"Lest you go away entirely." (CD)

"Well yeah, back to St Paul. But I don't know whether we were here or here. [Pointing finger on the map.] Now see, we were in the forest for about a week or ten days before we started attacking. So I'd guess we were in here some place. I don't know. And we attacked here. And Sandler – he was a nice boy – he wasn't a boy, but he was killed in here someplace. (D)

"And all for the hill over here?" (S)

"It's quite high." (CD)

"Yah. We must have been up in here someplace. And then someone ordered us to walk down to Strass to relieve, I believe, it was our third battalion. And they peppered us. So we went back and stayed in there and maybe this was all woods, I'd guess." (D)

"The firefight at the brick house. Do you remember the brick house as being outside of Strass?" (S)

"The brick house was, I would think, something like this." (D)

[More map.]

"OK." (S)

"And we were going to attack. Where's Untermaubach? Here. Well …" (D)

"The closest house is the one we passed" (CD)

"Well, the stone house is not brick but it does have kind of a fence around it. When your mother and I were there it was just a big wire fence. And I think this is it. Some shrubbery. So yah, we … Oh, I think ... See, we were in Strass and we were going to go … Where's Untermaubach? Yeah, here's woods here. [Bent finger to the map.] So we were going to go here, yah, and we did. We were going to go here and then go into Untermaubach. And we got some firing, some firing from over here. We had a firefight. That was the brick house thing. So then the brick house was, I think, here someplace. [More at the map.] And I think we started back here. We needed to go there. And we ended up here. Then, the next morning, early in the morning, we went into the woods. They weren't there. And we went through the woods and they were here. (D)

"This is the hill, huh?" (S)

"This is high ground. Where's the town?" (D)

"This town is actually Untermaubach, this whole thing." [With sweeping gesture.] (CD)

"There was high ground here. And we walked over, out of the woods, and it was high ground for a while, then it sloped steeply down into the town. So ... and then we went in the town. And spent three days ... shootin' people and being shot at. And uh … (D)

"We were all going ..." (W)

"We can all go home now. Aha!" (D)

[Laughter and applause, and pause.]

"Oh here we go, back to the same place." (CD)

"I remember … We were in this place. I thought we were fighting in a church. Well it turned out, I think it was a chapel. Some sort of monastery, or something like that. And …" (D)

"Do you remember where this was in relation to where the monastery was, in relation to the other, other parts of the city? In other words, were you …?" (S)

"What I recall is that we finished this off and then we had the open field where I had my diarrhea program, and ah …" (D)

"Your heroic diarrhea." (W)

"Yah, heroic. Yah gee." (D)

"You almost got the DSC because a colonel was watching the attack as you were coolly walking across an open field under fire." (S)

"But there was nothing else I could do. I had the GI's and I was weak and it was my turn to cross and I couldn't run. But some kid, I suppose, said, 'You were put in for a DSC for that?' And then, I think, I speculate ... Why didn't I ask Bob Packer who was the other officer, the company commander? And then, it's impossible, you couldn't ... And then he'd probably say, 'of course not' or something, or he'd never heard of it, or tell me, 'You didn't do anything.' Yeah! And so …" (D)

"Shut up and here's another roll of toilet paper." (CD)

"The best I heard about it, I think. No one ever said you did a good job or a bad job. Especially ... Except Colonel Foster, when I lied to him, was unhappy. But, you know, you'd think sometime someone would have clapped you on the back or kicked you in the seat of the pants and said, 'Why didn't you do better,' or, 'You did a good job.' No one ... I never heard that. And, uh … (D)

"Did you ever get a chance to see Courtney Hodges, General Hodges?" (JB)

"No." (D)

"The General? He was a general." (JB)

"He was …" (D)

"At that time?" (JB)

"Well, I think he was a lieutenant general probably. But then they had a lot of them, full generals, I think. No. Hell, you know they say these generals …" (D)

"There were so many out of the Hürtgan Forest at this period of time." (JB)

"Well, and you understand why they weren't up to the front. But our regimental commander, I'd say, and I can say this specifically, got hit right near my CP. My CP was a hole in the ground, you see. But I … After the war was over, the colonel calls, called me on the phone, and see, I'd returned from the hospital and I guess I had ... I had H Company ... And the colonel, who had then not got down to Strass yet, but he was in the forest and got hit. See? And he said, 'Well, you weren't there,' or, 'How did that happen?' So I was able to say to him, 'Sir, you were hit about a day before this happened. You were up in the forest.' He said, 'Oh, oh.' Well at least he didn't chew me out again for lying to him. I didn't ever hear about it. Were they going to relieve me? And I had thought that I would be disgraced. And this colonel, Norris who was battalion commander, I think he liked me and I certainly liked him. Well, I don't think he ever said ..." (D)

"What happened to him? Norris?" S)

"He stayed in. He stayed in. He was a West Pointer and he stayed in, and when I got called back in '51 I was down in Fort Riley, Kansas. And I was up in the tower running the firing range and a group came along, a bunch of people headed by the colonel, a full colonel, and it was Colonel Norris. See? So he was a full colonel. And I think now, why didn't I?…" (D)

"Did he remember you?" (S)

"He didn't see me. I'm not sure. And I saw him, and I think now I should have asked somebody to have ... Anyone can do it, or at least any officer, and I didn't. So I should have ... because he was about the only fellow that I really ever was in a way close to ... or at least recognized that I might have done something right. See? Uh, so that's it. And

I have since learned that he died. He was no kid then. But I think when I knew him he was, I'd guess, maybe thirty years old or something like that. And he was a lieutenant colonel ... But it took Eisenhower thirty years to make lieutenant colonel, and he probably got it in five years. Wars will do that." (D)

"Yah." (W)

"Yah." (JB)

"You move faster then." (CD)

"I'd be kind of interested to take a peek here and see what this is and see what we can see." (D)

"Yeah?" (CD)

Stop the drive, a sudden halt.
Dismount, deploy.
Walk and talk; walk the talk.
"I'm sure it's a chapel now." (D)
Walking, walking; marching along.
Crunch crunch, crunch crunch;
Rhythmic rhyme under foot.

"Here. We had a firefight here. Now, I don't remember any details at all. As you know, I don't remember firing in anger except that one time. I suspect that I did some. I don't know. But here it is. And we got inside. And I think they have a chapel in here so I had thought we were in a church." (D)

"Within this courtyard?" (JB)

"Within this courtyard. And we went in and there were windows overlooking the river. And, ah … well, somehow they surrendered, the people who were down on the other side of this building." (D)

Walk 'n walk,

Hut two;
Gravel, leaves;
Three four.
Crisp and manly shuffle –
Marching tread.
Column of twos.

"A civilian place now. I don't know. Don't remember that tower or any of that stuff. But then, of course then, I wasn't looking at architecture either. You know, it's a big thing to me. Well, I … It's obvious …" (D)

"Of course, Daddy. Of course." (CD)

"The priest's house was, I think, over there and on the other side. I think it's this chapel and whatever else." (D)

"When was this?" (JB)

"The fifteenth or something like that. Oh yeah, we finished most of our combat time in this town. Yah. So it was Christmas. We walked out on Christmas Eve. So this was probably about December 20th or something like that." (D)

"How bad was the ruin?" (JB)

"Well, we left it standing, as far as I can tell. Was it intact? I'm sure there must have been some bullet holes or something, and I … See, there are windows up there. Maybe it's still a ... a monastery." (D)

And then the moment hard at hand –
That for which we came.

We turn from the chapel, pass through the archway and find ourselves in a courtyard, seemingly deserted. But then espy someone in the shadow of a shed. I salute, approach and explain. Workman, he is – German Russian – Stalin relocated to far off and foreign Kazakhstan, finally repatriated here to Germany. His accent is tough for me and mine for him, but we both show interest and reach an understanding. He waves and calls to a woman who now exits the main hall and approaches to be introduced. She says her mother-in-law owns these grounds, as has her ancestral family before.

This castle.

The Countessa.

And then:

"19 …" (D)

"19 …" (Countessa)

"… 44." (D)

"… 44." (Countessa)

"November, in this building." (D)

"Oh ja." (Countessa)

"Was this a monastery? Ask her, do you speak English at all?" (D)

"Sprechen Sie English? Was war Diese? Eine Kirche?" (CD)

"Immer eine Burg. Ein Castelle, ja?" (Countessa)

"A castle." (JB)

"Ja." (CD)

"Es ist nie, nie …" (Countessa)

"Old world …" (JB)

"1944 in Herbst sind Sie nicht hier angekommt?" (Countessa)

"Ja ja. Mein Vater war hier." (CD)

"Ask if there was a chapel in here, if there was a castle?" (D)

"A castle." (CD)

"There was always a castle." (Countessa)

"Always a castle." (CD)

"Twelfth century." (Countessa)

"Yes, but did they have a chapel in there? A church? But inside here I remember a chapel." (D)

"No, no, it was ... it was ... the first time it was the chapel of the castle …" (Countessa)

"Yah." (D)

"… and then it became chapel for all people." (Countessa)

"Yes." (D)

"This … this …" (Countessa)

"But they didn't have a little room there which … I thought it was a chapel, a little church." (D)

"No, no, no." (Countessa)

"Well, that's my story." (D)

[Much laughter.]

"He wrote a book." (W)

"He's an author of a book." (JB)

[And more laughter.]

"Yes, before I met the politisden. Wie heißt politisden? Ja, Politisden." (Countessa)

"Politicia?" (W)

"Politician?" (JB)

"Gendarmes." (Countessa)

"Polizei." (CD)

"Polizei." (Countessa)

"Ja." (W)

"Ja." (S)

"I mention it … In south Germany … And then they tell me that we war alive only because they went in the church and …" (Countessa)

"Prayed?" (CD)

"Prayed? (JB)

"Yes, prayed. Also, but …" (Countessa)

"They were down. They were crouched down. In the pews. Hiding." (JB)

"Hiding." (W)

"In, in Altar." (Countessa)

"Altar?" (JB)

"In every church there is Altar." (Countessa)

"Oh, an altar!" (CD)

"Oh, an altar!" (D)

"An altar, exactly." (JB)

"And they were behind the altar. And they ... they were alive." (Countessa)

"Mm …" (CD)

"Oh." (JB)

"Ausgezeichnet." (W)

[Laughter.]

"It's fantastic. And my mother-in-law, she war here still, and the soldiers gave to her Zigaretten. And they saw my mother-in-law going up the stairs and always wishing ..." (Countessa)

"Bad habits." (CD)

"The American soldiers gave your mother-in-law bad habits." (JB)

"Of course – shot at." (CD)

[Much Laughter.]

"You got that right." (CD)

"They were handing out cigarettes." (JB)

"Yeah, I know." (D)

"Cigaretten fo' Mama?" (CD)

"I came by my men. I let them kill themselves." (D)

"Er war dann hier." (CD)

"Ja, Ich verstehe. In my home ... in my home ... the home of my parents. They were in Urlich." (Countessa)

"Urlich." (JB)

"Urlich, you know?" (Countessa)

"And I live, I live in Brussels, Bruxelles, Brüssel." (JB)

"Ja ja." (Countessa)

"But they're, they're from …" (JB)

"You speak your ... speak ...?" (Countessa)

"I speak French but not, ah …" (JB)

"Not Flemish?" (Countessa)

"Ah, no. Not so. No, I'm from the south, more from the south. Plus de sud. But I love this country. I love this area. I come here very, very often. Germans and Americans were killing each other with a horrible casualty." (JB)

"You were in Hürtgenwald?" (Countessa)

"Yeah." (D)

"Ja." (Countessa)

"Gramma?" (D)

Daddy gets to tousling the small boy's head (heir presumptive or apparent?):

"Ja." (Countessa)

"Gramma. Doo doot!" (D)

[Laughter.]

"We Germans sometimes like to have very much children." (Countessa)

"Ja. So do the Irish. We're Irish." (W)

"Eight. We have eight." (D)

"Eight children." (JB)

"I have 26 grandchildren." (Countessa)

[Laughter.]

"Whew!" (S)

"Ausgezeichnet." (W)

"We're up to 18, I think. I can't …" (D)

"26 grandchildren." (JB)

"Now do you people live here? This is where you live?" (D)

"This is my …" (Countessa)

"Daughter-in-law?" (D)

"Daughter-in-law. And she is in the family's house here. The others have other … andere Häuser." (Countessa)

"But all of your grandchildren live in the area of the Eifel?" (JB)

"No no." (Countessa)

"No, they're all over. No one in America? None?" (JB)

"No. We went to America to see it but …" (Countessa)

"You can't stay there." (JB)

[Laughter.]

"Yes, yes. One of my daughters-in-law was much, a long time in America. In the east. And yes, and she likes America but she is very happy to stay …" (Countessa)

"To come back here." (JB)

"To be here with her husband." (Countessa)

"Ah ja." (JB)

"Here there are five children." (Countessa)

"But do the young, do the young boys ... do they have ... do they get English in school now? Do they learn English in school?" (JB)

"Ja ja, yes, und Joseph und Florin are learning ..." (Countessa)

"At what age?" (JB)

"I didn't even know about English very well!" (D)

[Laughter.]

"I like very much to read English books if they are not too kompliziert." (Countessa)

"I'm not sure …" (JB)

"Complicated." (CD)

All talk at once.

Back and forth real fast.

I cain't tell.

"… Oh, he's dead." (D)

"He's dead." (Countessa)

[Confusion.]

"… Gräfin von Spee. The Countess von Spee." (Countessa)

[Voluble confusion.]

And then she is gone.

And she spoke with us, the old woman almost Daddy's age who had been a little girl cowering on an altar in a war.

And it had been at the place of her people. Daddy's men were fighting in her courtyard and in her house, despoiling and destroying that what lay before them.

And she was kind, very kind. She offered us postcards of the grounds. She invited us back when the younger woman's husband would return from Bonn, and that he himself might be interested.

And for God's sake, how could one ever again be that – after having been through all that – to cling to life by but a prayer to an absent god.

Shellshocked, by way of denouement, we continue amongst ourselves as before in the now chilling lee of the high-arching stone portico.

"… the chapel, and this is their own, their own private ..." (D)

"This is their …" (W)

"Their …" (D)

"When those people were groveling down, down in fear in that church to survive, to live." (CD)

"Was this what she was talking about?" (D)

"You guys were doing the shooting." (S)

"Yah, was it this church she was talking about then? Yah, that's right. I was one of the … We were down in… I was in charge of it, I guess." (D)

"Did you? … You didn't knock the top off. You didn't artillerize the top of it like that?" (JB)

"You know, I never had anything to do with artillery and ... and …" (D)

"The one time. It wasn't going so well." (CD)

"Yah." (D)

[Laughter.]

"And you have a forward observer in the company, see, and our … Every rifle company had three 60 millimeter mortars, but that was ... that was in the weapons platoon. And I was a rifle platoon leader, and I didn't have much to do with these guys. And you'd think …" (D)

"You'd work together." (JB)

"Yeah, well. Well yeah, you'd think so." (D)

"Like you would with the tank guys." (JB)

"Yeah, I think so. Well, tanks, we trained with tanks and I had a little experience. Got knocked down once." (D)

"You just didn't have an opportunity here to bring the … to really use tanks as they should be used." (JB)

"Oh they ... We had 'em in town though. We had a couple tanks." (D)

"I remember one: You had a Sherman tank." (JB)

"Yah, yah. We had a couple of 'em. One was in town here …" (D)

"But almost everything here is new. It's all been, really been …" (JB)

"Oh, what I'd guess ... That house … I'll bet it's that one which is the stone house and I just don't remember and that's that." (D)

"There's a new fence around it." (CD)

"A new fence, and its stone instead of brick. I say brick 'cause that's what I remember." (D)

"That's 'cause, I think, everything is more ... In that period of time, it was typical of this area" (JB)

"Yah, but you see, the part that is confusing is that … I'm sure I saw it when I was with your mother. And I don't remember such an elaborate place. But that was 19 years ago. Ah, but my recollection that it was brick, and I wrote it as brick, and I would assume that I was going back to my time with your mama there. So, I don't know. Now it's stone and that's what makes me wonder. It's kind of in the right spot though. And ... but it's near an open field. See, we had to cross an open field." (D)

"If you were targeted on that map it would be between Gey and Strass, and that was right where we stopped, and that's where it would be." (JB)

"Well no, beyond Strass, toward…" (D)

"Strass and …" (JB)

"Untermaubach." (D)

"Untermaubach." (JB)

"Yah yah." (D)

"You know, at some point, maybe we can do this tomorrow. I want to get out in the forest and walk back up to where the rest of the platoon was." (S)

"That was up pretty close to the edge there." (D)

"The 88's started coming in. You hit the deck. And Futch and Couric behind. A big piece of shrapnel took off the top …" (S)

"Yah." (D)

"… of Futch's head. And Couric was badly wounded in a number of places. And Futch was obviously gone but you were counting on moving him. You were standing over this guy, this kid from Alabama …" (S)

"He was a nice boy." (D)

"A kid or two back home. Only 19, 20 years old. And he was a bible guy and always stopped people from cussing." (S)

"You never forget that stuff, huh?" (JB)

"I know. So we're not going to be able to find that, but it would be interesting to walk in the forest and see the kind of …" (S)

"I sort of thought that too. But look, you know ... I can say I'm going to walk over to California or something from Minneapolis. But it's worth a try." (D)

"… An area that's similar, in the woods. We're not gonna …" (S)

"We'll have time. That's a good thing. We've got four days here rather than in and out in one or two." (D)

"We'll look …" (S)

"In fact, other than that …" (D)

"Can you imagine? Life in a foxhole. When I read that ... I've read it in so many other books…" (S)

"Yah." (D)

"You can't imagine if you've never done it." (CD)

"I don't remember. I really don't remember. You know how they talk about how wet it was and all that, and I just don't remember the weather being terribly bad. And we were there … We got there December third. And it …" (D)

"But the cold?" (W)

"Well, I don't even remember that. Now …" (D)

[All talk at once.]

"You were worried about something else." (S)

"The 88's." (CD)

"Surviving." (W)

"Well, these guys, these guys tell stories about how bad the weather was. And I understand that. I just … There was a little stuff down there that might have …" (D)

"But I remember this friend who was a combat veteran in the 75th Infantry. He said the thing he remembers most is the cold." (JB)

"Yah." (D)

"December and January. That was a record cold." (JB)

"Record cold?" (D)

"Record. Record snow." (JB)

"Yah?" (D)

"We haven't had snow like that since." (JB)

"The only time I really remember the weather was in the Bulge that one day, and digging that hole, ha ha, about this deep. And spent two or three hours doing it. And I think I did it by myself. I must have shared it with somebody. And I was a high ranking officer in the US Army." (D)

[Laughter.]

"I could say, 'You dig a hole for me.' Oh, I never did that. But I shared a hole. The little guy, what's his name, was killed, my runner?" (D)

"Elliot." (W)

"Elliot. And I'm sure I spent time ... And we didn't talk about school or relatives or anything, I don't suppose. I don't even remember …" (D)

"Conversation." (CD)

"Conversation or being in a hole and I'm sure I was in lot's of 'em. Ah …" (D)

"You wouldn't survive if you weren't in a hole?" (JB)

"Oh no. That's right." (D)

"Especially holes with logs over them." (S)

"There were the tree bursts." (D)

[Much muttering.]

"That was interesting. I never thought about that." (JB)

"Yah." (D)

"The way they were hitting the tops of the trees. You know, you don't see a lot of trees that aren't damaged. I kinda look at that since I read your book. I never realized that was a tactic for artillery." (JB)

But the dog of disaster is never far afield,
But comes hard, fast hounding bounding –
You don't even have to whistle:
Sick. Suddenly and without warning Daddy suffers attack – the GI's of yesteryear are here to haunt again. Sick.

"Make it back to Monschau?"
"No."
"Stop in the town or on the road?"
"No."
Knock knock.
Sheepishly gain quick admittance.
Shit-storm then;
Shitty now.
Shitty-shitty bang-bang.
The glorious glorious afternoon of unlikely magic.
But Daddy bad gut.
Back to Monschau.

Amazing, miraculous,
Astonishing, astounding;
Wonderful, wonderful afternoon in Untermaubach.
Full of ... full of wonder.
To find the place, to find the church,
The castle where the fighting was.
And what would be the odds?
The gambler's Vegas bettin' line?

It is,
It was,

She was
And still is
A countessa,
The Countessa.

Back at the Hotel Royal. Daddy a bit bushed. The dirty digestive problem after such a fine day. Lie up in the bed, quiet, sleeping for several hours now. Hope, of course, OK.

All for the best, and maybe better later, he said.

Willy, Sean, Chris (The Boys) meander here and there in one grouping or another. Espresso at the Konditeri next door.

Try some wine –
Fine and fine.
But there is the botheration;
One can't help but worry.
And then it's time –
Time to meet the creature.
Sean and Willy walk together.
That's a good thing,
I think.

Ah'm steppin' out.
To walk about to walk it off.
It's so …
It's dark now,
Just past sunset.
The made for postcard lights are up
And I walk the medieval street of stone.
Hallucinatory mist is on.
And all is opaque.
Life is never clear.

There's the proprietress with her little dog, Fifi.
And lookin' good to step on out.
We have the word.
On she goes.
On go I.
Beauty never gets old.

There are the old Roman ruins outside and above the ancient little village.
My thought is to climb, to ascend.
Opulent architecture of yesteryear.
Broken down stairs make it easier,
Or maybe make it much harder.
Got to find it.
But lost.
Somewhat.
So what.
Maybe I should head back to the bar.

Walk around, look around;
To sip the naughty nip.
Wonderful day in wondrous way.
Amazing, astonishing, astounding, awesome, eye-opening, fabulous, miraculous, portentous, prodigious, staggering, stunning, stupendous, sublime, surprising, marvelous.
Man, O Man.
The out-and-out day of thunder.
Whatever thesaurus might say.
The countess,
The castle.
Cobbled over cool,
Slippery tip-tap.
I move on.

I scratch my way, way up the hill,
But he's but more than just a hill;
Though no damn damned D-Day today,
No deathly dirgey surge foray –
Grim guns de Pointe du Hoc.

The craggy switchback upheaval. Almost reduced to hands and knees. There is a handrail; I have my stick. To the ruins, the theatrical architectural up lighting. Don't know what it is – Looks Roman but maybe it's not. Could be somewhat later, Gothic maybe.

Ah ... but the Beauty. I look down over the unsuspecting town. It's dead ass black before the lights. I hear the sound of the rushing river and its tributaries and, God help us, sewage or whatever which flows beneath the buildings – aqueducts and viaducts and such run fast and make noise underneath.

To tip over now would mean to die. I'd fall flat on my face and be dead and fuck it.

You need your tripod now. But I can stand – f1.4, dead quarter second, and be there. And thank you very much, Monsieur Cartier-Bresson.

Shoot what seems to be what's left of a castle. From down and low and below things look close and similar and familiar. From up on high they are vastly separate, disparate, different.

So get down now;
Next man up.
To see what's seen and next in line –
Be onrushing Abentauer be.

So high as hell and lost as well.
Can't tell the steps from the path from perdition.

The blinding glare of the theatrical lighting robs me of what scant sight I can rest from the barren blackness.

But bare and barren me –
Homeric hero He forgot.

Surrounding sound of rushing Ruhr.
Sing hard and soft water river.
Got to get down.
No panic yet.
In fact:
I'm tough;
I can take it.

So, standing weak-kneed here, high over the stark soft-glowing city of lovely lonely lovesome Monschau, by myself and all alone – I seys to meself: “I wish my girl were here.”

With me.
And could see.
And be with me.
You never know when the sadness must strike you.

Almost fall far, again and again,
And alas and alack, make it back at last;
Touch down for soft solo landing.
What the hell.

Stand on smooth and rough and wet, slick shiny cobble in city center Marktplatz. At last on even ground. There's a surprising plastic sculpture of a monumental green foot, big as a small elephant. Photo-op, of course. O yeah.

Assailed by sound of music. From where does it come? It's, by God, Jazz. We got the sax and trumpet on it. You can hear it.

I walk to the music.
Lost.
Lost as hell.
I hear the sounds,
I feel the groove;
But I can't tell direction.
But there is of now the babbling, bubbling brook –
The sweet sound of jamming water,
The funked up groove of time and tune.
Jazz.
It's all and always Jazz.

So where am I?
Where is it that I find myself?
Look for and to my father and my lot.
Where?
Where art thou?
Oh, I see. Over there – now over here.
Suddenly and full-tilt un-assèd!
I'm lost but now I'm found.
I'm back.

Daddy still feeling badly – the GI's, the dreaded diarrhea. And in the war, the colonel on the hill with the glass remarked favorably upon the brave young lieutenant advancing under fire with such sangfroid.

"Give that man a medal." The Bronze Star, it proved to be.

So, Willy and I in same style step out to down a drink and try to find some take-out food for the old guy lying in the bed. Imagine such a thing as that in Europe! (The nature of the serving of the food, not the sleeping apparatus nor the disposition of the gent .) Well, we manage actually to do exactly that and then all is well and swell.

Debacle deferred to the near or distant future.

Disaster forestalled for just an itty-bit.

Daddy

Chapter Twelve

Friday, October 19, 2007
Monschau

After you've spent the night walking back and forth between the bed and the biffy, it's hard to know when you've gotten up for the day. But I did.

The boys were worried. At least one of them was with me all night. I needed the help. I was limp from the GI's. Someone found a liquid medicine to help. No help.

One of the boys stayed with me in the room all day. They brought me breakfast, lunch and dinner. I could barely stand looking at the food let alone eating it. I was sick. What little food I got down to my stomach, soon thereafter exited from one of the body's apertures. Since I had planned to write about the trip after we returned home, I might have been delighted to have the opportunity to compare my current diarrhea difficulties of October 2007 with those of December 1944, both commencing in Untermaubach.

As I lay sick in my hotel bed I'm sure I had no delight in anything, but now, two years later, I can compare the two "GI's" experiences.

In 1944, the GI's first occurred either while I was in a frigid two-man foxhole or the cold basement of an abandoned house, either within talking distance of the enemy. With the aid of one of my men, I was able to walk back a few hundred yards to the battalion aid station, where I was given some medicine and allowed to sleep the rest of the day on a cot. After the sleep I walked back to the company. The next day I joined in the attack and firefight across the open field in Untermaubach.

If any of my men had been asked about my GI's problem, I'm sure he would have noted how lucky I was to be away from the fighting all day while being able to sleep on a real bed.

In 2007 I was more than 60 years older than in '44. The years delayed my recovery.

So, I am in bed this morning bemoaning the fact that I am again sick with the GI's and cannot visit the open field outside of and overlooking Untermaubach, the location of a memorable firefight.

I'm remembering December, 1944, and how, after our battle at the brick house, the now fewer men of E Company advanced without opposition through the woods east of the brick house.

We reached the east edge of the woods overlooking Untermaubach with orders to attack across the open field above the town and thereafter to proceed into it.

From "Shavetail":

"A few mornings later we... moved through the woods to its eastern edge, which overlooked Untermaubach... We still had only one rifle platoon (40 men), and I was the leader.

A dense fog covered the town and the approaches to it. At about 8:00 a.m. the company commenced to attack, leaving the edge of the woods in two parallel single columns... I waited in the woods, intending to proceed after the first few men had advanced.

After the scouts had advanced about a hundred yards out of the woods, the fog lifted suddenly. The scene before me was a flat open field for about 150 yards, and then the land dipped downward into the town. The Germans had dug in at and started firing from the 150 yard mark. Because the terrain changed from a flat surface to a rather steep downgrade into the town, this was the last place from which they could defend against an attack from the woods. Our men returned fire. By that time I was in the middle of the field. I crawled over to one of the squad leaders, a sergeant, and told him that he and I would run up to the front to direct the attack. 'Sergeant,' I said, 'we've got to get up there right away. You go ahead and I'll follow. We've got to knock out that fire. Move fast and keep your head down. Good luck.'

The sergeant ran ahead of me, under enemy fire, across the field toward our most forward position. About halfway there he fell to the ground. I thought he was hit, but he got up, shook his head, and ran forward. I followed him. He showed me his helmet with two holes in it – one where a German bullet entered and a second where it came out. A near miracle!

Inside the steel helmet was a fiber liner. The bullet entered the steel helmet, traveled within the fraction of an inch between the helmet and the liner and exited the helmet without hitting the sergeant's head. Impossible? Almost, but not quite. I saw the whole thing. It's true.

During the fighting I called for a Sherman tank to fire at a German position. When it pulled up, I stood at the front of the tank to show the target to the tank commander who stood in the turret. Before I backed away, he closed the hatch and fired the 75 millimeter cannon at the target. The muzzle blast knocked me to the ground. I got up, and I've had ringing in my ears ever since.

But today, in my hotel room in Monschau I don't even notice the ringing. I mostly notice the diarrhea and find it ironic that today I will not visit, as I had planned, the fifth location on my itinerary.

I am remembering December 23, '44, our third day in Untermaubach, and how we had taken most of the town except for the buildings close to the Roer River and the bridge crossing the river. For the past few days I had been battling a severe case of the GI's (diarrhea in civilian parlance). I even walked back to the battalion aid station where they gave me medication to slow things down. I don't think it helped much.

From "Shavetail":

"We decided to try to take the bridge first. It was located about 100 yards north of the center of the town and had only a few buildings near it. In order to get there, it was necessary to cross an open field fifty to 100 yards wide. While some men fired, others sprinted across in a single dash to get to cover on the other side. The German fire was light, so the first few men reached the other side safely.

Then I decided to go. I was still so sick and weak from the GI's that I could not run, but instead walked as fast as I could. Unknown to me, Lt. Colonel Norris, the battalion commander, was observing our operation from back on the high ground. I learned later that he remarked favorably about the brave lieutenant who calmly walked across the open field in the face of enemy fire. Of course he didn't know that such "bravery" was aided, abetted, and directly caused by a severe case of the GI's.

Lt. Colonel Norris recommended me for the Bronze Star medal for walking across the open field. I got the medal.

The colonel never told me to my face that I had done a good job. In fact, during my four and a half years of active duty in the army, I never had anyone compliment me for anything. I suspect that I never earned a compliment, but I can't help but think that the law of averages or some other unknown factor would have caused some unsuspecting human being to let slip some sort of statement resembling, "Devitt, ya did all right."

The Bronze Star medal was introduced during World War II. It was awarded to soldiers for either "heroic" or "meritorious" achievement. The heroic achievement medal was the lowest medal for bravery in combat, followed by (in order of importance) the Silver Star, the Distinguished Service Cross, and the Congressional Medal of Honor.

I don't know if I ever knew what achievements were classified as meritorious, but precisely the same Bronze Star was awarded for both. This failure to distinguish between the two caused many men who had been in combat to criticize the Bronze Star for heroic achievement since it was no different from the one for meritorious.

I recall that soon after the war in Europe had ended, when numerous Bronze Star medals were awarded for activity during the war, many infantrymen would laugh at a buddy who received the Bronze Star for heroic achievement, while pointing out that it was the same as the one received by a fellow for non-combat achievement.

At some later date the experts who worked on medals added something to the Bronze Star to indicate if it were for heroic achievement in combat. I received my Bronze Star before the addition was made.

I'm sure that in the medal-distributing business it was helpful to have the recommendation come from a fairly high ranking officer such as Lt. Colonel Norris. The next ranking officer who saw what I had done was probably myself, a lowly second lieutenant. I'm sure that the rules proscribed a soldier from recommending a medal for bravery for himself.

When I decided to walk across the open field, I had no thought of bravery or medals. What was I to say, "Men, I've had diarrhea for the last three days, so I can't run across the field with you. I'll wait for you here. Good luck!"

To the men, that comment would have gone over, as was said at the time, like a lead balloon. It was like telling them that since walking might increase my risk of injury, I would not walk across the field. Yet they must run across.

What moved me to walk across was not bravery, but duty, something I was obliged to do. I had sometimes ordered my men to obey me, to do their duty and risk their lives while having little or no risk to myself.

Now the situation was reversed. The GI's increased my risk this time. I had to walk, making me an easier target. It was my turn. As the leader, I had to apply the same principle to myself.

It was not bravery, but duty which compelled me to choose to walk across that battlefield. Surely, however, while crossing the field, I did not think of duty, or bravery, or medals. I just wanted to make it across that open field while remaining in one piece.

I'm pleased to have received the Bronze Star medal. I might have deserved it. But if I deserved it, so too did all of the other of my men who crossed the field that day.

In the hotel room in 2007, my sons were more concerned about my health than I was. When asked how I was doing, I'd usually say "Pretty good," but towards evening I'd let slip out "Not so good." I'm sure that increased their concern. The boys had nothing to do in my room except help me out of bed, to help me into the biffy, or bring me a glass of water. While in bed, I'd try to sleep (usually with little success), so there was not much talking.

The baseball season was ending. I don't recall if the Minnesota Twins were in the playoffs, but if they were, I had somehow lost interest in the Twins. I was really sick!

The boys would bring me picture magazines with the hope, I guess, of getting my attention off myself and the GI's. No luck. I'd whisk through a forty page picture magazine in sixty seconds.

We'd chat a bit. But mostly about my health. If one of them tried to distract me by trying to discuss baseball, politics, or any of my other usual topics, I'd defeat his endeavors by turning his discussion into a monologue in which he was the sole participant. No one was going to deprive me of the comfort of feeling sorry for myself!

I hope I was not quite so self-centered as it sounds, but the GI's had a grip on me. But because I spent almost all of my four days in Monschau in my hotel room with the GI's, Chris, Sean and Willy were able, while taking excellent care of their father, to explore and discover that fascinating medieval town.

Willy

Monschau day 3

Up and down all night using the latrine, Daddy feeling poorly. We're starting to worry. It's agreed by Chris, Sean and me to keep a close watch, and always have one of us here at the hotel at all times.

Dolly calling from Minnesota to commemorate the first anniversary of Mama's death.

Uncle Bob has died as well these last few days. "The last of the Mohicans," says CD. Daddy's younger brother. Daddy now the last of his tribe.

It couldn't be that Daddy has come back to this land, over a half century later, to die. And of the same sort of ailment that he suffered shortly before his near-fatal wounding in these killing fields.

Surely that which we call God wouldn't be so cruel, so perverse.

Things looking grim. A not so subtle change in our outlooks, our plans. It may well be time to focus on getting home. And soon.

Daddy can't possibly make it to the Huertgen Forest. The Ardennes likely out of the question as well.

Sean will go, check out the Huertgenwald, and deliver a copy of Daddy's book to the Countess in Untermaubach.

Out exploring the town alone. A funny yellow choo-choo train runs slowly down the narrow main street. For sightseeing. Very few automobiles, people moving under their own steam. As they were meant to. A fine thing to see.

Popping into shops, have a look-see. Old-World style toys, merry-go-rounds and wind-up music boxes, beautiful hand-made things, but pricey too. Shop woman talks me into buying some sort of linen table thingys for me sisters, made here in Monschau, which it seems has a long history of linen manufacture, similar to Belfast. Some caps and shot glasses, touristy crap, and back to the hotel to check on Daddy, relieve Chris. But first have bit of lunch. Stop at this Imbiss, order three long wursts with Pommes frites – two for me, one for Daddy. Hope it's not too heavy for his stomach. Gosh, these are good... just take it out of the bun for Daddy.

Daddy sleeping. Just settle in here, do a spot of reading – Bill Bryson's amusing and informative tome "The Mother Tongue," about the etymology of the English language in all its eccentricities. Very apropos for this excursion.

A wee dram of this excellent Apfelkorn. Looking out my window. See our proprietress out on the street below, outside the fire station next door, helping to unload a delivery truck into her bakery and café, which is also next door.

She seems always to be in perpetual motion, this fine and athletic woman. Always doing something or other whenever encountered. Most wonderful service she and her husband provide. Sending up pots of tea for Daddy, genuine concern for his condition.

CD returning now from his walkabout.

I, down to have a smoke, sitting at a patio table outside our front door.

An old American approaches. I've seen him and his pals before, talking in the hallway about their wartime years in Germany. Their talk crass and oafish. This one now, Daddy's age. Trying to get in the front door of the Royal, which is kept locked, all guests provided with keys.

"Goddamned Germans... how ya supposed to get in this place?... damn Krauts..."

Mumbling to himself. 3 o'clock of an afternoon. Can't figure out how to get to his room.

I consider offering him my key. Maybe while instructing him to get his shit wired together. And to remember to bring his key with him when he steps out.

I think better of it. Pretend I speak no English. Should he enquire. A true "Ugly American." One of those, he is.

He wanders off, still cursing our marvelous proprietors and the German volk in general.

Most of these, our present neighbors – these younger and civil denizens of Monschau – were not even alive during the war. Abhor it and their country's culpability in it with a great passion. Many frankly ashamed of their national past. Do as many Americans reflect on theirs? Admit to themselves that all nations, all peoples, have certain things to feel ashamed and regretful about...?

Fuck him.

Back upstairs, Daddy awake and not feeling much better. Eats a bit of his bratwurst, most of the fries. I offer him some Rolaids, which don't help. Keep him drinking fluids, says Chris' wife Marilyn, an RN, when Chris calls home. On a telephone that actually works.

Down to the market for bottled water and juices.

Sean returning from the forest. He and Chris out and about. To a bistro it seems. Having a bit of the karaoke. Funny stories CD tells...

Myself on Daddy duty.

Brothers returning some time later, time to consider dinner. Only one thing for it – back to our pub.

Saturday night in the Rhineland. The place livelier than last night. CD and I here to fetch the comestibles. Placing our order at the bar. Our dad still not feeling well, and if we could get what we had last night... danke.

Not the usual thing to get carry-out food here, but they agree again tonight. After all, we *are* big men from America, and we surely like to spend money. At this fine establishment.

The barmaid's daughter. Not working tonight. Instead here with friends. And a young bloke. Aaah... well... Should I just check out that jukebox? Maybe a Stones song. Or Otis Redding. Give these Teutons a bit of the olde hoodoo voodoo. Dance on the tables. South Minneapolis style. "Don't you mess with Cupid. 'Cause it's aaaaaalll riiiight, now. In fact it's a gas..."

Our man Garrett at his usual stool. Looking like he hasn't moved since last night.

"What say, man? Abend!"

"Ja, Abend, guys."

The usual bi-lingual blather. Garrett seeming to know everyone in the joint. Has several conversations going at once. Chris involved in other various convo. Much reflective staring off into middle space for me...

"Noch ein Bier, bitte."

Another shot of the Ells, courtesy of your man. The odd furtive glance at my Germanic queen. She waves. The boyfriend looking unsure of himself and his standing. Oh aye, laddie, I remember. Being young. Universal. Ritual and emotion. The ever present heartaches. Oh, they'll find you two. Set your clocks by it. And dreams and ambitions. These young Germans. The same as those in 1939? The same as all others in the West? Does good really triumph over evil, beauty over ugliness? They say we are all really the same – the blood red, the bone white. The heart so round. And so often blue.

CD laughing. People like him. Wherever he goes.

I light a cigarette.

Our food taking a little longer than last night. Really should be getting back. To Daddy.

But these here – are they the daughters and sons, the grandchildren – of his former mortal enemies, the one-time enemies of all mankind?

Up now, say goodnight, gathering food containers, effects. Shuffling towards the door.

God wants us to be happy. At least occasionally.

A wave, a bow. To those here. Who brought some cheer. And me. Just that much closer. To an understanding. The heart of the world.

Into this good night we ungently go. Me with large plastic bag of food containers, balancing that whilst smoking and steadying CD.

"Whoa, there! Easy now, son!"

"Oh, aye, just you never mind me. Blow winds blow, hearty old buzzard and all that."

The cobblestones glistening and slick in the drizzling rain.

"Steady, lad, steady!"

"Whoa! Whoops! Still standing... You can count on me!"

Laughing our proverbial arses off now. Pausing for a spell at the little bridge which runs over the Rur. Sharing my cigarette. The gentle flow of the river also seemingly laughing.

"Daddy and Sean are probably starving. Hope they're not mad at us."

Chris tap-tapping with his walking stick. These ancient cobbles a bit of a test if one isn't used to them. When squiffy.

The yellow street lights mimicking the moon. And here, an odd and whimsical sculpture in the town square, a huge foot. Toes and all. What's it mean? Why here? Who bloody cares! It's a big foot! And seems about right. This Chaplin-esque night.

Fumble for keys. Through the hall and up the stairs. Oh, geez – steady, man, steady.

Home sweet home. Aaah!

Daddy and Sean indeed famished. Daddy nibbling at his food, still feeling lousy, maybe worse.

It's decided to look for a doctor tomorrow, a Sunday.

Back in my room, readying myself for bed with a smoke and a nightcap. Wee clock-radio on low. Radio Luxembourg I think. Long and beautiful piece by John Coltrane – 'A Love Supreme' – re-mixed with Gregorian chant. Strange and compelling it is. Chris dozing off in his bed, sleep through anything. And a thing that makes me quietly laugh.

When I was eleven or twelve years old, Chris came home for the first time on leave from the Army. He was quartered in my bedroom, it having a set of bunk beds.

Later that night he came home from where soldiers go when on leave. I was still up, and thought it good gas to play for him a cassette tape of a George Carlin comedy album.

Chris stretched out in the lower bunk, still in his clothes, laughed along with me to Carlin's description of the Seven Deadly Words and going to Confession at his childhood church in New York City.

I was laughing myself silly when I asked Chris a question, and lo and behold, the man was fast asleep. With his mouth open in laughter. Never seen anything like it. 'Til this night in Germany.

As Coltrane's tenor sax melded with the monk's singing, Chris had dozed off to sleep. With a beatific smile on his face.

And though our concern for Daddy's health was paramount – we having decided to forego visiting Jim in Brussels and the Ardennes Forest, where Daddy barely survived being blown up by a German mortar round in '45, and cut the trip short and head for home – it struck me that this was a good way to comport oneself. Even in repose.

And to my father and brothers, I silently wish all the best. And, with the closing coda of the Coltrane piece signaling Last Post, I retire.

Perchance to dream.

CD

10- 20-07 8 O'clock

Creaky Yoga in this morning.
Daddy poorly, up at night ill.
And I not well – what with the worriment.
He won't die now or soon, will he?
The irony would be too much.
Has God such a sense of humor?

Out for the morning march.

Call it a constitutional.

Some things never fail to give satisfaction, grant pleasure, or even to tender succor.

Smoke, pause and reflect on yesterday's yesterday.

And after one's fashion, on all and every.

At some fuzzy point in time, called Marilyn and Cally, the wife and the daughter, and actually and really and with the minimum of madding fuss and without deploy of one-winged widgetry – made the hotel phone work. Right from my room. Just dial the number. Truly risibly incredible.

Well, knock me down with a noodle!

Despite the desperate fog of battle, hunt down and capture the obligatory postcards. Now to dutifully find the Postamt. Would it then be Saturday this fine day all day?

Look up at the ruins that I gained last night in the dark.

Think of that: With intent and on purpose to achieve ruin. Didn't guys used to shoot themselves behind that sort of thing? God damn!

Hope against hope that Daddy's OK. Hope all has been fine for him. Or maybe only most. What was or is to be expected? Or maybe only hoped for. Whatever that it might be that we all, all of us hope for.

It was a truly fine and magnificent moment at what he calls the church in his book, but which turned out to be the castle of a countess. And a grand one at that.

German breakfast in the hotel dining room. Only Sean makes the scene. Daddy and Willy don't come down – Daddy laid up, Willy lays up. We talk quietly and seriously of this and that, and decide to bring up the cornflakes or something bland or some such.

There is a party of gray-faced guys who loudly complain of something stupid in strident chauvinist southern American voice. My good brother and I do what you do and I've done before: Switch to another tongue and deign to feign ignorance of the Ugly American.

Have direction – Walk the walk to the Postampt. Everywhere I look is on canvas with a frame around it. I hear the soothing and stimulating self-help recording of wind and stream and birds chirp-chirp, and click-click heal and stick on the old-school paver.

Manage to mail the two cards with no fuss and little prompting, and embarrass myself thinking the old saw about German efficiency. And oh my goodness, there's a gift shop there. The pretty dirndled girl helps mightily and she flirts in fine and proper Saturday morning fashion.

For the girls back home I score two pendants and two bracelets and a cutesy bag to put them in. All my shopping woes and worries over in an instant.

If you go somewhere, you must bring something back as souvenir. Pause to sit on new old stone wall. I couldn't be happier, he said.

Back to the hotel. There are the lads with the Lieutenant. Daddy up and about but he'll not venture forth for fear of the embarrassment. Wouldn't want to win another bronze star.

To market to market to get some vitals: Pernod, couple bottles of Apfelkorn, a few beers, can of nuts and some apples, and I'm set up and set.

You bet.

Not to sally forth on the driving tour, so it's off for the solitary walkabout. Try to find the castle that is said to overlook Monschau.

Walk about, walk about, walk about.

Rock 'n' roll and twist 'n' shout.

Not only can I not reach the castle, but I can't even discover it.

Try the cigarette automat – Try to make it work. Son of a bitch – I think I'm robbed. But ah … I finally get, while not the cigarettes themselves, at least my ventured money back.

Off along the little streets, it's sunny and schön. Even sport the shades today.

Seek hidden castles; joust with windmills.

I find myself on a small narrow street, straight out of a movie – Two cars could never come abreast.

Up up up I climb, up and up –

So steep as to roll your ass down.

At last and with much exertion I out of breath get to the top.

Missed it, missed it again.

For there is no castle, at least not here. But there is a tiny chapel. Not much bigger than the red English phone booth. Only four people could fit inside it. Out of stone it is. No one is here. No electric light. I step in. The candles are lit. It's a "Chapelle for the Devotion to our Holy Mother, Mary" – Worn insculpt, it is upon chiaroscuro wall.

I contemplate, I pray;
Somewhat sacrilegiously steal some photo likeness.
And then the magical miracle:
To pause outside the holy chapel
And see the sought hidden castle.
Like a mirage, it's really there.

It looks as though it might be used as a modern person's modern home. But certainly not in the modern sense (if that can have postmodern meaning).

To take my bearing and head back down and see if I can't descend to depth.

Again.

Holy Mary, Mother of God,
Pray for us sinners
Now
And at the hour of our death.
Amen.

Nearby is an old graveyard – necropolis, if you will. It is small. I enter. Most of the tombs are new and beautifully upkept. There are several sepulchres though, four or five, that are old. Very old. For age, one cannot read what it says on the stone. Wear and care have worn the script. There is one grave that looks to contain six or seven soldiers. It gives their rank and the type of unit they were in. It is still-life still and quiet of the dead. Supplicants busy themselves in silence to maintain the hallowed graves.

Walk slowly and carefully with grace, show respect.

Time to head down. I find a path, a walking path. And I can see the ruin (indeed, anticipate the ruination). The castle dates from the thirteenth century. The old Catholic church was built in 1650. An old engravature tells me, and the

German tongue both serves and fails me. I determine that Daddy and I shall attend Mass tomorrow at 11 o'clock. He'll be pleased and surprised that I have chanced upon the enterprise.

Dig out a pathway and some stone steps down. It's tiny, wild, overgrown with green. There seem to be sectioned plots where some people camp. Other times I pass directly past someone's back door. I fear I'm on private property (whatever that might mean). But now I reach the wider flagstone street (by wide I mean 12 feet). And now down to the bottom and into the town.

Time for something to eat.

Zig-zag up and down stone stairs, directly back of hotels, people's houses. Enmired in labyrinthian maze. I think this back-stairs restricted but can't tell. What the hell.

Back in the burg, the city itself. Walk the narrow streets by little shops. Find another chapel, much larger than the other though still miniature model small.

Carved in stone as though forever is a prayer, saying, slogan, ejaculation of some sort – another devotion to Mary, Mother Of God. It tells to take five minutes to reflect and pray, and Mary will intercede – guaranteed. It seems a cult, no? God knows of what those medieval characters may have been capable.

So it's deep breathing bright light
To airless meditative black,
And back to eye ache cobble tap.
Après the ascend and descend,
The up and down,
The in and out –
Breathe fresh fall air and look for the little Imbiß joint.

O look, there's Willy! Same thing in mind, I see. Brothers heart-to-heart in open air, smokin' an' jokin' in the delicious sun. Time to take the picture-pause, smell the smell of sizzling sausage, frying spuds, fresh baked bread; and gobble Currywurst, Pommes frites, and amble loose joint and jolly back to the hotel.

Call Sister Dolly from the hotel room. The phone works. It is the anniversary of Mama's death. Uncle Bob is indeed now new dead too.

And so all go that way some day.

Commiserate a salty bit,

A bitter season taste of jive.

Hang up.

Roll on.

As always and now and forever.

Amen.

Daddy still sick.

But bumps with the boys.

Long, strong and late into the night.

At some point in the proceedings it is decided that we best and must push out and get our downed man something sick-food light to try to get down. We huddle up and play dietician: salad, omelet, hold the greasy meat, better no bread? We all head out in pack together. Check the drugstore for whatever would be in it, but by the time we get there it is closed and we're too late.

Shit.

We council on the street in the dark by the naked light of the amber lantern. Sean to retire to tend to Daddy. And two strongs scout for a Gasthof for the drink and what Willy curiously calls the "take-away."

Seek and find a fine enough bar.

In fact, it seems that it was found last night and now we dramatically return.

The girl for whom Willy looks and wants just isn't there. What's new?

We drink and drank – the grand rousing time.

Chat at length with German chaps. Talk of war and other dire and awful things, somewhat to my embarrassment. But Willy enthusiastic and seemingly so the others. Cards are exchanged and someone says he'll show us about tomorrow.

Long and strong, late into the night.

Bumps with the boys.

We'll see.

We will see.

Daddy

Chapter Thirteen

Sunday, October 21, 2007
Monschau

This is the third consecutive day I've been stuck with diarrhea – the infamous GI's. I've had this before, but in the past I had recovered in three days. But today I think I am worse. I had to go to the biffy more often, and I was having trouble keeping my balance while walking there.

The boys asked the proprietress of our hotel where to find a doctor. They were afraid I was dying. She gave us the address of a clinic in town. The clinic was in an office building with two rooms full of medical equipment and occupied by a receptionist, or nurse, and a young male doctor. With Chris as my translator, I discussed my complaints with the doctor. He examined me, said that I had diarrhea, and gave me a prescription for medication. For the half hour visit the charge was 20 euros, 30 dollars in my money. Not bad. Not dying.

We drove back to our hotel and asked the proprietress the location of a drug store to fill the prescription. Rather than telling us the address of the drug store, she insisted, yes insisted, on going herself, which she did. I think she let us pay for the prescription.

I'm thinking again of yesterday and have decided to write to the countess in Untermaubach. I was too ill with GI's, so I sent Sean to deliver a copy of "Shavetail" to her, along with the following note:

Dear Countess Von Spee,

Thank you for your exceptional kindness in our visit to

your home on October 19. I was one of the American soldiers who, in December 1944, invaded Untermaubach and your home. In fact, I was the lieutenant who led the platoon.

Until yesterday I had thought your home was some kind of monastery. In December 1944, it made no difference whether it was a home or a monastery. We had orders to attack, and as I'm sure was true of the brave young German soldiers who opposed us, we obeyed our orders. Yet I'm sorry that circumstances called for including your home in the battle.

I'm happy to learn firsthand that a German family, whose magnificent longtime family home was invaded and damaged 63 years earlier by a platoon of American soldiers, should greet and treat the leader of that platoon with such goodwill and kindness.

God bless you and your family,
William L. Devitt

I went back to bed. The boys had stopped having one of them stay in my room. They rightly thought that staying in the room was unnecessary. Instead, one of them would regularly come to my room, open the door slightly and, if I was not sleeping, ask if I needed anything. If the old sleeping giant needed help, he got it. I still remember several of the times when I was awake and looking at the door and seeing it open slightly. And there was the face of one of my dear sons looking in to be sure that Daddy was all right.

But I wasn't all right. Not only the GI's, but I was concerned that I might not make it to my <u>seventh location</u>, our final destination. Namely, the cold, bald ridge in Belgium's Ardennes Forest where I was seriously wounded on January 3, 1945. In July, 1988 my dear wife Mary and I made our one and only trip to Europe to visit the places where I had been in battle in World War II. On that trip we did not attempt to visit the seventh location because at the time I didn't know exactly where it was.

However, in planning the October, 2007 trip, I did some homework and found a map of the area. The map showed the line as it was on January 3, 1945, separating the Americans to the north and the Germans to the south. The front line followed a road running east to west and going through the Belgian town of Bra. My division, the 83rd, was on the line.

I knew that my company, E Company, had not been as far west as Bra. I recalled that on January 3, 1945 we had walked south on a gravel road to reach the bald ridge. Voila! I had the solution to finding the ridge!

All I had to do was follow the southbound gravel road, cross the Bra (east-west) road, and within a mile or so would appear my elusive ridge – the one on which, in January, 1945, a German mortar shell exploded delivering a piece of hot shrapnel into my belly and ending my war.

In 2007 I was too sick to go. A major disappointment. Again, the GI's.

From "Shavetail":

"The Ardennes was heavily wooded, with many tall pines. It was memorable especially for the deep ravines that cut through the area. The roads meandered along the sides of the ravines so that while walking along a road we had high ground on one side and lower ground on the other with trees towering above us on both sides.

On the morning of January 3, the company left the bivouac area and started to move to the front. We trucked to within a mile or two of the front and then walked from there. As we got closer to the front we could hear more incoming artillery shells going over our heads, and we heard their explosions on all sides of us...

It was three o'clock in the afternoon when we arrived at our position at the front. The incoming fire became heavier, and we were told not to go beyond a ridge ahead of us.

We were to take positions along a low, treeless ridge beyond which there was an open valley and more forest beyond that. The Germans were in the forest. The weather was getting colder. The snow was coming down harder, and there was a light dusting of it on the ground. We did not go to the top of the ridge because the Germans could have seen us. Instead we stayed on the reverse slope. As soon as we arrived, everyone started to dig slit trenches for themselves. Apparently the Germans did not know that we were on the ridge, since their artillery and mortar fire was falling a few hundred yards to our rear. The realization that the German fire could come closer at any time was sufficient incentive to dig as quickly as possible.

As soon as it got dark, Packer (E Co. commander) and my new platoon sergeant and I went to the top of the ridge to see what faced us. This is called an 'estimate of the situation,' namely, an inspection of the area to see the intricacies of the terrain and the location of the opposing forces, with an eye to determine what action to take.

When we got to the top of the ridge, the German artillery and mortar fire was falling within 200 yards of us. As a precaution, I stood in an old German slit trench that was two or three feet deep. I figured that a little protection was better than none.

Packer, and the platoon sergeant and I, talked quietly for a few minutes. Although the German artillery and mortar fire was close, we didn't think we were in immediate danger. We had the problem of when and how we would attack the German positions the next day. Of course we knew generally where the Germans were–in the woods–but we had not as yet even seen a German. We also had the usual problems–feeding a large group of men and protecting ourselves against incoming fire. But in war, as in ordinary times, it's funny how quickly one's plans can change.

Without warning, there was a large explosion. The war was over for me.

About thirty feet from where we were standing, a German mortar shell exploded with a flash of light and big bang. The entire ridge was brightened momentarily by the flash. I immediately felt a sharp pain in my stomach. The platoon sergeant fell to the ground badly wounded. Packer said he was hit slightly, and I slumped down into the hole to protect myself against any further explosions.

The Germans did not realize that we were on the ridge. The artillery and mortar fire was landing two hundred yards behind us until that single mortar shell (known as a short round) got all three of us. Shrapnel from the shell sliced into my belly and left hand, but all three of us survived.

I was carried out on a litter to the aid station where the doctor stopped the bleeding and said to get me to the hospital. Although my hand was numb and not hurting, it was bleeding, so I waved the hand at the doctor. He had just not noticed it. He wrapped it up and sent me to the hospital. – the diagnosis, "penetrating wound, abdomen."

I was in hospitals four months. The belly wound was the real problem. It turned out okay. "All's well that ends well."

Two weeks before my collision with the mortar shell on January 3rd I had a much less serious meeting with a German "potato masher" hand grenade.

We were in the town of Strass, near the Hurtgen Forest. We were trying to dislodge the German infantry from a brick building. They retaliated by throwing the grenade at us. The explosion seriously wounded my platoon sergeant who was nearest the grenade.

With the explosion I felt a slight sting near my right eye.

We finally prevailed. The Germans surrendered. The fighting stopped. Our first sergeant noticed that my forehead was bleeding and asked what happened. I told him it was nothing important, that I was nicked by the grenade.

The first sergeant mentioned the slight wound on the morning report, and I was awarded a (cheap) Purple Heart medal.

For years I've sort of apologized about receiving what I called the "cheap" Purple Heart, but now I think that good luck, happenstance, or some other factor came into play. If that tiny piece of shrapnel from the grenade had been one inch to the left, it would have hit my right eyeball. Result – a penetrating wound – and a dramatically different outcome to the cheap Purple Heart story.

"Penetrating wound, abdomen" reminds me of what the outcome would have been if the shrapnel in my belly had penetrated another inch into an untreatable organ thereupon leading to my death.

Stop speculating! It didn't happen!

In 2007, my plan was that, as we walked or drove slowly along the gravel road, I would remind the boys of my experiences, which they first learned about from my telling them and their later reading of "Shavetail." I would tell them again, but on the very spot where the German artillery opened up and the shells landed, at first harmlessly well past our location, while walking on the gravel road toward the ridge. And how then, with the forest's trees surrounding us, the shells started landing closer. It seemed as though the Germans knew we were coming, though they certainly could not see us.

I recall some of the men hitting the ground when they heard an incoming shell that might have been headed for us. I considered myself adept at judging the proximity of such incoming fire and continued to walk while the shells fell harmlessly a good distance away from us. There was, however, a flaw in my thinking. Although my cockiness saved me from hitting the ground on several occasions, I only had to be wrong once, and the incoming explosion could have been fatal.

My imagination in planning the 2007 trip brought me to

the top of the ridge where I hoped to find (with no sense of reality) the German foxhole in which I was standing when the mortar fragment sailed into my belly and ended my war. I think I felt that this would get the boys as close to the war as possible, while having some sort of similar effect on their father.

Finally, the GI's. I did not even try to find the ridge. The plan did not come to fruition. The ridge, wherever it might be, must linger on without me.

Surprisingly, it was not, as far as I remember, until the last few days that I speculated about what might have happened to me if the mortar shell on the ridge had not exploded near me and ended my war.

Why were there only three of us (the company commander, my platoon sergeant and I) on the ridge? Where were the other three or four officers in the company?

They had been with the company for only a couple weeks, having been added as replacements soon after the company had walked out of Untermaubach with a mere 40 men and needing another 150 more for a full rifle company.

I think that the company commander and I thought that since the three of us had the most combat experience, we would get the "lay of the land" before bringing up the other officers to view the terrain.

The new officers had not yet been in combat. Probably the nearest they had come was the preceding afternoon (as we walked toward the ridge) when the incoming German artillery fire kept landing near us, but never near enough to cause casualties.

Perhaps the thinking was not nearly so profound or thoughtful as noted above. The company commander saw (and knew) my sergeant and me and merely told us to join him on the top of the ridge. No profound thinking.

If the mortar shell on the ridge had not gotten me, I would have remained with E Company as a platoon leader in further fighting. The law of averages would have found me as a later combat casualty, probably seriously wounded, but substantially less serious than a mortal wound which would have left me languishing, yes, dying, on some cold, foreign battlefield.

CD

10-21, I think

Sunday morning, Mass in mind.

Then of course the chewy breakfast.

I wander to the drugstore to see what time it would open. But it does not indicate. Back to the hotel. Unsettled with the circumstance.

But fine fresh morning – You want to live.

Always in Monschau surrounded by the sound of water. Unending music for the soul. Bet they don't need self-help sleeping records here.

Happen upon our wondrous proprietress at breakfast. (I fail to mention that she's really very pretty.) Ask about a doctor for Daddy. The woman is astonishing, astounding: She not only recommends a doctor who would actually Sunday morning see us, but jumps in her little car like an Amazon and drives there leading us urgingly on.

Small and simple set-up: Bantam reception/waiting room, single theater not much bigger. No tricky beeping equipment. It seems almost primitive but I'm sure that it is not.

We see the doctor (and he sees us). I am proud and pleased as punch that I can help with translation because Der Herr Doktar's English is lacking. Daddy duly examined and I attend. It is thought that he will be fine and it is only the "traveling sickness" with the diarrhea. So, script in hand, need but to cop the dope.

Back to the town square. Unload. Daddy to the hotel and in. The boyos outside, standing around and talking about going to the next town (and where would that be?) to get the prescription filled, when our Patron Saint (whose name I stupidly still don't know) appears and insists that she might have that medicine as a result of having been recently ill herself.

We wait in the street like louts while she investigates.

Finally she comes out. It's not the same stuff so we make to hasten off. Yet she accosts us and says that she will herself fetch the cure and bring it back to us. We all protest of course. To no avail.

She also offers to do our laundry when we inquire after a laundromat. She must think us, I suppose, so simple and muddled, or perhaps even entirely incapable of washing our own clothes, and insists on doing that.

So we scurry to assemble same. Lo, poor Daddy's laundry is back in the car that Sean has just now sped off to park.

We fumble and fumble. One of the cleaning ladies is downstairs waiting, while we wonder and wander.

Finally Sean appears and we get it all together.

I say we would pay, which seems normal and to be expected, required even. No, she insists, no. So we're owing this woman and I'm not sure how we make it up. Awfully, oh so sweet, I say.

So, knock me down with a noodle.

I'm simply bloody dumbfounded.

Back to the hotel. Sit around without aim. Daddy sleeps. We fumble with language books, compare notes, and try to figure out how to communicate and what to do. The why will become apparent later we hope.

Bit of a bite of a chill this day of gray.

I look out the unshuttered window, as some might watch TV.

This – one of life's long-standing enduring hoary pastimes.

Keep calm and carry on.

Here we be.

After Daddy's morning episode, the trip to the doctor, the laundry shuffle, and the unnatural niceness – I am exhausted, stretch out on the bed, stare at the ceiling, listen to the sounds and the voices from the street below.

As a post-war French existentialist novel.

Bourgeoisie take their holiday. Weekdays, it seems to be mostly tourists. This is the weekend and the Germans are out in force walking about in groups, taking the tour – the families, the lovers, the oldsters, the motorbike comrades in their elaborate and theatrical costumes.

Snap decision to hunt for food,

And grind the gears and turn the wheels and walk.

Daddy unconscious naps.

The boys are anxious, already out and about in the mist.

Excellent little lunch at a small café. Step in out of the soft rain. There are maybe six tables in up-tone yellow. Omelet, fresh green salad, milk the savory cup of coffee. The waiter-cook-owner, the only one there, asks where I'm from and we talk. He has a little English; my German is strong today. Asks what I do for a living (somehow they always do) and I tell him I man the Fotoapparat and we consider that and discuss art in general. He even asks for my advice (oh, God help him) on what to get and which.

The rare and jolly exchange.

A little bell tinkles and a pretty blond girl enters.

Soon others follow; I check out.

Outside – the soft but persistent rain.

Maybe hide back to the hotel,

Maybe some God-forsaken stroll.

Maybe I don't know.

Run up on Willy who lounges on the patio off the street outside the hotel. So we sit on steel chairs at a black iron table with red-brown patterned pavers under foot in the lee of the old artful edifice, just on the edge of the suddenly smiling sun.

"Procure the vitals for later?" say one.

"Surely sure," say t'other.

“Would that be vitals or viddles?” say one.

“Surely sure,” say t'other.

And it's off to nearby city center Marktplatz that I go it alone.

Let's see. Shoppin' 'n' scopin'. Small and alien print. Beer, wine, vodka, Pernod (the evil Pernod), can o' nuts and an apple. That should do it but it don't.

Five drunken German women day trippin'. One grande dame slams into me.

"You are Frenchman?"

"No."

"Englishman?"

"No. American."

"No."

"Yes."

She makes to pay for cigarettes when pocket change explodes to floor. She bends to retrieve – shiny black spike heels, tight but low-cut jeans, loosey-goosey top. You can see, not the top, but the bottom of her black and red thong; and that's a lot.

Wink grin to the cashier – I bend to help and to help the play.

Her friends descend, cluster about, and whisk herself away.

Thusly is she saved and spared.

And thusly so meself.

And what one tries to pass off as honor.

Back to the grand hotel.

The infantry up'n at'em. Feeling better, which is good, 'cause he couldn't feel much worse and not be dead.

He sits in his chair, composing a note to our hostess. Along comes one of the – I was about to say – the servant girls, but I don't mean that – ah ... one of the room help with laundered laundry in hand. They'd finished our washing, primarily for Daddy. Everything sweetly neatly folded. The shirts and pants hang on hangers. She put it all away and hung them on the hooks and in the closets. (I, of course, throw everything in a bag and leave it there and live out of a tawdry and desperate box.) Ah ... I must and want to pay her. It seems you ought to pay for the service. Isn't that how we show respect, give thanks; transact Papa's "simple exchange of values?" Maybe even how we show affection?

She refuses the Geld, say not to pay.

Well then. I mean to tip her. Grab a five euro note, hand it toward her. No. She won't take that either. A bit confusing. Feel a fool. How friendly and kind and helpful these volk are. Ah … the smiling and the laughing and to forge ahead and effectuate fine kind things, even though you try to stay them.

What's wrong with these people? How different from and at odds to the usual general life in which you try to make people be proper and decent; and they desist from that, persist in not that. Flummoxed I be; but heartily heartened, truly touched.

I fight off welling burning tears
And hope I'm not seen as a chump.

But I don't care.

I really don't.

Really.

This fine lot bring to bear the same vigor and enthusiasm to do kind things, that is usually reserved for people who are trying to fuck you over.

May God now and always bless 'em.

Gray afternoon fizzle drizzle
Gives way to evening rolling rain.
I shiver and watch from the window above
As figures clutch umbrellas to hand
And strike their stroll in promenade.
Lights now lit glisten from off the street
As though some one would shoot the scene.
Faint fog cuts a slight diffusion.
It's early yet as tolls the bell.

And then it's time for some wriggling and writhing, a bit of the kung fu fighting. Hope not to strike the combative air among my brothers. Certainly mean not to. When in public and doing hard, aggressive-looking boxing exercises and people happen upon me, I would stop and do stop, lest it seem threatening. Not so the public tai chi. Though discovered, I continue unabashed, even with an audience – since it is usually slow and seemingly gentle, and not thought to be dangerous but rather a curiosity.

But so it goes.

Even Sean moves around a bit – pushups and shadow boxing.

Tighten up;
Loosen up.
Good stuff.
Good for him.
Good.

Unabated drizzle drum tattoo.

Cocktail Hour – The Hotel Royal.

Daddy lying up; he comes to. Quick trip to the WC. He looks better and gives the tentative encouragement and, dare I say – hope.

Telephone (can do it) Marilyn and Cally, wife and daughter, the girls, my loves (I seem to think). Never thus far this long apart, I fear ... Ever?

"Pump the liquids."

"We will."

"Keep him pissing."

"Thank you, Baby."

Look out the window once more:
Shiny street stones wet from rain.
The sun, such as it is, has dimmed.
Crowd thins.
No one there now.
Solitary stalker.
Heel on stone (Tun-Hut!) –
You can hear it.
Street scene lonely lovely.
Sole coughing motorcar traverse.
You hear it in your sinking soul.

Still moist chill but now I run hot.
There is the searing cutting fear
Of the upcoming day and days.
(Never mind the hard advancing weeks and months and years –
Parading pitiless and ungentle.)
Yesterday I crowed: Yeah-yeah –
I can take this tour,
Make the scene,
Go the distance,
Survive to fight another day.
Shit-happy hubris now it seems.
And now I'm so worried, out and out scared –
Maybe Daddy the one who won't.

We are all alone and separate and disparate and desperate together, and then stomach cramps attack and again the call to duty.

Look to get me gone.
Reconnoiter, live off the land.
Drink up, saddle up;
Find the food for Father.

Daddy still ailing. Sean mounts guard. Willy and I, our own bad selves, race off to the bar to get some take-out, or as he would have it, "take-away." Back to where we been before – a hangout already almost. Hope to cut the heroic figure and to be well loved by all and sundry but it's sorta slow tonight. Girlie tending bar not love me, nor Willy too. Buddy of previous eve not eager either. Order the chow but it's a long time a-comin'. And yes, that is a distinctly American uncouth practice. Sorry. Don't mean to disgust.

But we drink our drinks; we stand our rounds well met. Have and had a few between us too. They feed us Els, the native liqueur of Monschau and damn – it's fine, and I wish I could get it in US. Restorative effect, folklore has it, it has. And by George, I feel better already!

The food, it finally comes; we drink up and go, bring it back to Daddy.

But there is the question of balance en route.

But Brother Willy lends a hand.

So what's up tomorrow? The next day? I never understand the plan nor ever even what to do – much less the long game – what it means.

The Long Con, I call it.
I don't want to know what it is;
I only want to learn to live in it.
Tactics over strategy.
Well, there it is.

Here it is.
Goodnight.
"Aw geez, guy." (Willy)

O God In Heaven, please save us.
Or at least Dear Old Dad, if You please.
All day and night the drizzle without end.
By open window I can hear it.
O God, please grant, please give us strength.
Sorry we missed mass.
Give us strength.
Give me strength.
But would You not give Daddy health?
Give him strength.
Give him life.
Grace!
Aw Geez, Guy.

Willy

Monschau day 4

Daddy must see a doctor today. A Sunday. This could prove difficult. Possibly more so than finding food in France, or telephones. That work.

Yesterday Chris and I had a walkabout. All over town, up steep tracks to the main highway – 399. And then to an ancient castle overlooking Monschau. All its depths we explored.

Would this ancient town, with all its Old World beauty and charms, provide us with that most vital of modern conveniences, indeed, necessities – health care?

Frau Propper, our proprietress extraordinaire, has been following Daddy's illness with great attention and concern. And her actions thereof are extremely moving.

After talking with Chris and Sean, she recommends a doctor in another town a few miles away. Then insists on driving ahead of us to make sure we get there easily and in short order.

She asks the hotel staff to launder our clothes. And deliver them to our rooms. Which is done. Free of charge, though we hide euros in places where the staff women will find them. As they refuse to accept any payment. For helping our father.

Out to find the clinic, a couple towns away.

A receptionist, sweet and receptive to Daddy's humorous anecdotes. The doctor, a tall, good looking youngish chap and a nurse. Their English, not so good, Chris accompanies Daddy to the examining room. A short time later – a half hour or so – they're finished, with the verdict being that

Daddy merely has the “traveling sickness.” The GI’s. A common medicine, well known in USA, is prescribed.

Now the bill.

35 euros.

About $45 US.

For a doctor visit.

And you know what?

Within a day, Daddy will be feeling fine. A bit tired, as we all are, but fine.

In the U.S. such a visit would cost $200. And that’s with health insurance.

So the nation, the society which brought the most horrifying slaughter and barbarism of the modern epoch to the world now provides health care of the highest order to old American soldiers, for the price of a meal at a restaurant. To those same who once helped bring that society with its obscene leadership to its knees. In the hopes of building a better one.

Which was done.

And this is one result of that Herculean effort.

Would an old German tourist get such treatment, at such low cost, in USA? Without the services of an Emergency Room? On a Sunday?

I would hope so. And that there are things to learn from a former enemy. Now such a staunch friend. That might help big men from America. To be more. Of that goodish way to be. Which we call:

Civilized.

Vielen Dank, Deutsche Medizintechnik Industrie. Gott segne Sie.

Later that afternoon. Daddy composing a letter of thanks to the wonderful Frau Propper and her quiet, friendly husband. A copy of his book will be given, as well as flowers, which Sean seeks out. As tomorrow we leave for Belgium. Neiuport, up the north coast.

Having a smoke out front of the Royal with CD. Here's one of the hotel staff. A middle aged woman, short dyed blonde hair, exotic makeup around her eyes. She hails from Turkey. Pauses for a smoke with us. Has the aspect of anyone who does physically demanding work, when having a short break in the action – tired but talkative. So easy is her manner, her English good. She being the housekeeper, the one who washed our laundry, folded it neatly or hung it up in our rooms while we were out to the doctor with Daddy. Chris now offering her 15 or 20 euros, she waving a hand as she coughs on a drag from her cigarette, won't hear of it, and continues talking of some other thing entirely unrelated to our fawning praise of herself and the hotel staff in general.

Such people are these. Money alone doesn't usually buy you such humanity.

Chris observing that these fine people go about the business of treating us with such decency with a vigor and conscientiousness as is usually reserved by others for treating one shabbily, for fuckery.

The term 'grace' comes to mind.

The evening spent doing this or that, shopping for gifts, exploring, who knows what. Daddy, no doubt, having a well deserved nap.

And of course the dinner hour will soon arrive. And you can bet we know just where to get it too.

Down to our local, as we have done nearly every night in Monschau. This night, though, not nearly as crowded. Bit subdued, it is. And our erstwhile friends there not so welcoming as before. Our man Garrett sitting at the end of the bar with an old boy, a crusty codger, playing cards, not looking happy about his immediate fortunes. Not looking too happy to see CD and yours truly either. We buy him a round, he reciprocates with a shot of the creature, the good Els, and that's it for the night.

Our food takes longer than even last night. We are nonplussed, and stop ordering drinks. Have a big day tomorrow anyways. Driving north to the coast.

And it's "so long, 'twas swell to know ya." And back to our rooms. To gather our bearings. For the final stretch of the journey. Things winding down now. As they inevitably must. On our stay in this magical fairy-tale town.

CD

10- 22 8:20

Deep sleep – Up an' at'em – Qigong.
Worried for Daddy; who wouldn't?
Will he survive this tour, this tall travail?
Or will I eat my heart out?

Still hope to find the site of The Great Man's wounding – picked off a hill by cannonade in the Bulge, and busted up his belly and almost killed him.

Bring Daddy's book, "Shavetail: The Odyssey of an Infantry Lieutenant in World War II," to the Countess along with his carefully composed personal epistle.

Sean wants to walk in the woods – What was it like for those then?

There is the computer café to be found and the booking for Belgium to be made. Sean will drive, the booking seems to fall to Willy who also wants a bank, and maybe I can help.

It falls my lot to stay with Daddy. Fine, well and good. Happy to help.

And by all that's Holy (or not) I will – I shall.

But alas, the terrible task befalls me too, one I never thought perchance to perform: I must seek out, search for and find something called "Depends," diapers for adults, for him, he who spawned me. I'm sure neither he nor I never thought it would come to this, this nor anything like it.

God, Oh God please help us.

O won't You deign to do?

And what hast Thou, like a bungler in a kitchen, wrought?

Out for to walk the walk. Weekend's over and done. At early hour in post dawn monochrome – the Teutonic workmen abroad and rampant, shouting gruffly, totin' ladders, talking in loud and strident tone to one another. Riffing as drudgers do. As I in my turn do too.

Late season cool and brisk and damp,
The fog envelops and blankets
The picture postcard little burg.
I clutch me to myself.
I walk.

Quick march along the well-spring river,
My hands are cold.
My heart, it's cold.

The sound of the coursing tributary had previously calmed, made happy, amused me even.

Not now.
None of those things.

Tap tap, my stick on ancient stone.
Up and out of town.
Turn around.
Back on down.
Breakfast.
Hope to God,
Hope to God
That Papa can turn it around.
Fog.

Walkabout walkabout. Get a few things done.

Try, for once in your life to be useful, helpful, efficient.

Scout up a corner store with all you could want and much that you don't.

Embarrassing diapers for Daddy. Disturbing. But there's no real shame in it, is there?

There's the needed bank for Willy's business. And hope there is some money left.

Back to our home away from home, skip the elevator, two stairs at a time.

Ah, it's that we're busy people, friendly people, moving about and getting things done. The whole day freight train underway.

The sun now peekaboo out; better change to the lighter trousers.

Our Da looks a little bit better, sitting up and writing cards for the Countess and for the Cunning Concierge.

Carry On Carry On.

So Daddy ensconced at the hotel with his business, Sean on the driving tour, Willy and I head out – maybe find the storied castle, maybe not; but have the agreeable afternoon, no doubt. No, none about that.

We'll pick up flowers, have a spot of light lunch at the Konditorei;

Present the flowers, the book, the card, the note;

And then perchance we're on to evening activities.

Things are looking up. Or at least not now so very much down.

Here's to hoping Daddy will be well, fit, strong, and maybe even to astonish and be big – big as life itself.

He seems a little bit better.

Will a little bit be enough?

Willy and This Silly Sod out hiking in the warm and aesthetic life giving sun. In shadow of the buildings or outcropping of rock it's cold.

Quixotic searching for the castle.
Up upon up we scramble over rock and through brush.
Call it The Ascension.
Reach the rim round the town and view Monschau way down below us.
We're not driving, we are not looking for banks nor exchange machines nor information nor telephones. We may be a little lost but we do not mind. We have the castle for which we sojourn and seek in our sights, and …
We walk.
"Swell." (CD)

Willy and Yours out tramping – to roam the civilized wilderness. We actually and really finally find the castle – not just pretending. It's of a pretty good size (as your vintage castles go). Built in the thirteenth century, it had been in disrepair; restored, then I think, in the 1970's or 80's. Looks as though some are living here now. There are signs in German that I can't completely understand that seem to discourage one from going various places and doing enumerated things. And the courtyard shows a sign that says "Private," so I'm convinced somebody lives here; but wonder at the history, the hidden story.
O look: Such as I've never, not ever seen before – a permanently mounted ping pong table made of concrete, right there out of doors and in the keen hearty breathing breeze. (But maybe it's a but a sculpture.) And of course we sadly lack the requisite sporting utensils. (Much less the proper togs.)
And all of a sudden: A stampede, a cavalcade of squealing children. Must be Kiddie Day or a day care of sorts. 40 or 50 of 'em, running around, thither 'n' yon, and playing at wilding. Chaperones scramble to ride herd, with some slow schmucks in tepid pursuit. It's quite possible that we're not supposed to be here but …
What the hey.

All back together; we all hold court.

So Sean and Daddy are off for the big dinner-outing extravaganza, which they both quite like. And God Bless 'em, I think it a fine thing, and good and great that they can spend some time together.

I stick and stay with Mister Willy –

Chit-chat, lolligag and bullshit.

Tomorrow and tomorrow and tomorrow:

We'll be on the road for Belgique and hope to roll expeditiously along, undeterred and undismayed. But there is the worriment that no place to stop has been planned, found and booked; and, as it were, I'm under the gun, since consensus has it that it is I who ought to have made the arrangements.

What? Find computer and phone gadgets and the tasteless cafés that quarter them and fuck around, fuck around without any end.

Why? They finally bought my theory of roll up, look about, ask around – find the flop, get the crib, just go there. Just like ever and always.

Well, that's my system (such as it is), though there is indeed the counter thought, vociferously voiced and universally held.

If it goes badly,
Then I'll be the goat.
And if it goes a little badly,
It will go real badly.

How? Like to sleep in the car in a ditch on the side of the road with the vulnerable Old Man in the damp with the cramp all night long till the very bitter end.

In any case, we roll tomorrow.

Tomorrow and tomorrow and tomorrow:

Daddy

Chapter Fourteen
Monday, October 22, 2007
Monschau and Nieuport

The day we left Monschau I sent the following note together with a copy of "Shavetail" to the proprietors of the Monschau hotel:

Dear Herr and Frau Propper,

Thank you for your exceptional help for my sons and me during our stay in your lovely hotel. Finding a doctor for me in my medical emergency and then driving to the pharmacy to pick up my prescription were together a service beyond anything I have ever seen from a hotel proprietor.

Having our soiled clothes cleaned for us is another example of your generosity.

My sons and I will always remember the kind, gentle and outstanding service of yourselves and your associates at the Hotel Royal in Monschau.

Sincerely,
William L. Devitt

Nordic hikers. The morning we were departing from the Hotel Royal in Monschau, we came upon a scene which, if it had been in winter, would have looked familiar back in Minnesota. Coming out of the hotel was a group of six–three couples, wearing warm jackets and hats, pants, backpacks, hiking boots, and in every hand a ski pole. They reminded me of Nordic skiers.

I don't know if they were local folk taking advantage of their lovely and interesting countryside, or if they had flown in from Berlin to explore the ancient towns and sites of the Rheinland.

As a Minnesota boy, I could see that the group was missing two items, skis and snow. The boys immediately engaged them in conversation. They were German, and yet somehow we called them "the Nordic Hikers." They told the boys that they had hiked twenty kilometers the previous day and expected to do better the next.

In snowy Minnesota, from December through March, cross-country skiing, with the usual foot or two of snow, is a major pastime. But I have yet to hear in Minnesota of "cross-country hiking."

Since most of the time on the trip was spent in France or Germany, the question might be asked as to my impression of the French and German people.

The people with whom we spent most time on the trip were the two women who owned and ran the hotels we visited in St. Lunaire, France (two days and one night) and in Monschau, Germany (five days and four nights).

Both women were slim and attractive and I'd guess in their mid-thirties. They ran their hotels well and were particularly diligent in satisfying the needs of their guests.

Each hotel had three floors and fifteen to twenty rooms. The tiny hotels had no lobbies and only a small cubicle at which to register. Both had a few workers including one husband apiece. They did not introduce their husbands who fitted in as part of the working crew.

St. Lunaire. We entered her hotel not to rent rooms but to use a phone to locate the bed and breakfast we had reserved in St. Lunaire. She let us use the phone and helped us try to locate the bed and breakfast. No luck. So instead, we rented two rooms from her for the night.

One room was across a bridge from an area of two adjoining rooms. Willy and I were in one room. The other was empty. Chris and Sean were in a room on the other side of the bridge. All four of us thought that it would have been nice to have Chris and Sean in the empty room, yet we didn't say anything to the landlady. But that was not necessary. Soon after we unpacked, she realized how pleasant and important it would be for us to share the adjoining room. So she opened the other room for Chris and Sean and helped them move their luggage. I cannot forget the thoughtful and selfless action of a French woman for a few American strangers whom she will probably never see again.

Monschau. Our original plan was to stay two days and three nights, but when I became afflicted with diarrhea (the GI's), the stay was extended to five days and four nights. Our Monschau lady had more time with us than did St. Lunaire. She offered me medicine and led us to a doctor to treat me. She insisted on driving to a nearby town to fill the prescription which the doctor gave me. Her concern for me was so great that she treated me as though I were her father rather than an unknown old foreign geezer whom she would never see again.

Both ladies were always friendly and responsive to our every need. They both treated us American tourists with kindness and generosity, quite different from the rather impersonal treatment we'd receive in most American hotels.

It would be a magnificent world-changing achievement if all people in the world would learn to treat all of the world's other people with the same kindness and understanding which these two ladies from France and Germany displayed to four fellows from another far-off country.

Upon leaving Monschau, the revised plan (since I was still so weak from the GI's) was to drive northwest past Brussels to the English channel coast and find a place for the night. The next day we would drive to Calais, leave our car, take the ferry to Dover, and train to a hotel near Gatwick airport. Last day, plane from Gatwick to Minneapolis-St.

Paul International Airport and home. The revised plan worked without a hitch (I think).

We reached the channel coast in the afternoon and started to look for a place to stay. After inquiring at a few hotels near the water, we discovered that the Belgians, not surprisingly, have an affinity for water, and place a substantial premium for the use of hotel rooms located in the vicinity of the English Channel.

So we drove into Nieuwpoort, which is a town only a short distance away from the coast. The name reminded me of the city of Newport, Rhode Island, which I have never seen, but have been aware of all my life. It is known for the summer "cottages" built near the seashore overlooking the Atlantic Ocean. They were built in the 19th century by prosperous – no, rich – no, VERY rich people from New York. The cottages were in fact thirty room brick and stone monoliths built as summer getaways from their even less humble New York City dwellings.

I saw no "cottages" in Belgium's Nieuport.

For an hour we drove up and down the town's narrow streets. There were several small hotels, but no rooms available. Finally, a bit before dark, we found "bed and breakfast" which had two rooms. We were the only guests. The owners were a middle-aged couple. As a sort of greeting, the wife served us tea and cookies. They sat and chatted with us for a while. I don't recall what language or languages were used. But the boys seemed to be able to communicate no matter what the language of preference at the moment. I did a lot of mumbling.

I remember only one thing from the conversation. The wife made some critical comments about her fellow citizens who live in the south of Belgium adjoining France. Nieuport is in the north, near the Dutch border. My understanding is that in Belgium, several languages are commonly used – Flemish, Dutch, German, and probably others. Perhaps the Belgian people could learn something from my sons – just be friendly and try to get along with everyone.

The most memorable experience in Nieuport occurred that evening. After dinner I went upstairs to my bedroom and lay down. After a while I heard a dripping sound. I opened my eyes and saw drops of water coming out of the ceiling and starting a small pool on the floor. I got up, put on my shoes, and went to the ground floor. No one was around. The owners had gone visiting to their daughter's house. The boys, possibly thinking that I could handle my nap without their help, had walked up the street probably with the prospect of finding some bottles of Belgian beer.

What could I do? I stepped out the front door and noticed the lights being turned off in the small grocery next door. When the store lady came out of her front door, I explained to her the problem. She said she would call the owners at their daughter's house.

But I was not finished. What if the store lady somehow failed to talk to the owners? My solution? Call the fire department. Somehow Willy appeared on the scene. We walked across the street to an office building and told a man the problem, and he called the fire department. I later learned that Chris and Sean had also phoned the fire department, which responded promptly. We had things well covered.

The owners thanked us for our help and offered to allow us to stay another day at no charge. I, of course, declined since we had to get back for our flight home. It did occur to me to suggest a rebate of part of our one night's stay. Both of our rooms had wet floors, and we had to move all of our luggage and clothing to other rooms. Despite my penurious inclinations I figured the owners had suffered enough (considering the cost of repairs and house damage), so I resisted the temptation to add to their financial woes.

Since the language I use is pretty solidly restricted to the English tongue, how could I have communicated so well with my Belgian friends? The answer is that I should be thankful for the Belgian penchant for multi-linguistics. Is that a word?

Willy

Our last morn in Monschau. Bags packed. Pay our bill. Oh. We can't. Get money from the cash machines. Nice. Maybe we won't be allowed to leave. Fine with me. CD, however, saying not to worry: he has the ready, ready. In his shoe. Yankee dollars. In the hundreds.

We figure out how to get money. Somehow. Chris and Sean deliver flowers, book and thank you note to our proprietors.

Now it seems we have nowhere to stay once we hit Nieuport. Sean orders me to find an internet café for to find some lodgings online. He's as tired of fuckery as Chris and I, Daddy being mostly imperturbable, for better or worse. Mostly for better.

CD says "Fuck it. Find a place when we roll up. We'll find someplace then."

Now there's a novel idea. Okay. We will.

Standing around outside the Hotel Royal, our gear stacked around us, Sean down the street to fetch the car.

Final goodbyes to the Proppers – thank you so much, we'll never forget our stay here – and along come some amusing folk. Four older Germans, two women, two men mid-60's early 70's age-wise. With ski poles in each hand, backpacks slung. Stopping, they smile and tell us their story, this hearty lot. "Nordic hiking" is what they are engaged in. Having hiked 15 miles the day previous, they hope to do 20 today. I avoid making a tasteless joke about the German military's historical ability to march long distances. These friendly volk may well have been alive during WWII, very young children they'd be. And seem so happy to chat with the B.M.f.A., as we are with them. Something there is about meeting the old ones, the ones who were on the opposing team, as it were. Their parents or grandparents – what are their stories? What were their politics? Back then. Did they think it was a good idea? If only for five minutes... The question of genocide... Do average people fully comprehend it while it's actually going on, if they are even aware? What it means? And Hitler was a great fan of American westerns, cowboys and Indians, films, the history, theory and method, the Trail of Tears...

Forgive – perhaps.
Forget? Never.
War is over.
If you want...
Auf wiedersehen.

CD

10-23

Last day in Monschau, so I'm told. Up early, 5:30 aufstehen. Qigong, soft and sweet, and kungfu with a vigor. It's still pitch black outside, you see.

The agreeable evening last night – lounge around the hotel room with Brother Willy, chatting, drinking and looking out the window – always perennial favorite. Bit of a drop of the Pernod, the pernicious Pernod – standing in, pinch-hitting off the bench for the evil, evil (but absent) Absinthe.

Sean and Daddy together, out and about on assault of dinner. Daddy maybe better.

Must solve the puzzle of the bill.
Damn cards won't work, persist to fail.
But pool our regal real money
Of which we have (O Joy!) enough.
Of which we may just have enough
For the next bad bill to be paid,
And the next; and the next, and the next and the next.

The time of wonder here in Monschau, this beautiful little German burg of gracious magic. And to think: Picked at rankest random from a touring map but for the centrality to the locales we had hoped to visit, which we didn't due to illness.

Such hopeful, helpful happenstance!

My father and brothers sleep yet.

Forgo the early morning constitutional (unconstitutional day that it will be), hang out the window like a Russian Revolution rider and smoke the smoke like it's my last.

It's dark, black, and achingly cold.

All packed I am; won't speak for The Others.
Am I my Brother's Keeper?
Or even then the Father's?
Off for Belgium; we're not sure where. To Brussels or points past.
No finish line yet determined.
We don't know where we sleep.
Nothing booked nor carved in stone.

There has been the simmering controversy: Who will find and book the bed? Everybody wants everyone else to do the deed. Do it now, do it now. I won't. I suspect that none of us may even be able.

Never discovered the rumored, heralded, vaunted internet café. Nor would know how to comport one's bad self, nor how to make the computers work at all at all.

It will be to me in person and on scene and in situ to find the bed and the breakfast and to surely secure them.

If I fail, I'll be an asshole.
The Everlovin' and God's Own Asshole.

So what's wrong with the old system? – Just Go. Round about death of the afternoon, start asking for a place to stop. If nothing there, no room, drive on. Check the next, and so on and so on.

Should be OK. It always is. But I'm under the gun, down and dirty. But excellent breakfast draws nigh.

Bon appétit.
Bonne chance.
Bon courage.

To break the fast at early hour,

What with the cold cuts and the ham and the cheese and the hard bread and the granola and the yogurt and the tricky juice, don't know what it is but it's great. Even eat the ceremonial egg in the funky little silver egg cup which I can't quite figure out how to work, and it turns out unfortunately to be of the soft boiled sort, but eat it and eat it anyway.

And we're set and ready to roll.

Hope all the little plastic cards will work today. Some times they do; sometimes they don't. Entirely capricious. Failing that, there is the actual capital, real money stashed in a shoe.

Liquidity not the Gordian Knot.

But about to blast for Belgium.

And wowie zowie; gee, gee wiz!

Pater Noster seeming somewhat a bit better today. Looks more alive. Up and on his feet and making to move around. He doesn't come down for the breakfast but we bring him up yet another bowl of cornflakes.

Mmm. Hoffentlich schmeckt.

Pay the bill,

Do the deed.

We have, as it would be, the problem of paying, of course. The cards won't work. As is their wont to not. Ahhh ... but now I bring the coin, the cash, the stash, real money, the folding stuff of green, the paper, next best thing to bite-with-your-teeth specie; go for the gold.

The heartfelt salutation all around – meet and greet and goodbye. Manage to get through the ordeal without the tears. But not so easily done at that.

Run into to some old folks outside the hotel while waiting with our luggage for the car. They had gone and done 30 kilometers yesterday and would go 20 today. They were, it seems, indulging in "Nordic walking." Which involves using ski poles as you traverse on foot.

Much fun and mostly high spirits;

Hooray, hurrah, huzzah!

The volk of Hotel Royal very friendly, very fine. I'll never forget. Not now, not soon, not ever.

And now we clamor to board the car to resume our role

As bumbling clowns on move and go.

Now we drive

The driving tour.

High Ho!

Set to go:

To rock, to roll.

Final farewell.

But alas, it takes half an hour to cram into the car.

You know it don't come easy.

Now we find a bank and play with plastic.

Wonder if it will work – again.

Then we hit on a post office

And send things somewhere.

To rage again against the contretemps.

There is the contentious and disputed but primitive attempt at navigation.

More fuckery with maps,

More obtuse observation,

More pre-emptive aggressive remark and suggestion – some of which physically unlikely, biologically unnatural, and if the laws of physics still mean anything at all – truly and starkly impossible.

And yet we forge intrepidly on.

Drive on.

Right on!

So here we find ourselves in Nieuport, having journeyed through Germany into Belgium.

Beemer wheels keep rollin' and so do we.

Find a place, a B&B, as I foretold and knew we would (not to gloat, but to gloat [anyone would]) – a place, a crib, an abode, a bed and a breakfast. No smoking here, up front portentously pronounced. To which I've unfortunately and with some mild irritation become accustomed.

Nieuport – Not the one of jazz that I know.

Things are looking up.

Homey middle-aged couple offer coffee and eats by way of welcome. Pleasant talk of language and history. But then we get to social concerns: They don't like the Walloons. Or is it the Flemish? And the vehemence – Dirty lazy bastards prevent Belgium from forming a government and are responsible for all the ill you can think of.

Sounds like Good Old US of A with The Blacks, The Whites, The Mexicans, The Muslims, and everyone else you can think of.

But even so and in spite of same, most pleasant in the sun saturated nautical day room as light then is slowly lost, and the Euro black coffee is bitter and fine, which contrasts and amplifies the sweet chocolate hazel Nutella on thick brown bread. Willy and Daddy and Meself, Sean napping – but look, here he comes; he's got food in his mouth, he's bending over the sink, he's had his nap.

And just now, now this, and in this:
This transitory evanescent moment,
This rare high shutter speed snapshot,
This warp, this time-out of time –

Life at large is good.
If you pay close enough attention.
I pause and look and pony up.
But giddy-up a go-go.
But ah ... Yeah ...

Then Willy and I unpack and procure the hidden potables, and sit, chat and drink. Something evocative of something (je ne sais quoi) in fiddling with luggage in hotel rooms new to you, but that you'll never see again.

Daddy and Sean – they sleep next door.

Gradually, then suddenly, it's later.
Time to hit the street.
We scatter.

Daddy and Sean for I know not where. Willy and Yours to hunt some'at to eat, we know not what nor where.

Step and stride on brick pave in the wind by the sea. It feels fine to swing shoulders and hips, and move and groove.

There's a well lit crowded corner café – quiescent little families and great groups of laughing boisterous young. And in we go.

Meet the friendly family with the Alsatian, I think it is, (or is it that the humans were from Alsace?).

The smell of food is overpowering and we order, but not sure just what. Find out in a minute, I guess; and here it comes, a feast – kabobs, kabobs and mounds and mounds of steaming mountainous fries. Dig in.

Down the hatch. Exeunt, out the door. And there's Sean of a sudden. He's rushing around looking for something – a phone, I think. Says, out of breath, there's water coming through the ceiling in our rooms.

Jesus Christ! Rush back to the crib, check it out, and no shit, it's the rip-roaring flood of the bible. Pipes are busted somewhere, everywhere, and we better do something fast. But what?

Rush around, rush around – What to do?

Where's Daddy? Jesus Christ! Break huddle. Sean and Willy manfully break to save him. Where is he?

There! There, wandering across the busy street, with his chin up, feisty.

I bolt back to where we were. Get help. Find a phone.

Cause a big scene but it's friendly and it's cool. They all would help me but what do we do? Everybody seems of help and sport – the customers, the countermen, a cook from the kitchen.

Do you call the fire department?

Yet the heroic fire brigade

Faces fire,

Brings water.

But we have the water.

Bring fire?

I call the fire fighters, or rather, someone does it for me since I lack the technique.

Bust back up the street to the stay.

Sean and Willy rush around, to no end I can discern. Daddy merely muddles with intent, of which I can't tell too. We've got a flood. Great God. Somehow, it seems, the water heater, main something or other is busted. We run around. We Whirling Dervish cartwheel. Who do you call and how? What do you do? (Let's skip the When, Where, Why.)

Finally the fire department comes like the cavalry with lots of lights, noise, and aplomb.

They somehow do something to make the water stop coming. Of course there's still plenty still there everywhere, soaking and drenching and making a horrible mess. With relief Daddy and Sean off to look for food.

Mr Handyman returns at last, aghast, but gets down to it – the cleanup.

Willy and I breakneck upstairs to salvage our gear. Alacritous help out cleaning up. Quick, steady the ladder as I climb up into the attic.

Ah, so fine and friendly, really robust.
The Action Jackson Americans.
Our Odd Duck Dude proffers apology.
Accept, of course; what else to do?
And no hard feeling; What The Hell?

Well, now over and done – finis.
Big breakfast tomorrow, they say.
Step off and out to clear the head.
It's "hut two thee four" – take the tread.
Savor the sip from silver flask.
Just a geste to trip the trigger –
Sump'n' for the final supper.

Daddy

Chapter Fifteen
Tuesday, October 23, 2007
Nieuport, Calais, Dover and Gatwick

After a nice breakfast at our bed and breakfast in Nieuwpoort we drove to Calais. The food at breakfast was good but not especially memorable, so it might have been

Flemish, French, Dutch, German, or even Minnesotan.

In Calais we had to return our rented car and then take the ferry to Dover. The car rental agreement provided that the car must be filled with gasoline immediately before its return. Although that's a common sense and fair provision, it still upset me that I paid for gas that someone else would use. A rational reply to this is that when we first took the car out of the rental agency, we used gas that was paid for by someone else. But only minutes after the gas payment, came the rental bill for two weeks use of the car – a healthy one thousand seventy dollars.

I can hear someone who wants to take a trip but can't afford it, saying to me "If you didn't want to pay for it, why didn't you stay at home?"

My sincerely humble reply is, "The cost was no surprise, and I'm very, very happy that I took the trip."

For a fellow from the largely land-locked state of Minnesota, a ferry boat should be similar to a Mississippi River paddle boat. Instead it is comparable to a luxury ocean liner, in both size and amenities. Although the channel trip from Calais to Dover was only an hour, there was enough stuff on the ship to keep one amused for hours. There were restaurants (plural), bars (plural), snack bars (plural), souvenir shops (plural), cash exchange windows, English pounds for European euros (plural), and more and more.

The boys spent their time on the ferry exploring the numerous attractions. I soon found a comfortable easy chair and enjoyed watching the occasional ferries which passed us heading in the opposite direction toward Calais. It was a convincing reminder of my earlier days enjoying watching the small boats sailing on the large, lovely, home-studded Lake Minnetonka outside of Minneapolis.

When we arrived in Dover, we immediately took a train to our hotel at Gatwick airport. I chose a pricey one.

All four of us shared a single large room with four beds, only the second time on the trip (Luxembourg being the first) when we shared one room. Unlike the cramped quarters of the youth hostel in Luxembourg, we had two windows, lots of room to walk around, our own (unshared) towels, and no limitation on our use of water in the bathroom. Some might say, "Real luxury."

But the most memorable time that evening was our final dinner of the trip. A problem with this is that to be memorable, one must remember some memorable thing or things. I don't. But I'll try.

I do remember before dinner sitting up at the bar with the boys and ordering drinks for all. It had probably been years since I last sat down at a bar and ordered drinks. With eight hungry children, a father quickly learns how many days are often left in the month after the money runs out. I always had a job, but the kids were always demanding, through the cajoling of their dear Mother, such luxuries as shoes, socks, underwear, and even for a few, eyeglasses, topped off by insisting on three meals a day. It wasn't quite that bad, but for years there was no money left for hanging around in bars.

So when the barman told me the drinks were four pounds apiece (a total of 16 pounds), I paid it, while reminding myself that we were on vacation and that money isn't everything. I was, however, still thinking back to my younger days when a drink was only two dollars. So I think I thought at first, that prices had doubled from two to four dollars a drink. But wait! One pound equals two dollars. So the £16 drinks were $32! The price not only doubled once, but doubled once again.

When time came to pay for a second round of drinks, I reached into my pocket to peel out £16 ($32) plus tip, and announced that it was time to proceed into the dining room for dinner. I'm sure the dinner was excellent, but I cannot recite the contents. I think we shared a single bottle of champagne, but without the anguish I felt in paying for drinks in the bar. In paying for the dinner and the champagne, I simply signed with my credit card and avoided the agony of reaching into my pocket and peeling off numerous pound notes and then handing to the waiter that pile of hard-earned cash.

Months earlier, when planning the trip back home in Minnesota, I had hoped to discover the seven most memorable locations described earlier, and to walk with Chris, Sean and Willy over those darkened forests, treeless and coverless open fields, and through ancient towns with ancient buildings seemingly designed to invite young American and German men to kill each other in house-to-house battling.

But even the best laid plans (of which mine were not among) often do not end up going as anticipated. My less-than best laid plans to visit the seven locations resulted in satisfactorily visiting only one of the seven (in baseball, at least, a feeble .143 batting average).

That one of the seven was Untermaubach, the place where I'd engaged in three days of house to house fighting in the war. That is what I described earlier as our last objective – the buildings near the Ruhr River, in our third day in Untermaubach.

Since six of the seven locations were in or near the Hurtgen Forest, I had planned to visit them first and to visit the seventh (in the Ardennes Forest) on our way toward the airport and home.

While driving on our first full day (October 18) in Monschau through the Hurtgen, we drove by the first two locations (both within the Hurtgen). The plan was to walk through them in the next two days. The walk through did not happen! (The GI's). We next drove to Strass and the brick house (the third) and did not stop for long. From there we drove by the fourth location, without stopping, (site of the fire-fight outside of and overlooking Untermaubach). The same for the fifth, the open field in Untermaubach over which I walked and got the Bronze Star. At the castle we got out of the car and visited the sixth of the seven locations we had planned on seeing. As to the seventh location, the Ardennes Forest – the Battle of the Bulge, we did not even go near the place.

Why did we fail to visit the other six? Those who have read my earlier quotations from "Shavetail" might recall that in December of 1944, while E Company was attacking through Untermaubach, I was stricken with a severe case of the GI's and I was so weak that I could not run, but was able to walk across an open field lightly defended by German infantry. Any student of military tactics would not consider that an appropriate method of advancing upon the enemy.

So – 63 years later, in the same location, near the same ancient castle, the same affliction stopped my walking and positioned me to my bed for the next three days.

Willy

Nieuwpoort

Heading north to the coast of Belgium. We had given some thought to making a stop at the site of a certain concentration camp along the way, at Sean's suggestion. When we had planned to meet Jim in Brussels, this seemed an appropriate way to end our journey. By bearing witness to the best, and perhaps only, reason for making war. Daddy's war. Which had, for the Allies, ultimately, a moral center. Rather than the customary nihilistic economic concerns which inform most armed conflicts.

But it's not to be. Again, we are hurried and harried.

We will need lodging soon. No place booked. Must needs keep, as Mr. Wodehouse would have it, the "big, broad, flexible outlook." Or BBFO for short. Maintaining this will stand us in good stead. Maintains CD.

Arriving in Nieuport, a grey and dreary afternoon. Sleepy town, this. Driving up and down the streets, Chris or Sean hopping out occasionally to check out a hotel or B&B. The BBFO in full effect.

Much sooner than anticipated, we find a place, right across the road from the Channel.

Nice enough joint. The main coastal highway outside being torn up for construction work. Daddy and Sean both immediately take naps, Chris and I both immediately take drinks.

Hunger arrives unusually quickly, so it's down the stairs and out the door, look this way then that, and decide to go that way.

Dusk upon us, very few cars on the blocked-off main road, God be praised. Damn nuisances. Promenading down the street, the only sounds our voices and feet. And the almost imperceptibly dull roar of the sea, always audible, always there. Even when still.

Let's check this place out. Standard deli-type café, the menu up on the wall behind the counter. Some sort of something or other with the ubiquitous pommes frites, and something for Daddy too. French spoken here. Have a sit, dig in. And here's a couple with a dog, big Alsatian German Shepherd, curled under its human's feet. Dutch, they are. Perfect English. Chat amiably with them. Friendly folk.

After a quick beer, out to the street, walking back to our rooms.

Up the street comes Sean. Determined gait and unamused aspect.

"Hey hey! What's the word?"

"Water... coming down from the ceiling... Daddy still up there, proprietors out for the evening... looking for a phone... hope they have that sort of thing here in Belgium..."

Oh, geez. Okay, hustle on down the road, to the B&B, Chris stopping back to the café we just alighted from, Sean continuing up the street.

In the door, up the stairs, and here's Daddy. Have a quick look-see. Sure enough, water drizzling down from on high in Daddy and Sean's room. Quick – move some luggage, then follow Daddy to the street. Tell him Chris and Sean are in search of communication devices. To call out the Fire Brigade. If there is one. Daddy going next door to the Aldi's supermarket which is just closing up. I down to the café to find Chris. Meet him on the way. He's asked the friendly denizens to phone the proprietors, whom everyone knows. We back and up the stairs in a flash, move all Daddy and Sean's gear out of the room and into ours. Back downstairs, CD back down the street, wondering if the Fire Brigade is who we really want, as if there is fire, they will surely bring water. But seeing that we have now water, shall they bring fire?

Re-meet Daddy, who has met a shop girl, who has called the proprietors. Now Daddy would call for the Firey Brigade.

A place across the highway. Glass front design studio. Daddy moving rather too quickly. Oh geez. Wait, Daddy – look out, it's dark. Oh boy, there are some actual cars coming and not much light. Mother of God, there he goes. Must hurry on here, a quick sprint to outrun the damned automobiles and catch up with D. Daddy into the studio showroom, I watch him through the window. One chap on his mobile phone, much gesticulating. Out comes Daddy, back across the somewhat quieter Highway of Death to our hotel, wait for salvation. Or something.

Have a much needed smoke. Daddy of course does not. Here. A fire truck. Arriving with not a great deal of speed nor sirens. We wave. They wave back. Dismounting from their rig, putting on coats in a leisurely fashion, no headgear for them tonight. Hope not due to budget cuts. Hi, guys.

Just now another geezer shows up, a nephew of the proprietors. His wife has just had a baby, yesterday it seems. Young guy, mid 20's. Crowd of five firefighters entering the hotel, not looking overly concerned, as there is no fire, and they volunteers from a nearby town. I try to appear helpful. Saying important sounding things. In bad French. Which they ignore. As they all speak English quite nicely, thanks.

Sean and Chris arrive at some point. The water mains are shut off. Everyone smiling and smiling. The captain, the only real fireman, had been on an exchange program with the Los Angeles Fire Department. And in fact is wearing a ball cap from said department. Nice guy, much laughter and it's thanks, gents, sorry to break up your poker game. Which is, the captain tells me, in fact what they were doing.

Daddy and Sean decide to have some dinner, that being one of their favorite pastimes. Down the road they go.

Chris and I chat with the nephew. And here comes the proprietor, the husband – big guy, a bit confused and embarrassed. Seems he was having dinner with four generations of family. Poor dude. Feel bad for him. Chris and I upstairs with him, up into the attic on a ladder, CD up there too. Myself holding the ladder. Guy comes down, taking it all pretty well. CD and I decide to be nice, as opposed to the other. Gathering towels and mop and bucket, cleaning up as much water as we can. Move effects to a new room. Commiserate a while with our host. Says we can expect a big-ass breakfast tomorrow. OK, no worries, just take it easy, see you tomorrow.

After cleaning up as much as can reasonably be expected, it's time to find D and S.

Down the street again. Here they are, a Chinese restaurant. Tip on in, Daddy and Sean just finishing dinner, order a quick bevy, disseminate the evening's crack. Sean insisting they should give us a reduction on our bill. Seems reasonable. Daddy deciding they've had enough misfortune tonight, thinks he'll let it slide.

Back to base, then. For a dryish sleep.

Next morning, down to the dining room for breakfast. Daddy and Chris already there, Sean not feeling well these past 24 hours, has a lay-in. Our proprietors chatting with D and CD. Middle aged sorts, rather suspicious demeanors it seems to me. Especially the wife. Who seems to wear the pants here. Walloons, they are, and tell tales of acrimony with the southern Flemish. Socio/economic considerations it would be.

I have an almost unbearably strong inclination to laugh when the term "Walloon" is uttered. The mere sound of which gives me great mirth. Always has.

"Wallooooooooooooooooooooooooooooooons!!!!!"

But I resist this urge. As they seem to not possess the same humor as I. Even though we try to laugh about the moist adventures of the preceding eve.

They offer us a free night's stay, knowing full well that we have to get back across the water to catch a plane. Oh well. Not bad sorts. But compared to some of our hosts and hostesses in France and Germany, not the most helpful either. No wonder they're always getting invaded by – OK, stop. Not funny (tee hee).

And now we leave the Continent. Or try to. Sean has some parcels to mail, gifts for Georgia and the wee bairns. Then out come the maps. Not this again. Can we just go back to Monschau?

From this time on, until we arrive at Calais and get on the ferry, I may as well have been asleep. Though I'm sure I was actually looking at maps and signs. Fortunately it's just a short hop south into France, down the coast, past Dunkirk, and soon we'll be seaborne again. Back to Merry Olde. Blighty.

CD

10-24-07 8:30A

The wide-eyed yoga this morning,
Up and out for the walk.
I quick-march along a canal,
Past bleak industrial dry dock
To the bobbing small boat harbor.
It's brisk and blowing and painful.
Bow head and hunch bold shoulders,
Move briskly and fight cold wind from the sea,
The North Sea,
La Mer du Nord.

Yet all the rest repose abed.
Sweet sleep surfeit, the well earned rest.
I rouse and roust them.
All rise and rally.
We'll soon and some time see.

The promised big breakfast laid on
And due to extra credit due –
The help
We lent
Last night
In the slapstick big adventure.
Sweet suet breakfast post bitter wind walk.
The four square of stout squad fall in.

The lights with a flash blink suddenly out.
And I like it; I like it a lot.
We have only the artist window light

On a pea soup subdued grey day.
The poised North Light begs a portrait.

Am I the only one to relish – to camera-jock countenance – the painterly luminescence, artful aspect and Old World canvass phrasing?

And then the lights blink back again.

Daddy much better, though Sean a bit of the malady himself. Willy more or less OK, or at least no complaints, and I myself feel fine. And why not? – He said with a smirk.

Then Sean would post some presents or such, so he and I hustle off. And then ensues the standing around, milling about, waiting for him to do what he does, and then the inevitable driving and driving, and now the procedure of the post. Then we'll be back and hopefully before noon or two o'clock or maybe midnight be on our merry way.

(As they say.)

The premeditated planned plan:
Out of Nieuport, on to Calais.
Take the merry ferry,
Ride the ruddy train,
And to the swank hotel,
And gate-crash hubbub Gatwick.
Hot time on the town tonight.

Much motion and commotion here in this zone of Nieuport. Doomed to stay smack dab in the middle of a bristling construction zone, and try as we mightily may, we just can't seem to escape. And a hustle-bustle working port to make the head swim – lots and lots of quick moving serious workmen and plenty lot slow moving slugs of curious tourist types too. Although this would be the off season (it is said), it seems more on than off to me. Plus the far-out rum phenomenon: hotels and bed and breakfasts deserted, with no one there and the doors locked – abandoned like a lonely child at the bus depot.

On the driving tour once again.
On the road again.
Just can't wait to get on the road again.
We pay our dues
And bid our adieus,
And we're off to Savate Calais.
Return the car,
We hope;
Recover the deposit,
We hope;
Find the ferry,
We think;
Cross the water,
We will.
Then it's trains and taxis
To the Gatwick of all air ports.

And on and into Calais. Fairly easily done, though nothing in life comes easy. Somehow find the port. Find the Hertz rental – Of course there's no one there. We must drill for oil; discover gas. We have our instructions; given license. Not so far away, it's easy, it is said. So we're off to fulfill l'essence.

We'll see.

Sean sure kills the screeching stop-and-go nerve-wracking driving. Good man.

Loop-the-loop through endless complex circles: concentric, tangential, don't forget the figure eight. More high speed geometry than I can muster.

Better he than me.
Get the gas,
Park the car,
Perform the paperwork,
Get the tickets,
Go through customs.

Wait and wait and fiddly-fuck around, and we're now on the courtesy bus, stalled and waiting to see where we must be, hold the breath to board the boat. Luckily, the driver is in charge of all that.

Or so it seems.

We escape Gaul soon, and with that and with luck also all the japery at French expense too. Why so much drollery directed at those who extoll liberté, egalité, fraternité? I'll be most glad that it will cease.

We'll see what smites us in England.

On to Dover.

I savor now, and most likely,
My last tick of time On The Continent.
Somewhat sad – but so what?
I've my had fun in Europe
And Europe has had fun with me.
Think on my youthful adventures.
Blink back the shameful hidden tear.
The bus rolls on.
And we do too.
So do I.

We set to sail.
But there are no sails.
The engines rumble.
It's brisk on deck.

The sea is green.
The sky is gray.
There is white foam that follows us.
We pass another privateer ferry.
A loud sound shrieks to warn.
There is a small fishing craft close.
A helicopter circles overhead, flying low.
It hovers over the vessel, hunting like.
The little boat seems to list.
Is she in trouble?

The proud ferry rocks and rolls as of old –
But I with my iron gut.
Though worry about my kinsmen.
Fear deadly sickly confluence of quivering innards with all-at-sea outards.
Hang here with Daddy; brothers free to wander.
Tempus fugit. Fuggit (– The Naked and the Dead).
Back to here; time to reconnoitre.
Lust to find things free of duty
That one might smoke or sip.
Pip pip!

Make Dover, make landfall. Make it out of the boat, meander our way down the clip-clop ramp. Need to wait for Daddy – what with the minor emergency. Up and down the gangway, slowly and with care. Track and protect Daddy, strive to spare him his dignity.

But it's not our's to show him shit.

Depends donning yet daunting not.

Luckily baggy pants, but bulldog man.

Sean and Willy kindly and manfully tote and drag his baggage, lug his luggage. Up and down; pull, push and poke.

I chat with all and sundry. Hang back, Daddy watch; chit chat, lollygag and bullshit.

Semi-old English couple: side file, smile and profile.

"You look like an explorer," she say.

What?

"What?" I say.

"What with your hat, your cane, your grip – You look like an explorer."

Lost in the hustle-bustle crowd,
But find the port carriage service.
Now wait for straight-laced English bus
To take us all to train or tram.
And from there, the wrong way cab.

Reservations have been confirmed and we did this all, this last, through the cunning use of a crackerjack telephone. We put money in the machine; the telephone worked. We actually and unaccountably communicated.

Or at least someone did.

Train speeds through English countryside.
Looks like a BBC production.
First dusk,
Now dark.
Transfer.
Stand to the platform,
Walk about.
No smoking in this fair land
But you can squeeze through the turnstile and find a spot.
Spirits runnin' really high.
This is the way to travel, boys.
This is how you do it.
But miles to go before I sleep.
And one more transfer yet.
I think.

Willy

Seafrance brought us here, P&O brings us home. The sea a bit rougher this day. I get the sea sickness. Strange sensation standing upright, walking, but with unmistakable feeling that one is swaying, on the sea. Which one is. Rather unpleasant, that.

Scope out the duty-free shop. Buy a book on Brit Special Forces, SAS and that, and another on the last surviving British soldiers and sailors from the First World War, telling their tales, circa 2006. The youngest one being 104 years old. 'The Last Post' it's titled. I'll read this on the train up to London. Very apropos. And very moving.

Back now in Britain. The usual ass hauling on foot, shuttle-bus and cab to the hotel at Gatwick Airport. Where we'll stay the night.

One biggish room we share. Donning our finest evening wear, we repair to the hotel bar. As is done.

Our last night abroad, for most, if not all of us.

Pakistani and Indian bar staff. Christ, I hope they reserve social convo to the footy and Amy Winehouse's latest difficulties, lest there be war of the un-civil sort. In this busy metropolitan travelodge. But they're awfully good to us. Big men from America. Or, as it transpires, Europe.

On the train up from Dover, waiting on a platform for our connection, perchance to chat with a gal, my age, plain, working class, but with an openness and humor about her pretty face, so typical of British women.

Told her my tale, asked where she would disembark, etc. Wondered why Europeans on the Continent thought ill of

Great Britain. Not in the historical context, but in the more contemporary sense.

She laughed and said it was true, it's mostly the French, but seems to be general.

I was bewildered – after all these years, indeed, centuries, that such chauvinism should still exist. In such a place as Western Europe, especially now that the European Union was in place. Why, I asked – Is it because you lot haven't adopted the euro and still retain the pound?

She chuckled, said perhaps, but for other less obvious reasons. Some of which she was equally baffled by. I recall thinking to myself, the old adage: "As goes England, so goes the world."

When the ravens quit the Tower of London – watch out.

CD trying to convince the barman that he, indeed, *really does* want two double shots of vodka. To complement his Guinness. A bit of a tall order, this, as such imbibing behavior is not generally done here. On these shores. Where civilization was born and reigns. Unlike our land. Where barbarism rears it's parochial head and manifests itself in, amongst certain other principles, practices and preoccupations – uncouth drinking habits.

My dear CD – perhaps one day it will please you to order a fine and simple gin and tonic. The creature is still the creature. Just with a bit of tonic. As a tonic. And even a pleasant lime. Oh, aye, laddie.

Any and all ways, we soon shift to the dinning hall. White coated waiters. Patient, waiting for our orders. As Chris orders another round – two doubles, thanks. The usual confusion offers a bit of hilarity as CD explains very patiently to our waiter, who listens and absorbs, with equal patience, this startling request:

"Ah, my good man – two double vodka sours. But withhold the sour. And then you'll have it. Neat. Just like whiskey."

“Yes sir – I see. Two whiskey sours with double the sour.”

“Ah, well. Not quite. If you just pour some vodka in a glass – and *nothing else* – that will do nicely.”

“Yes sir. And you would like four of these?”

“Uhm, no no – just two. And make them doubles, please. Just – never mind. OK, sure. Four of them.”

Daddy is intent on everyone feasting to their hearts’ content, he’s buying. Have at it, boys.

Looking over the menu, I consider a fine traditional English Shepherd’s Pie. But opt for a leg of mutton with mash.

After dessert, another drink, and a certain amount of recollection about what we’ve just done, where we’ve been. It’s time to retire. And Sean and I have an argument about snoring, as we must sleep in the same bed tonight. I insist I do not snore, and that he most certainly does, and to a window rattling degree. This goes on a bit, and I decide to record his nocturnal detonations on me little tape recorder. Which will later produce the sound of, along with cats outside our window doing battle, the hotel plumbing and central air system heaving and sighing, and general white noise – four big men from America. Snoring. As one does.

Can’t sleep, and not for snoring. Out of bed and gingerly take me backpack out the door and down the hallway to the lounge. Salute the bar staff, step outside for a smoke. These same stars, this moon over London, on view everywhere in the known world. On this night.

Back inside. Take a couch.

The big screen bar TV showing Turkish armored columns rolling into Kurdistan on Iraq’s norther border. Our NATO brothers – our allies – met at last.

As Armenian revenants bear witness.

Outside again. A few weary fellow travelers loading their luggage inside. Scottish accents. “I cannae’ get Martha on the phone... ach, weel – we’ll jis’ haveta kip doan here the night an’ see yon the morrow...”

Velvety black sky above. Just me. The lights on all over the world. Don't put them out. This big man from America not so big now.

Back in the lounge. No images of horror on the TV, just football and grinning marionettes. I've seen three wars unfold in real time – Vietnam, the Gulf War, and the current wars in Iraq and Afghanistan. Eerie green images from night-vision goggles, high-explosive artillery rounds, missiles and bombs, naval ordinance from offshore. Like falling stars. Shock and awe indeed. Surely the BBC would tell us if things were hotting up in northern Iraq.

My 21-year-old nephew Liam in Iraq now. When will they stop? Can't a B.M.F.A enjoy a few pleasant weeks abroad without open warfare popping up on television screens everywhere? (Or in Liam's case, outside his barracks.) Is it true that all human enterprise and progress is based on friction, on conflict? Daddy's war never really ended. Just shifted a bit. Sideways. So this is what we are. Human beings. "If you want peace, prepare for war."

But I'm tired, not just physically. Can't read my book. Eyes glued to the TV screen. Where the Turkish armor? Heavy infantry units? Did I imagine it? Is it not so important, or is it just the start – not much information yet..."intelligence"...

Does this mean Liam can come home? Does this mean I can't?

I remember this from 1991 and 2003 – late for work, not being able to sleep. But I must. For it will never stop.

Saint Francis of Assisi loved all animals. And not just the human ones.

"Lord, make me an instrument of thy peace..."

And I have a plane to catch. My home.

And promises to keep.

And miles to go.

Before.

I...

CD

10-25-07 7:15

Out for early walk. Nothing much here. There are roads and roads everywhere, freeway or highway, just like US of A. So, set out for the constitutional – pilgrimage to, in and of a "car park."

Daddy up and about early too today, briskly performing the morning ablutions. He seems of good cheer and high spirit –

If not good, better;
If not well, weller.

Last night, the drinks all round at the posh hotel bar and then on to the tony restaurant for the big dinner, but I of course (bad man) would only drink.

Black tie, starched white shirt, pomade hair and prominent practiced painted smile of barkeep and all and every. None speak the English (never mind American) but I. All of previous province, e.g. India, Pakistan, Malaysia, China. Better best but do it to it– Order strong and sure: "Vodka. Double vodka." But everybody sweats it; then I do too. As though they'd never heard the terms before, or maybe my diction is bad. End up with two Guinness, two Martini – double or otherwise.

Back from adventure at the bar, into the civilized dining room in conclave with my kinsmen, meaty English fair. But none for me – Only the drink would do – What with the jolly hearty repartee and raillery, toasting and boasting, the pointed and suavely put riposte, (was there the Champagne? [if not, there should have been]); and the inner self-sadness and reflection. What little I remember was memorable.

Back then to the room, all four of us. Just a bit cramped and crowded (but clubby) but we're OK.

What's for breakfast? Don't know.
Missed it. Missed it again.
Hours early and ahead of time,
Walking and waiting and pacing.

Not quite so cold this morning here in England, as I step it out to stretch legs and lungs before the forced immobility.

Yet fresh and fine as the first thirst drink of water in the morning.

The English folks so fine and friendly,
Outgoing and forthcoming –
Though that's not what you often hear.
Now utter the English;
Soon articulate the American.
Euros and pounds to rest;
Back again to bucks.
Had enough specie; my money made it.
No one went broke; no, not today.
Did my duty; performed the duties.
I think.

Was reasonably cheerful and jolly, and hopefully contributed in some way, shape, form or fashion, in some manner (or what?).

Look forward to Marilyn and Cally,
The wife and the daughter at home.
Hope they've not forgotten me.
Hope they like me some.
Whatever will the dogs do?

So on to the big top airport
For that wild and woolly showboat.

Eat the anti-freak dope,
Chew the anti-smoke gum.
Ride the wind.
Hope for the best.

Gatwick airport.
Final smoke.
Through customs.

Very crowded. The dangedest I've ever seen. The most crowded airport ever.

Two hours to kill. What joy.

Daddy OK, more or less, but confused and disoriented and has the tough time to grasp meaning; he can't understand. That's all right; it's OK – I am always confused and seldom understand anything at all.

Daddy finds a quick opening spot to sit among the menage. One brother must stick to The Old Boy's side, the others range and rove. We are, after all, explorers. I draw first Daddy duty. We sit with our effects, our affects; with baggage, each other, our selves.

In time, it is my turn and of my wont to wander.

Lotsa duty free shopping. That, I've always thought a funny turn of phrase. I generally don't go in for that sort of thing, but what the hey! – It's a new dawn today! (Until, of course, such time as it isn't.)

But walk and walk and swing the stick
And see fine folks from all over the world.
Verne: Around The World In 80 Days.
Prince: Around The World In A Day.
CD: Around The World In 15 Minutes.

The British signs are chucklesome droll and elegantly put, evocative of old time empire panache and another age altogether.

There is an inscription indicating an area devoted to "Shoe Repatriation" where one would re-don one's rides following the customary custom check.

There are also telling invocations enjoining one to refrain from attack of airport workers, and the penalties therefrom that might incur.

Voices over the loudspeaker constantly promote security. Bags must never be left unattended, lest they be confiscated and destroyed.

Sean appears and kindly fetches juice and water for the thirsty.

There is the visitation.

At length we line up,
Shuffle shuffle, board and load;
Strap yourself in, buckle down.
Nervy sit and relax and smile for the fly-girl.
So we fight our way through fog
And lift
To light.

Willy and Daddy doze. Sean and I conspiratorially confer and determine to bug Daddy to frequently ambulate and ingurgitate the water. We be happy with our own bad selves – to thus, and thusly boldly make command decision.

I switch to Minneapolis time. It's now 7AM. So, at 8AM Minneapolis and airplane time we'll all indulge ourselves in a jolly walk.

I check the shitty glossy magazines in the pouch adjacent, play with the headphones, listen to music – maybe there are movies, should I see fit.

You don't get much action on a plane in flight,

(Not unless you're in a dogfight).
Nor smoke.
Bing!

Eight hours and change,
I fear the ordeal endures.
Take the dope,
Pound the gum.
Made it before.
I'll do it again.
Do as I've done.
Lordy, Lordy, O what fun!

Sky high aloft we are we are.

The trolley comes with drinks. Mine would be double vodka with Heineken back. The brand of vodka – oddly and ironically and poetically called "Skyy" vodka.

So now on high I sip the Sky Vodka.

Then the awesome A1 airline food, so much maligned. But you know – not so bad at that: chicken, rice, vegetables, salad, coleslaw, bread, crackers and cheese perhaps for later – but mine for me right now. Too, I devour Daddy's bread, his rice, Willy's bread, Sean's slaw.

I don't feel so bad after all.

Catch the girl on the rebound, policing the dead soldiers. Cop another double Skyy vodka. Also the fruity white wine with my meal.

Swallow the pill,
Pound the gum.

Be All in fairly fine spirit,
We are we are,
As high and fast we fly.
Daddy walks now at our insistence.

We fill out something called "The Re-Entry Card."
Wrongly,
Then rightly,
Then I don't know.

Sean and Willy sleep.
To finish my wine, give sweet dreams a shot –
May be can I rest torturously too.
Would that I hadn't ditched my flask to the non-carry-on luggage. Faked out again by vulgar lumpen dominion.
'Cause I could use that right now.
But thought it wouldn't fly.
But, you know what?
Right now it would fly –
Real high.

Fly high over the Atlantic,
The great circular route.
Now past Greenland, hard over Labrador.
We've hit landfall.
Two thirds there.
We're gettin' there.

Sean watches a movie. Willy reads. I attempt to listen to music with those pesky little bugs in the ears and simultaneously chat with Daddy. (Even though every yogi knows that you can only do one thing [well] at a time.)

We talk (alleged) literary endeavor: I struggle to concoct a tome of bad stories and worse verse. The Great Man muddles with a volume of history to follow up his fine book, "Shavetail." Of course, there has been of late little opportunity and no impetus to work, what with the tour and the motion and commotion.

I feel real close to my father

In the hyper here and now
In the quiet of the clouds.
They say that such for which sons yearn,
And maybe it's true,
But at this very moment I do.

Should arrive Minneapolis – 3:00, 3:30, or so.
Get myself back to the castle.
What will happen?
Who will be there?
Am I missed?
Do they love me?
Will the dogs know me or bite me?
What will life be like?

I got the goods – the gifts, I mean.
I think them good. Or at least good enough.
But not that that means all that much.
Any short money gambler knows –
There's no such thing as a Hundred Percent.

The funky retread airplane air –
The menthol when you don't want it.
Squished up again like stacked and packed pillows.
The queer faint humming buzzing white noise.
Develop the powerful thirst.
Bonne journée.
Have a nice day.

The Old Boy sadly says he's a bit disappointed. Thought he could do more physically. Bad luck to get sick. I murmur wordless sounds meant to convey commiseration and encouragement.

But what the merry hell –

We all always want to do more.

"I think we did and do plenty lot o' something, Daddy. And the meeting with the Countess was magic. And I can feel it still."

Fortuitous,
Serendipitous.
Wondrous and beauteous.
It was indeed something at that.

To fail to find the spot where he was badly hit and almost killed doesn't surprise me. Nor he – lo, the decades on year after year. Even had he been healthier, heartier, more mobile and spry; I think it almost impossible, certainly improbable and, after some sadness and over-regret – the logical lawyer knows that too. Unfortunate, but not the crushing disappointment. And for this I'm heartened and happy.

But Daddy is a doer – he likes to do things. (And, just a taste peevingly, likes to pronounce that phrase.) If you have half a day free and of no particular account, he thinks you ought to make plans, carry on, follow through; you ought to do something, go somewhere, see stuff.

While not entirely inactive, not a slug – that's not my way. I'm just not buying; don't subscribe to that post.

Live and let live, one always says. (Even if trite and hackneyed.)

I love the aimless, endless hiking abroad.
Some times in day.
Some times in dark.
In day or dark, let come what may:
Gad lunch where you happen to land.
Shop for groceries like a local,
And as though you long-time live there.
Seize exercise like a fighter, as ever.

Swig and swill like a nobleman –
Toast and boast with the most.
Entertain the rich persiflage.
Go out, walk about –
The Wild Wide World of Peregrination.
Loquacious at hotel for all to see.
Solitary silence on road, on path, on street.
"These are a few of my favorite things."

We mostly managed to work together –
Stay together, play together;
Of course not always in concert.
"The team" (as currently irksomely said).
Thus were we bound, were we not?
Hope none feel anger,
Nor bear sour rancor.
No sharpened hard feeling either.
But sup o' the milk of human kindness.
As the French say: Fraternité.

I'll never take another road trip like this again – no more long run auto shows.

I relish the rail parcel, rolling back to Gatwick, through artful English backyard scenery as of an inkhorn novel or 20th century cinema. Love the rocking in rhythm and the urging surging musical motion. Like a varietal Blues – by turns sweet, sad, sexy; poignantly high and low, consecutively and simultaneously.

We sit and sit and talk and joke and think.
I planned ahead; I have my flask.
I had (and have) the boon companions.
Sometimes that's all you need or want.
How often do one pause to pray?:

It's good to be alive.

So maybe I'm all through with travel.
Travail and hunger, to rage and ravel.
Old apologue ended of me.
Loved it so much so many years aback –
Long, long aeons ago,
A lifetime of lonesome longings.
I never knew how to trek with others,
Or even ever just to live with them.
Never did it very damn much.
Ah … always so low and lonely.

So what did we make of it? What do I make of it? What it is?

Did it, does it mean anything? Does it bear and boast the consequence, the magnitude, the weight? What does it mighty signify? Or does it? Or will it ever will?

It certainly wasn't all fun and games.
This life of ours never is.
Not life along the long long road.
“Die lange lange Straße lang.”

So there was the laugh. There were the laughs. There were the spirits, high and low. And so they always are. And so it always is.

Till death the pain, the human refrain.
I knew it would be and it was.
And so it always is.
It is, it is, it is.
'Tis.

Neither Willy nor I had been eager to attend – Too busy, too tired, too broke. Sean, stout fellow, down from the get-go. 'Twas something The Father just wanted to do. For reasons you must read novels to know.

But we went. And that's that. That's it.

Make the best of it, Brother!

I think we largely did.

And it was and is an honor.

And a time I'll never forget.

Will our kinship be affected or effected or for good or for ill?

How would one view one's self, one's fellows, or even history itself – current, recent, or past?

Don't know. Do you?

Anytime you find yourself in and amongst an assemblage for a certain some time, cheek to jowl, hand to mouth, hand to hand at the front –

It's always good to get away.

To bound outside the circle,

To run and hide from the pack.

Yo, Yours to feature that.

Hope and pray Daddy hasn't taken a big hit to health. That he might bounce back.

I know I will. I shall. You know I always do.

And hope, trust, and think Sean and Willy too.

And indeed, bounce back like a Super-Ball – whose second bounce is said to be bigger than it's first. (But best beware: It is prone to break in half!)

Dulcet colloquy with Daddy of all manner of things: that of life, that of a lifetime.

Of war and peace, and life and death, of hope and fear, and all things past and to come.

Of Mama – his dead wife and mate; my mother, my mama; seminal figure in our (or anyone's) life – O Mama!

We both shed the tear unashamed.

O Daddy! O Mama!

Turn off the devices,
They say they say.
Finito.
Comin' in low, hot an' hard,
Dancin' prancin'
On a wing and a prayer.
O God,
Bless me,
Give me a break.
Let me win once with second take.
And
By God
Score
The winning touch down.

Willy

Gatwick- last day

Up early and outside the hotel waiting on a cab. Soon cruising down the motorway at a pretty good clip, airport bound. Suddenly a car barrels directly at us.

"Mate! Watch out!"

The car sails past us. As they are meant to. On the right-hand side of the road.

Laughter erupts. My foggy state making me forget where we are. Where the rules of the road are reversed.

"Sorry, mate. Bit of temporary madness there. Comes and goes. I'll be a good lad now."

Our Middle-Eastern cabbie chuckling. "No worries. Happens to the best of us. Even Americans!"

Usual long wait at the airport. Very crowded. Searching for a seat for Daddy, set up our little base while we wait.

Here's one. Chris, Sean and I taking turns wandering about the terminal, perusing the duty-free and all. I'm in search of a bite to eat, something for Daddy as well. Several restaurants, all very crowded. Hell with it. I'll do the dastardly deed. McDonalds. Also very crowded. Can't believe I'm going to eat this shit. Daddy probably won't mind though. Some fries and just take the soggy bun off the burger. Fill the belly a bit.

After a wait of 15 minutes or so, order and soon get my "food." Awfully hungry, tear right into my burger. And what do you know! It tastes different somehow, from that in USA. Not very good, but not as ishy as I recall this slop being. Only very moderately pleased. But I was famished.

Back to give Daddy his. Off now for a walkabout. This girl over there. Looks like a young Kate Bush. Good Lord, probably still in high school. Clearly that's her da with her.

Catches me gawking and doesn't look pleased. Probably happens a lot. To that lot. As she's obviously one of the great beauties of Great Britain. Sorry. Sorry. Sorry, sir. Won't look anymore. I'm a very bad man, I know this. Just avert me eyes and move along. Back to where I bloody well come from. Sir, it is to my profound regret and disappointment. That I will soon do that very thing.

Announcement comes that we should go now to an even more awful part of the terminal, to check luggage and all that sort of nonsense. We will be boarding soon.

Out with your personal effects, now. Place them in this tray. Off with your shoes now, hurry up you lot. Off with your belts too. Right this way now. Keep moving, that's it.

Me trousers coming down a bit. Fine with me. Give these limeys a bit of a show. These geezers here, security sorts.

"Canwecheckyabag,suh?"

"Pardon me?"

"Canwecheckyabag, suh."

"Sorry, mate. I'm not reading you."

Thick Cockney accents. These two blokes holding me backpack. Want something of me. And here a largish chap. Red faced. Thick northern accent.

"He said: CAN WE CHECK YOUR BAG. SIR."

"Oh! Yeah! Geez! Sorry. Go right ahead. No problem. Sorry... stupid American, ha ha... sorry, mate..."

Security gents have found me flask. Whoops. Opening and sniffing it. Probably seize it, as is proper. These days.

"Very good, sir. On your way."

Wow. Top blokes, these, for sure. Probably figured a moron like me could use all the help he can get.

Daddy close behind me, holding up trousers, having a sit to tie his shoes. Telling his story to a big, hard looking security man. 60-ish, grey haired, not to be trifled with. He seems to ignore Daddy's cheery banter, how he was here so long ago. Fought in the war, you know.

As Daddy claims his carry-on bag and we head to the gate, the security man turns his head.

"Thanks for helping out, Yank."

I give him a look, but he's back with the next passengers. Too young to have served in WWII, but not too young to have lived through it. Probably served himself, what with the post-war National Service. Malaysia? The Middle East? Africa perhaps? A definite military air about him. And must get tired of having to speak to people all day. And boss them around. As is necessary.

But that small bit of acknowledgment, that touch of gratitude, of recognition. For Daddy. Will stay with me always.

Close to boarding, yet another line. Daddy in high spirits. And here another security man. An Indian with turban. Daddy chatting him up.

"Ah ha! You're a Sikh, then!"

Daddy moving very close to him. Oh no. Please don't do it, Daddy. Oh geez. He's going to.

Daddy pats the guy's turban. OK, here we go. I can see it: Daddy wrestled to the floor, we intervening, and then Heckler & Koch MP-4's pointed at our heads, hustled away to where they take naughty passengers. Who pat security men's religious head-gear.

Fortunately our bearded Sikh just nods and attends to other passengers. Tragedy or mere embarrassment averted. Courtesy of these reasonable Brits. Who, like the Israelis, really know how to do airport security. And these here at Gatwick. Doing it with such good humor and politeness. Bless'em.

Soon on the plane. Soon in the air. Nothing of interest happening. Which is a good thing. Whilst airborne.

I watch the filum "Wag the Dog." A bit serendipitous, that. Considering last night's fright at Turkey's saber-rattling in Kurdistan. Still wondering what is going on with that situation. Maybe, as in this amusing film I'm watching, it was all made up. By government media experts for some form or other of political gain. Gee, I hope so.

As our man Hughes said to Daddy in Dover –

No more wars for you, mate.

Hours later, touch down at Twin Cities International. Waiting in the usual lines. Having a quiet word with CD. And here's Homeland Security. In our face. Asking for identification. Didn't like our private conversation I reckon. OK, boys.

Still on line. Here comes the dog, sniffing for bad smells. Sean's back pack on the floor next to him. Must surrender his apple. That sort of thing not allowed into the country.

Hours later, upon entering my apartment and unpacking me gear, I find a smooshed up McDonalds hamburger from the Gatwick terminal in my backpack. Which was on my back at the airport. Dumb dog, could have been a bomb.

Greet Dolly with a kiss. Load into the car.
Drive to my house.
Out the car.
Greet Anne with a kiss.
Inside now.
Lie down on my bed. Drifting off. Exhaustion.
Our journey. Daddy's journey.
My journey.
Hasn't ended yet.
And as sleep comes
This fine fettled 25 October
On the feast of St. Crispin –
I imagine it never will.

Daddy

Chapter Sixteen
Wednesday, October 24, 2007
Gatwick, Minneapolis-St. Paul

The final chapter. What to say? How to say it?

My answer is – to start with a story.

The story has little to do with the trip, but is about my favorite girl, Mary (who was also our children's favorite mother).

In comparing the two trips (the one in 1988 with Mary and the one in 2007 with the boys) the boys will not be surprised nor chagrined to learn that my happy trip with their mother in 1988 clearly outdid the sometimes stormy one with themselves in 2007.

Now the story.

After my meeting with Countess von Spee and after seeing and praising her matching pearls, I am reminded of my dear deceased wife, Mary, and – lipstick.

Quite frequently in the sixties and seventies after our family dinner, Mary would say something like, "Let's drive over to Southdale. I'd like to see a few things."

The Twin Cities of St. Paul and Minneapolis had two claims to fame. The first was something not in the bragging category, namely having the country's coldest temperatures among the heaviest populated metropolitan areas. The second was Southdale Shopping Center, allegedly, the first fully enclosed shopping center in the country.

I'd usually agree to go to Southdale, hoping to exercise some restraint to Mary's willingness to buy things, but mostly because I just liked to be with her.

We'd go to the make-up and lipstick counter of the shop, and I'd sit at the counter and watch and listen. I, of course, had the option of wandering elsewhere in the shop, picking things up and setting things down. But when I go shopping for myself, I go to the area that has what I want, buy whatever it is, and then go home. No wandering. As a result, I stayed with Mary and became quite familiar with lipstick.

To a man, at least to one man, lipstick is another world. The sales lady, after greeting Mary and me, would ask Mary what she was wearing. Both women knew they were talking about lipstick. I might have thought they were discussing underwear.

The saleslady would search behind the counter for the little round lipstick containers holding the different varieties of the product. The containers would be labeled, I presume, to describe the product to the woman buyer. The labels consisted of descriptive words such as Cinema Pink, Power Pink, Belfry Rose, Island Red, and Really Me.

For half an hour Mary would sample the lipsticks, usually, I think, applying a bit to her lips and perhaps a dash upon her wrist. All the while, Mary and the saleslady would be chatting in, to me, a nearly unfathomable tongue. Often, but not always, Mary would purchase one of the sampled lipsticks.

Mary would leave the store pleased and happy to have added a new color to her lipstick collection.

The only problem is that despite the labels and women's expectations, all lipsticks are the same color – red. Ask any man. He'll confirm that all lipsticks are red.

I, of course, never sought to dissuade Mary from her strongly held belief that lipstick comes in many colors.

With wars going on in Iraq and Afghanistan, and the world-wide threat of terrorism, Gatwick Airport requires stringent security inspections. So all passengers including myself were required to remove our clothes and answer questions before getting on the plane. Not surprisingly, the airport security man allowed us to reclothe before emplaning. They could have avoided all that delay by simply asking me if I were carrying a bomb or any other prohibited item. Anyone can tell that I have an honest face.

The security check took about ten minutes, and I spent the time relating to the security man a few of my World War II combat experiences including the Battle of the Bulge. He was probably not old enough to have been alive during World War II.

He showed little, actually no, interest in my war stories and obviously had no interest in the war. Nevertheless he seemed to realize that the old man talking to him participated in a war that saved his country from Hitler. Apparently with that in mind, he called to me as I walked away, “Thanks, Yank, for helping out.”

Our airline schedule called for us to depart Gatwick at 12:30 p.m. to arrive at Mpls.-St. Paul at 3:35 p.m. Does that mean that an eight hour flight from Mpls.-St. Paul to Gatwick becomes a three hour flight from Gatwick back to Mpls.-St. Paul? The answer is “No.” We are talking about two different clocks and time zones with the Gatwick clock and time zone eight hours ahead of Mpls.-St. Paul. Here is my layman’s explanation:

The earth spins in a counter clockwise direction, meaning that since Gatwick is east of Mpls.-St. Paul, it sees the sun eight hours before Mpls.-St. Paul, accounting for the eight hour difference in their times, with the Gatwick days beginning eight hours earlier. The speed of the airplane and weather conditions also affect the arrival time. So if a plane flies at 400 miles an hour, it arrives at Mpls.-St.Paul at 3:35 p.m. (Mpls.-St. Paul time). But if it flies at 500 miles an hour, it would arrive much sooner, perhaps at 12:15 p.m. earlier than the 12:30 p.m. departure time from Gatwick. Although lacking in verity, I still like the story that if you fly in a plane fast enough, you can arrive at your destination before leaving the departing airport.

One trouble with my determination to always arrive plenty early at an airport is the resulting endless waiting for the plane to arrive. London's Gatwick Airport must be among the best at adding to the misery of a long-waiting airline passenger. I've never seen an airport so large and so crowded.

Our plane might have been a bit late, so I managed to enjoy only two hours of waiting time.

After a ten minute wait for the elevator to take us up to the huge waiting area, the boys and I found ourselves in the midst of crowds of people milling around seeking and finding the very, very few empty benches and chairs. I'd been up for hours and needed a place to rest. I thought it would be impossible to find a place to sit, but the boys quickly found two adjoining seats and placed Chris and me into them. For the next two hours they took turns sitting by my side

While one brother would be sitting with me, the other two would be exploring the countless gift and souvenir shops, all sorts of stores selling all sorts of merchandise, as well as fast food and other eating and drinking establishments, all of which added to the overcrowded feeling of the place.

The flight home was not memorable. And that's a good thing. If we had rough, bumpy weather, I would remember. I'm always terrified when the plane in stormy weather bumps up and then settles downward. The downward move seems to last forever and makes me think of the ten or twenty thousand feet of thin air immediately beneath me. My prayers begin, and I resolve to never fly again.

It didn't happen. I think I slept through much of the flight.

After landing (surely not before landing) we went to the busy luggage pick-up area. The boys went to the place where they could find our stuff as it came in. I settled into a chair feeling a little grumpy that Dolly had not yet arrived to pick us up. Dolly is the baby of the family. The youngest of our eight. She has always tried to do just as I ask. I looked up and there was Dolly with a big smile. I stood up and hugged her, as she, in turn, hugged her grumpy father. She had been waiting and spotted us when we came in. Chris, Sean, and Willy came and hugged their little sister. Gratitude and love melted the grumpiness. We were home.

Afterward

About the time I had my diarrhea problem in Untermaubach, Chris, Sean, and Willy must have had a meeting in which they decided to "take care of Daddy." They probably agreed that their father's physical well-being was going downhill as well as a more precipitous decline in his ability to make wise decisions in everyday life. I saw on the trip that the boys were treating me with more deference than ever.

Daily one of them would remind me to call home to tell my daughters that I was doing all right. I think the boys probably thought that it was my time to be spoiled a bit by my children. Although I felt that the spoiling was not needed, I was inclined to go along with the boys' concerns and play the part of the helpless old geezer. Besides, I was somewhat proud that my boys cared so much for their Daddy.

When the boys and I became separated at the cemetery near Omaha Beach, I walked for an hour looking for them. Early in my walk I inadvertently passed by them when they were surrounded by the crowd gathered at the overlook above Omaha Beach. The boys did not see me walking by. They thought that I became confused and lost, and that worried them.

After the onset of diarrhea I spent much time in my hotel room. The boys would bring my breakfast to the room even though I could have protested to them that I was well enough to go downstairs to eat. But the foregoing does not include the times they brought dinner to the room when I was hardly able to get out of bed.

Sometimes in Monschau during one of my frequent afternoon naps, I would open my eyes and see one of the boys looking in on me to be sure that I was all right.

Although this kind of feeling is usually reserved by me in describing the feelings between mothers and daughters, mothers and sons, or even fathers and daughters, nevertheless I feel grateful to say with certainty that the most important memory I have from “the Trip” is that my sons care for, and do indeed, love their father.

CD

Subsequent Later – Life Remainder '08

Epilogue:

Had meant to hearty and well met meet
The very next fresh and whole-souled day.
But I caw called to no one
And none dropped in, stopped by for me.
Just a bit bushed it seems we'd be.
('Tween you and me and the fence post.)

What did it mean?
What does it mean?
How shall we proceed?
And what and how might all that seem?

Our One And Only Father,
True ikon of a doughty man,
Moves forward, always advances.
Though not unseemly self-aware,
Yet surely self-assured.
With Grace Under Pressure
He does what he will do.

He knows map-wise
Where he is,
What he's doing,
Where he's going,
What he means.

I, to compare and contrast,
(As they used to say in college blue-book test),
Never never ever know
What lingers long and late,
Whatever ever looming looms:

Fire for the back of the cup?
Or lag it haltingly up?
There may be many moments –
But there be but just two ways.

Daddy –
O,
Brothers three;
Heroes all,
Except but maybe me.

Where have we gone?
Where do we go?
Is it only futile?
Or maybe just might be for show.

So and then ...

Back to the grind, back to the day job, back in the studio – to make pictures that sell people things they don't need, can't afford, shouldn't want, and won't work;

For me.

And then ...

Return to Madison in the next state down to his fine girl Georgia and their swell young sprouts – he and she;

For Sean.

And it would be ...
Share the same roof – Filius sweetly to look after Patrem, cook his meals, cut his grass, shovel his walk, type his text, watch and mind his lot;
For Daddy and Willy,
Then and thus.

Of course and in time,
We've since met many times –
Have Big Bill Devitt and I.
He'll tell his tale
And I will mine.
Such is this.
Though might be that.

But it was He who planned and planed,
And cobbled and put together.
With Sean's and Willy's help, O yes.
And I can only tag along,
Play along,
Stay along;
And am honored and touched
To towering, trembling triumph –
To do so well as have done.

And so and then and thus, I charge:
Behold,
Look,
View,
See,

Regard.
There that stand before ye –
The greater man than me or we.

Ten Hut! …
There he goes.
There he is.
There he be.
No better man than he.

Fought two wars,
Reared eight unruly and rebellious whelps,
Husbanded Mama, such as none of you know,
Withstood the Depression,
Practiced Law, Catholicism;
Lived it he did he did did he.
And more and much of The Man –
Be He.
You might even call him a hero.
More marvelous man of Himself
Than I may ever see again.
Thank you, Daddy.
Thanks for the honor.
And indeed, thanking You for All!

Let us end with the childhood nightly prayer,
Some times still falteringly practiced
On knees in black and dead
Of fathomless coursing night:

God Bless Daddy, Mama, Chris, Sean, Mary, Anne, Nick, Matt, Willy, and Dolly.

I Love You.
Chris

– CD

THANKING YOU:

Jim Begg – For kindness and assistance on scene and in situ, and well beyond. Je vous remercie de tout cœur.

Paul Bard – For help in editing and formatting. Any irregularities (intended or no) that might appear are fault of my own self only. Go raibh maith agat.

ALSO:

Shavetail: The Odyssey Of An Infantry Lieutenant In World War II
– William L Devitt

Chaps & Chumps: A Youth In My Youth
– Christopher Devitt

On The Rail: To The Rock
– Christopher Devitt

Chapter And Verse
– Christopher Devitt

Bustin' Suds
– Christopher Devitt

Made in the USA
Middletown, DE
24 February 2022

61764014R00215